Workbook

COMPENSATION MANAGEMENT
Rewarding Performance

Fifth Edition

GRADE :

A-

Richard I. Henderson
Georgia State University

Michael Wolfe
University of Houston

Workbook

COMPENSATION MANAGEMENT Rewarding Performance

Fifth Edition

Richard I. Henderson

Prentice Hall, Englewood Cliffs, New Jersey 07632

Editorial/production supervision: Sally O'Grady
Cover design: Lundgren Graphics, Ltd.
Manufacturing buyer: Ed O'Dougherty

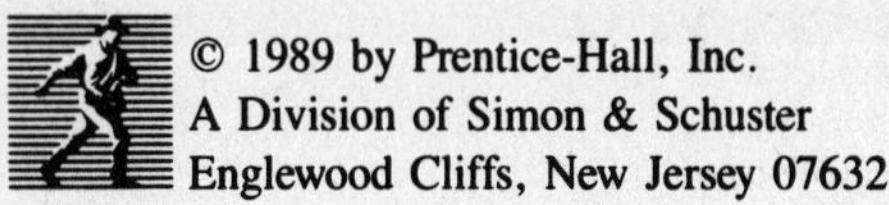

A Division of Simon & Schuster
Englewood Cliffs, New Jersey 07632

Printed in the United States of America

10 9 8 7 6 5 4 3 2 1

ISBN 0-13-155003-9

Prentice-Hall International (UK) Limited, *London*
Prentice-Hall of Australia Pty. Limited, *Sydney*
Prentice-Hall Canada Inc., *Toronto*
Prentice-Hall Hispanoamericana, S.A., *Mexico*
Prentice-Hall of India Private Limited, *New Delhi*
Prentice-Hall of Japan, Inc., *Tokyo*
Simon & Schuster Asia Pte. Ltd., *Singapore*
Editora Prentice-Hall do Brasil, Ltda., *Rio de Janeiro*

CONTENTS

Contents - continued

Contents - continued

INTRODUCTION

This WORKBOOK is an extended set of cases and experiential exercises that involve the student in many of the activities that are part of the daily life in a compensation department in a contemporary organization. In the cases and exercises to the WORKBOOK, the student performs a number of assignments that are similar to those practiced by compensation specialists. The text book, Compensation Management: Rewarding Performance, Fifth Edition, other readings, and research activities provide the data that will assist the student in performing the various roles of a compensation specialist. Responses to the cases will be more qualitative in nature and will be based on the assumptions and interpretations made by the analyst (student). On the other hand, the experiential exercises are designed to result in specific responses that are frequently quantitative. Where qualitative answers are appropriate, the response statements should take a specific form and contain specific content.

The student-compensation specialist is a member of Olympia, Inc., a large multinational conglomerate. The cases and experiential exercises (modules) are mirrors of real-world situations that provide students with learning opportunities gained through actual involvement in activities required of trained compensation specialists. In doing their part to integrate organizational objectives and goals with individual aspirations and expectations, compensation specialists lay a foundation for rewarding employees commensurate with their contributions to the success of the organization.

The cases and exercises follow in sequence the material presented in the text. Each module covers a different and essential part of the compensation-reward system and usually provides sufficient information for the student to accomplish the assignment successfully. However, it is possible that additional research will result in a better or more complete product. Valuable informational resources may be found in the references and bibliographies included in the text and in applicable literature in the wide variety of magazines and journals that discuss compensation issues. A list of some of these magazines and journals follows this Introduction. The underlined magazines and journals are those that consistently have articles of interest to compensation professionals. In addition, interviews with management and staff specialists who have compensation responsibilities may provide insights into acceptable approaches for solving module-related problems.

Compensation management is a dynamic, frequently controversial topic, and the student, like his or her counterpart in the "real world" -- the compensation professional, must stay abreast of current changes and learn more about each topic covered by a module.

JOURNALS AND MAGAZINES

Abacus
ABCA Journal of Business Communication
Academy of Management Journal
Across the Board
Administrative Management
Administrative Science Quarterly
Advanced Management Journal
Akron Business and Economic Review
Alabama Business
American Economic Review
American Federationist
AMA News Letter
American Journal of Sociology
American Political Science Review
American Psychologist
American Sociological Review
Annual Review of Psychology
Applied Anthropology
Arizona Review
Associated and Society Manager
Automator

Baylor Business Studies
Behavioral Science
Bell Telephone Magazine
Best's Review
British Journal of Industrial Relations
British Journal of Sociology
Business
Business Abroad
Business and Society Review/Innovative
Business Automation
Business Economic Dimensions
Business History
Business History Review
Business Horizons
Business Management
Business Quarterly
Business Week

Cadence
California Management Review
Canadian Personnel and Industrial Relations Journal
Civil Service Journal
CLU Journal
Colorado Business Review
Columbia Journal of World Business
Compensation Review
Computer World
Conference Board Record, The
Cost and Management

Datamation
Defense Management Journal
Dissent
Dun's Review

Educational and Psychological Measurement
Ergonomics

Factory
Financial Executive
Forbes
Fortune

Government Executive

Harvard Business Review
Hospital Administration
Hospital Administration in Canada
Hospitals
Human Organizations
Human Relations
Human Resource Management

Improving Human Performance
Inc.
Industrial and Labor Relations Review
Industrial Engineering
Industrial Management
Industrial Management Review
Industrial Relations
Industrial Relations Digest
Industry
Industry Week
Innovation
International Executive
International Labor Review
International Management
Iron Age

Journal of Abnormal and Social Psychology
Journal of American Society of Training Directors
Journal of Applied Behavior Science
Journal of Applied Psychology
Journal of Basic Engineering
Journal of Business
Journal of Creative Behavior
Journal of Economics and Business

Journal of Educational Measurement
Journal of Engineering for Industry
Journal of Human Resources
Journal of Industrial Psychology
Journal of Industrial Relations
Journal of Law and Economics
Journal of Management Studies
Journal of Political Economy
Journal of Purchasing
Journal of Social Issues
Journal of Systems Management
Journal of the American Hospital Association

Laboratory Planning
Labor Law Journal
Long Range Planning
Louisiana Business Review

Machine Design
Manage
Management Accounting
Management Advisor
Management Controls
Management in Action
Management Information
Management International Review
Management Magazine
Management of Personnel Quarterly
Management Record
Management Review
Management Science
Management Today
Management World
Managerial Planning
Manager's Magazine
Manpower
Mass Production
Medical Laboratory
Michigan Business Review
Michigan State University Business Topics
Monthly Labor Review

Nations Business

Occupational Psychology
Office Products
Operations Research
Operations Research Quarterly
Organizational Behavior and Human Performance
Organizational Dynamics

Pension World
Personnel
Personnel Administrator
Personnel Administration
Personnel Administration Journal
Personnel Journal
Personnel Management
Personnel Psychology
Personnel Quarterly
Pittsburgh Business Review
Planning Review
Plant Engineering
Plant Operating Management
Plastics World
Production Engineer
Professional Engineer
Psychological Abstracts
Psychological Bulletin
Psychological Reports
Psychology Today
Psychometrika
Public Administration Review
Public Opinion Quarterly
Public Personnel Administrations
Public Personnel Management

Quality Progress
Quarterly Review of Economics and Business

Sales and Marketing Management
SAM Advanced Management
Scientific America
Skyscraper Management
Sloan Management Review
Social Change
Southern Economic Journal
Spectrum (AIEEE)
Supervision
Supervisory Management

Tennessee Survey of Business
The Conference Board Record
The Consulting Engineer
The Director
The Executive (New Zealand)
The Foreman's Letter
The Manager's Letter
The Office
The Personnel Administrator
The Wharton Quarterly
Training and Development Journal
Training in Business and Industry

Worldwide Projects and Installation

Workbook

COMPENSATION MANAGEMENT
Rewarding Performance

Fifth Edition

OLYMPIA, INC.

Olympia, Inc., is a large multinational corporation which has its home office located in the United States. Over the past 30 years, Olympia has purchased or merged with a number of businesses that provide goods and services for a wide variety of markets and consumers. Currently, Olympia has annual sales in excess of $7.8 billion with more than 75,000 employees. It ranks among the largest 100 businesses in the United States. In 1987, its net profit exceeded $408 million.

The various businesses of Olympia are organized into 8 groups and 26 divisions. The divisions that form each group offer compatible products and have relatively similar technologies. Each group has a relatively free hand to develop its own strategy and structure. Considerable delegation of authority flows from Olympia's corporate leaders to the presidents of each group.

The two top corporate officers of Olympia are Chairman of the Board and Chief Executive Officer (CEO). At corporate headquarters there are also 3 senior vice presidents and a small corporate staff of professionals who are responsible for the analysis and design of the strategy, structure, and reward systems of Olympia. The planning involved in developing its strategy and structure assists Olympia in meeting the challenges of an ever-changing environment. The reward system supports the evolving strategies and structure and focuses the attention of all employees on the mission and objectives of Olympia.

A president heads each of the 8 groups of Olympia. Although each president has considerable flexibility in managing and leading each group, corporate philosophy and values provide the glue that ties together all groups and their respective divisions.

Central to the operation of Olympia are common values that are shared by all groups and divisions. These values emphasize ethical business practices, the dignity of human labor, and the critical relationship between profit and the performance of each employee. To ensure the continuing growth and profitability of Olympia, it is recognized that performance and rewards must be consistent with the strategy, structure, and objectives of Olympia.

The senior management of Olympia recognizes the complex issues facing managers at all levels to provide particular kinds and amounts of output within restrictions placed by (1) demands for profitable operations, (2) various government agencies to operate within requirements set by legislation, (3) customers, and (4) employees demanding a high quality of work life and rewards that make life away from the job more enjoyable and interesting.

To permit future growth and to promote continued improvement in productivity, the Board of Directors recently met with the key executives of senior management to formulate a mission statement for Olympia. Of particular interest to the key executives involved in compensation management were the philosophies and policy statements that relate specifically to the human resources of its various companies.

In formulating mission statements that relate to the management of human resources, the key executives of Olympia discussed a number of major issues. The following list covers some of the topics that are of particular interest to compensation specialists.

1. Values. Top-level managers have noted that the basic philosophy and values of Olympia are unknown or, because of communication barriers, become garbled when disseminated throughout the ranks. As Olympia becomes more and more involved in the measurement of employee performance from the highest to the lowest levels, it is imperative that organizational values are understood by all employees. It is equally important that the various systems that integrate individual effort with organizational requirements and rewards fit into or merge with the values of the organization. This is especially meaningful for compensation specialists because they have a responsibility to identify the knowledge, skills, and behaviors that are valuable to Olympia. It is vitally important that compensation management identify and develop procedures that promote the use and ensure the rewarding of desired and prized human qualities.

2. Quality of Work Life. Because of the wide variety of jobs, the diverse size and geographic locations of the various companies within the Olympia organization, and the mix of employee characteristics, qualities, and desires, it is impossible at this time to identify one specific approach that will improve the quality of employee work life. Olympia, however, will work toward promoting a positive partnership between management and workers. A major human resource goal of Olympia is to establish a workplace environment in which all human resource decisions involve a "due process" operation. In such an operation, management and workers have the opportunity to acquire full and complete information regarding certain actions that directly influence the work life of each person. Employees are not only permitted but encouraged to make inputs into decisions that affect their performance, safety, and health.

3. Human Resource Assets. It is because of the demonstrated skills and efforts of its employees that Olympia enjoys continued growth and increases in profits. Without a doubt, the human resources are Olympia's most important assets. Although top management recognizes and accepts this concept as fact, it also recognizes that there are many employees who could make greater contributions if they received better direction and were rewarded according to their contributions. A barrier blocking improved organizational productivity has been the lack of development and establishment of standards for measuring the output of employees at all levels. Without standards to assist in identifying job value and employee worth, human resource related decisions will not fulfill the needs and demands of the employees or the organization.

Although Olympia has for years permitted its groups substantial authority over the operations of their individual businesses, compensation policy and planning emanated from corporate headquarters. By the late 1970s, however, it became evident that compensation policy and planning, like other compensation functions, had to be decentralized. In 1980, Standards for the Design and Administration of Compensation by Olympia for its groups and businesses were issued. (See Standards at the end of this section.)

Within the past 5 years, the senior human resources officer has been promoted to Senior Vice President. Currently, the human resources/personnel department takes the following form:

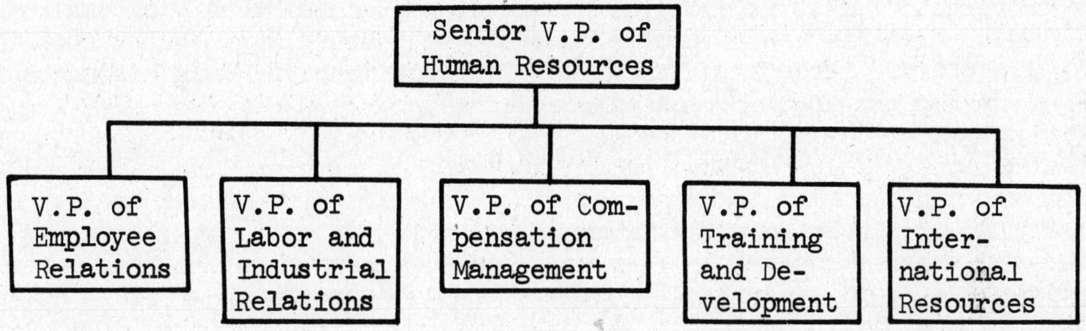

During this same period, those responsible for managing the various parts of the compensation system have been joined under one manager -- the Vice President of Compensation Management. The figure describes the configuration of the compensation department.

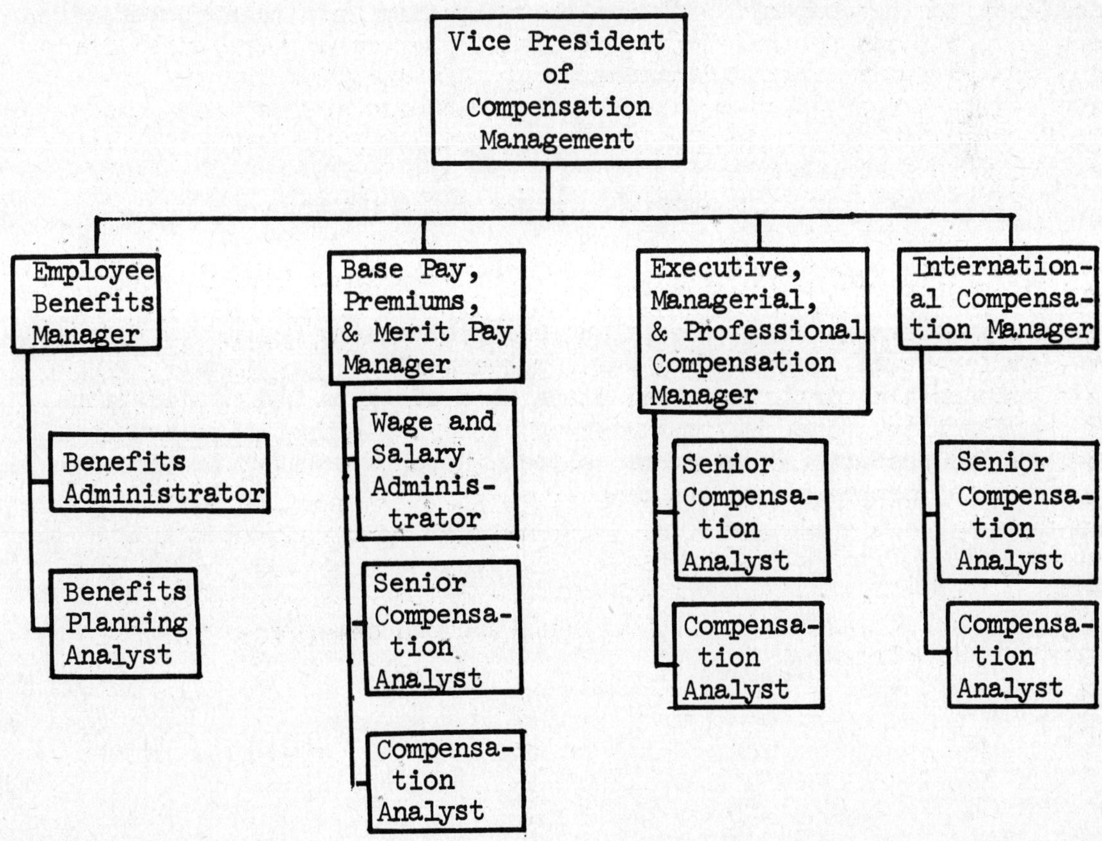

The following are thumbnail sketches of the jobs in the Compensation Department:

JOB CODE: 041

JOB TITLE: Vice President of Compensation Management

JOB SUMMARY:

Responsible for compensation and benefits programs for all categories of employees in all locations (including executive and international). Develops, implements, and administers programs which maintain the company's competitive posture while being cost effective. Reports to Executive Vice President of Human Resources (the top corporate personnel executive).

JOB CODE: 052

JOB TITLE: Employee Benefits Manager

JOB SUMMARY:

Administers all retirement, estate building, and protective (group medical, surgical, hospital, disability, and life) plans. Responsible for integrating benefits to avoid gaps and duplications as well as for providing coverages in such a way as to optimize the combination of benefit levels provided and the cost to the company. Insures that the firm retains a competitive benefits posture in the market place. Reports to the Vice President of Compensation Management.

JOB CODE: 055

JOB TITLE: Base Pay, Premiums, and Merit Pay Manager

JOB SUMMARY:

Administers all wage and salary administration, incentive, differential, perquisite, and supplemental pay programs. Responsible for integrating plans to avoid gaps and duplications and for insuring that the company retains a competitive compensation posture in the market place. Reports to the Vice President of Compensation Management.

JOB CODE: 042

JOB TITLE: Executive, Managerial, and Professional Compensation Manager

JOB SUMMARY:

Designs, implements, and administers compensation programs for executive, managerial, and professional employees. Programs include perquisites, incentive plans, stock related plans, long-term capital accumulation and estate building plans in addition to base salaries. Coordinates financial counseling for designated personnel. Reports to Vice President of Compensation Management.

JOB CODE: 043

JOB TITLE: International Compensation Manager

JOB SUMMARY:

Develops, implements, and administers compensation programs for international personnel, including expatriates, third-country nationals, and local nationals. Programs include pay administration, tax equalization, differentials, allowances, and employee benefits. Provides guidance to international management and may take policy level direction from them. Reports functionally to Vice President of Compensation Management, but also receives policy guidance from Vice President of International Human Resources.

JOB CODE: 053

JOB TITLE: Benefits Administrator

JOB SUMMARY:

Administers benefit programs. Consults with and advises employees on eligibility for insurance, hospitalization, and other benefits. Maintains benefits records and prepares documents necessary for implementing benefit coverage. Reports to Employee Benefits Manager.

JOB CODE: 054

JOB TITLE: Benefits Planning Analyst

JOB SUMMARY:

Analyzes and develops policies and benefit plans covering accident and health insurance coverage, retirement and pension plans, income continuance, holidays, and vacations. Maintains an on-going effort to determine and maintain equity with current benefit trends and legislated requirements and programs. Reports to Employee Benefits Manager.

JOB CODE: 056

JOB TITLE: Wage and Salary Administrator

JOB SUMMARY:

Formulates and administers corporate position/job evaluation programs and establishes procedures for the maintenance of an equitable wage and salary structure. Establishes job specifications and pay grades and conducts research on compensation plans in other companies. Conducts pay and compensation surveys and applies results to keep pay structure competitive. Reports to Base Pay, Premiums, and Merit Pay Manager.

JOB CODE: 057

JOB TITLE: Senior Compensation Analyst

JOB SUMMARY:

Assists in the development, installation, and administration of compensation programs. Evaluates salaried, middle, and top management jobs. Assists in administration of merit rating program, reviewing changes in wages and salaries for conformance to policy. Audits evaluation of jobs and application of existing classifications to individuals. Conducts compensation surveys and participates in compensation surveys conducted by other companies. Assists in updating the pay structure. Reports to Base Pay, Premium, and Merit Pay Manager or to compensation managers in specialized areas.

JOB CODE: 058

JOB TITLE: Compensation Analyst

JOB SUMMARY:

Studies and analyzes hourly or salaried jobs and prepares descriptions in standardized form. Evaluates jobs using established evaluation systems; determines grades and prepares records of the validity of the evaluations; may serve on job evaluation committees. Conducts compensation surveys and participates in compensation surveys conducted by other companies. Reports to Base Pay, Premium, and Merit Pay Manager or to compensation managers in specialized areas.

The upgrading and expansion of both the Human Resources Department and its compensation branch are the result of increasing government pressures and employee demands. These activities are also the result of realization by the executives of Olympia that if the corporation is truly to be a "people oriented company," it must provide the direction and support necessary to achieve this lofty objective.

1987 PAY SCHEDULE AND PAY RANGES FOR COMPENSATION PROFESSIONALS AT OLYMPIA

Job Title		Incumbent's Current Rate of Pay	Range Minimum	Range Maximum
		(Rates of pay in thousands of dollars)		
V.P. of Compensation Mgt.		81.2	66.0	99.0
Employee Benefits Mgr		57.1	46.0	66.7
Base Pay, Premiums, and Merit Pay Mgr.		54.2	46.0	66.7
Executive, Managerial, and Professional Compensation Mgr.		67.0	52.0	75.4
International Compensation Mgr.		54.1	42.0	58.8
Employee Benefits Administrator		28.6	24.0	32.4
Benefits Planning Analyst		36.4	28.0	37.8
Wage and Salary Administrator		35.7	28.0	37.8
Senior Compensation Analyst	(1)	34.5	30.0	39.0
	(2)	37.4	30.0	39.0
	(3)	31.3	30.0	39.0
Compensation Analyst	(1)	31.2	26.0	33.8
	(2)	27.6	26.0	33.8
	(3)	28.2	26.0	33.8

MODULE 1

DEVELOPING A COMPENSATION POLICY AND ADMINISTRATION MANUAL

The Corporate Manager of Compensation was asked to provide guidelines to assist division managers develop a compensation policy and administration manual that follows the values and philosophy of Olympia, Inc. To ensure consistency in application of the compensation policy among the 26 divisions, the Corporate Manager listed the following standards that must be met for developing a compensation policy manual:

Identify the compensation philosophy of top management;
Reflect the business environment;
Define the role of pay in total compensation;
Describe the method(s) used for establishing job worth;
Establish the competitive posture with regard to relevant labor markets;
Specify how performance is measured;
Relate pay to performance;
Commit the business to compliance with compensation-related laws; and
Communicate compensation policy to all employees.

A well-designed and properly implemented compensation policy is a critical component of an effective recruitment and retention program. Above all, it informs employees as to the compensation treatment they may expect. The guidelines set forth should be clear and easily understood. There should be sufficient guidelines to provide uniform and consistent compensation related actions. The following Table of Contents provides a model of an outline for a compensation policy manual:

POSSIBLE TABLE OF CONTENTS FOR A COMPENSATION POLICY MANUAL

Title Page

Table of Contents

Foreword (Introduction)

<u>Parts</u>:

I. Statement of Philosophy

II. The Purpose of Job Analysis (methods and procedures used by Olympia)

III. The Purpose of Job Descriptions (example of a job description used by Olympia)

IV. The Purpose of Job Evaluation (description of job evaluation method(s) used by Olympia and results obtained)

V. Recognition of Market Influences (description of compensation/pay survey used by Olympia and how Olympia uses collected data)

VI. Development of a Pay Structure (description or example of pay structure used by Olympia)

VII. Recognition of Performance and Contributions (description of performance measurement processes used by Olympia and relationship to various incentive/pay-for-performance plans used by Olympia)

VIII. Adjustment of Individual's Base Pay (description of process used to adjust an employee's rate of pay at Olympia)

IX. Benefits Provided by Olympia

Within the compensation policy, there are sections that identify the mechanics used for establishing an internally equitable ordering of jobs and the methods used for identifying and establishing competitive rates of pay. There is a description of what constitutes a work week and how pay is computed. This section includes a discussion of premiums and differentials and other special pay allowances. A time-off section includes pay policy regarding absenteeism, tardiness, and pay for time not worked that ranges from sick pay to leave of absence to holidays and vacations. The benefits section describes the benefits provided by Olympia, the major components or features of each benefit, and eligibility requirements.

The compensation committee of the Board of Directors of Olympia recently approved "Standards for Design and Administration of Compensation at Olympia." Corporate Compensation has developed general guidelines to assist each operating division comply with these standards. The standards and guidelines follow this module.

The Corporate Manager of Compensation also made a copy of the Table of Contents of the manual developed by Olympia Engineering Services (OES) and sent it to each division manager to assist in developing a manual.

ASSIGNMENT

You are the compensation manager of a division of Olympia that does not have a compensation policy and administration manual. You have the responsibility for developing the compensation policy and administration manual for your division for review and approval at corporate headquarters. Develop this manual and submit it by the end of the term. (As you progress through the course, you will learn about the various subjects to be included within the manual and be able to complete your assignment.)

STANDARDS FOR DESIGN AND ADMINISTRATION OF COMPENSATION AT OLYMPIA

OBJECTIVES

It is the objective of Olympia to establish and maintain compensation programs that will:

- Attract and retain qualified employees at all levels of responsibility who perform in a manner that permits Olympia to achieve its corporate objectives and goals;

- Reflect the relative value of the jobs;

- Be externally competitive and internally consistent and fair;

- Reward employees on the basis of individual performance and contribution to achievement of organizational goals;

- Foster good employee understanding and relationships; and

- Comply with applicable laws and regulations.

POLICY

I. Competitive Levels of Pay

It is the policy of Olympia

- To maintain levels of pay and benefits that are competitive with the average compensation of employers offering similar employment and competing in the same labor market for qualified employees;

- To establish such pay levels based on timely surveys of pay rates, benefits, other components of compensation, and all aspects of personnel administration;

- To make external comparisons on the basis of base pay plus other components paid in current cash on a regular, annual, nondifferential basis (such as nondeferred profit sharing).

II. Responsibility

Development of compensation programs, including job evaluation, market comparisons, and competitive pay structures, is the responsibility of each business profit center within Olympia. Within this decentralized framework, each Olympia company has the responsibility for administering its pay program in an equitable manner. Corporate personnel have auditing and monitoring responsibilities for the pay and total compensation program of each Olympia company.

The following general guidelines are offered to assist each Olympia company fulfill these objectives:

A. Job Evaluation

Each Olympia company is responsible for maintaining a job evaluation plan under which each job is described in writing and evaluated into a pay grade that reflects as accurately as possible the relative difficulty and the responsibilities associated with that job.

1. Job evaluation should be an orderly, systematic, and professionally acceptable process that provides a written record of the judgments in evaluating each factor of the job.

2. Each Olympia company should pursue a regular program under which the responsibilities and the duties for all jobs will be periodically re-examined by the compensation staff to ensure that job descriptions and the evaluation reflect the current responsibilities and duties of each job.

3. Regular reviews should be conducted of the application of job evaluation procedures by the corporate compensation staff to ensure that such procedures reflect similarities and differences in jobs.

B. Pay Structures

1. Each Olympia company has the responsibility for determining the number of pay structures that are necessary for the proper administration of its pay program. This determination should be based on internal policy considerations as well as external market considerations.

2. For office clerical, supervisory, and administrative employees, an Olympia company should normally have either a single, composite structure (generally 12 to 16 pay grades) covering all employees or separate nonexempt and exempt structures.

3. Pay ranges should vary in width from lowest to highest grades in recognition of the fact that lower-level jobs are normally highly structured and closely supervised, whereas higher-level exempt jobs are structured to require more individual thought and independent action.

4. Employee wages and salaries should be administered within the appropriate pay ranges. However, circumstances may exist which justify paying an employee outside of the stipulated pay range. In such cases, any payment below the minimum or above the maximum of the current pay structure in excess of one year requires prior notification to the Group Vice President of Human Resources.

C. Pay Surveys and Structure Changes

1. The pay structure(s) of each Olympia company should be maintained at a level competitive with the local and/or regional labor market as measured by regular surveys of competitive employers. Standards for the conduct of those surveys and for the presentation of pay structure data have been established by Human Resources at corporate headquarters.

2. Each Olympia company should participate, when possible, in broadly based community compensation surveys and should, if necessary, provide staff and other encouragement toward the establishment and improvement of such surveys.

D. Incentive Compensation

1. Each Olympia company should include within its compensation package an incentive plan that rewards individual contributions and work-unit results in a differential manner. Those individuals and work-units that perform in an exceptional manner should be rewarded through an incentive program. Economic incentives should be offered that encourage teamwork and increased productivity. The incentive program should also encourage employee growth and development. Each business should be responsible for developing an incentive plan that best fits its particular situation.

E. Pay Administration

1. Each Olympia company should budget sufficient funds to implement necessary structure changes and allow for pay grade penetration based on performance.

2. The responsibility and authority for determining all pay changes within the pay structures rests with the management of each Olympia company. Normally, pay increases should be a function of performance and productivity.

3. Each Olympia company should have a positive program of informing employees about job evaluation and pay administration programs with the goal of making all employees aware of the basis for their compensation.

Human Resources Policies and Procedures Manual

TABLE OF CONTENTS

300 COMPENSATION & REIMBURSEMENT	LATEST REVISION DATE
301 Salary Administration	06/13/84
– Scope & Objectives	
– Job Evaluation	
– Salary Grades	
– Performance Ratings	
– Starting Salaries	
– Types of Salary Increases	
302 Continuation of Salary During Absences	02/10/86
303 Pay During Jury Service	06/13/84
304 Relocation Expense – Transferring and Executive New Hires	08/15/87
305 Overtime Pay – Nonexempt Employees	06/13/84
306 Overtime Pay – Field Service Employees	06/13/84
307 Overtime Pay – Exempt Employees	06/13/84
308 Salary Payroll Budget	Section Deleted
309 Wage and Hour Investigations	06/13/84
310 Garnishments and Wage Assignments	06/13/84
400 TIME OFF	
401 Death in the Family	06/13/84
402 Holidays	06/13/84
403 Leaves of Absence	10/03/84
– Disability	
– Military	
– Maternity	
– Personal	
404 Vacations	06/13/84

500 BENEFIT PLANS		LATEST REVISION DATE
501	Matching Contributions Plan	06/13/84
502	Group Insurance Plan	07/11/85
	- Life & Accidental Death & Dismemberment	
	- Salary Continuation Plan	
	- Long Term Disability Insurance	
	- Short Term Disability Insurance	
	- Medical Benefits	
	- Dental Benefits	
503	CASH Balance Retirement Plan	10/05/86
504	Travel Accident Insurance Plan	06/13/84
505	Savings Investment Plan	09/27/84
506	Merit Scholarship Program	02/15/86
600 SAFETY & HEALTH		
601	ABC Policy Statement	06/13/84
602	Ohmeda Policy Statement	07/01/85
603	Emergency/Accident Reporting System (EARS)	
604	Employees with Communicable Diseases or Potential Exposure to Communicable Diseases	08/05/86
700 TERMINATION OF EMPLOYMENT		
701	Termination of Employees - Termination Pay	07/13/85
702	Termination Checklist	Section Deleted
703	Death of an Employee	06/13/84
	- Salary Payments	
	- Vacation Payments	
	- Death Allowance Payment	
	- Life Insurance	

800 MISCELLANEOUS		LATEST REVISION DATE
801	Public Relations - Media Contacts	07/15/86
802	Service Recognition	06/13/84
803	Retirement and Service Award Ceremony	06/13/84
804	Air Travel Restrictions	06/13/84
805	References for Former Employees	07/15/86
806	Operation of Private Aircraft on Company Business	06/13/84
807	Military Deferments	06/13/84
808	Coach Class Air Travel	Section Deleted
809	Access to Employee Files	06/13/84
810	Receipt of Honorariums	06/13/84
811	Floral Tribute - Death of an Employee	06/13/84
812	Sexual Harassment	02/15/86

MODULE 2

DETERMINING EXEMPTION STATUS AND PAY

You are the compensation manager at Olympia Manufacturing Company and you must determine the exemption status of the following individuals: (1) Mabel Jones; (2) Harry Norman; and (3) Rosie Hibbs. After investigating the work schedules and activities of the 3 employees, the following reports were written:

MABEL JONES

Mrs. Mabel Jones is the most senior employee in the office of Olympia Manufacturing Company. Mabel has worked for Olympia for 25 years, and her job title is Office Manager. There are six other clerks in the office. She has trained all six of them and, when they have a problem, they usually come to her for advice or assistance. Management recognizes her as a good and faithful employee.

Mabel's husband, Ed, who works on the other side of town, drops her off at work around 7:25 each morning. Since she is usually the first office person to arrive, her daily routine begins by making the first pot of coffee for the office staff. While the coffee is brewing, Mabel sorts the mail and places it in the appropriate employee's in-basket or mail box. (The production manager picks up the mail at the post office on his way to work each morning and, on arriving at Olympia, he places it on Mabel's desk before 7:00 a.m.) After sorting the mail, Mabel sits down and enjoys her first cup of coffee. While having her coffee, she reviews her in-coming mail, looking especially for checks from customers who have been late in paying their bills.

In addition to receiving $340 per week, Mabel earns from $3,000 to $4,000 in commissions each year for late collections that her telephone calls have helped to bring in. Many years ago, Olympia turned over to a collection agency all unpaid bills over 90 days in arrears. Mabel had mentioned to her boss that she thought she could help collect the money because, over the years, she had become familiar with many of their customers and had a good working relationship with them. They would talk to her about their problems with Olympia, and she was often able to assist them.

Mabel proved to be very successful in this assignment, so management decided to quit using the collection agency and instead pay Mabel a commission for all late payments she collected. The commission she receives amounts to about half of that paid to the collection agency.

During a normal work day, Mabel spends about 40 percent of her time posting to a number of different ledgers. She also spends between 5 and 10 percent of her time in conferences with higher levels of management. Seldom does a day go by that she isn't providing guidance or training to one of the six clerk-secretaries in the office.

The remainder of her time is spent on the telephone responding to client inquiries regarding shipping dates, quality issues, and other similar problems. Although she quite often cannot give the customer the desired answer, she is able to transfer the call to the individual who can provide the necessary information. If a customer isn't happy with the answers, he or she often checks back with Mabel who then attempts to obtain a better answer for the customer.

When not talking on customer-originated calls, Mabel performs her collection calls. She keeps a detailed diary of each past-due customer, noting the date and time of the conversation, what was said, and to whom she spoke. She quite often makes some of her collection calls while she eats lunch. All office people know they have an hour for lunch, and four of the ladies usually go off the premises each day, while two usually spend their hour in the company cafeteria. Mabel is a "brown-bagger," and eats her lunch at her desk. If no one else is in the office, she answers all incoming calls in addition to making some of her collection calls.

The office closes at 5:00 p.m., and all of the office help is usually gone by 5:02, if not a few minutes before 5:00. Mabel's husband, however, does not get off work until 5:30 p.m., and he doesn't arrive to pick her up until shortly after 6:00 p.m. During the time from 5:00 to 6:00, Mabel makes more collection calls, and is frequently able to contact some of those with late payment problems at that time that she couldn't contact earlier in the day.

HARRY NORMAN AND ROSIE HIBBS

A pay dissatisfaction problem has arisen with Harry Norman and Rosie Hibbs who are both programmers in the Data Processing Department at Olympia Manufacturing Company. Both are paid $560 per week, and it is not uncommon for both Harry and Rosie to work from 50 to 60 hours per week. Harry is a crackerjack programmer. His job description follows:

> Converts statements of business problems, typically prepared by a systems analyst, into a sequence of detailed instructions which are required to solve the problems by automatic data processing equipment. Working from charts or diagrams, the programmer develops the precise instructions which, when entered into the computer system in coded language, cause the manipulation of data to achieve desired results. Work involves most of the following: Applies knowledge of computer capabilities, mathematics, logic employed by computers, and particular subject matter involved to analyze charts and diagrams of the problem to be programmed; develops sequence of program steps; writes detailed flow charts to show order in which data will be processed; converts these charts to coded instructions for machines to follow; tests and corrects programs; prepares instructions for operating personnel during production run; analyzes, reviews, and alters programs to increase operating efficiency or adapt to new requirements; maintains records of program development and revisions.

The following summary describes the work that Rosie performs:

Analyzes business problems to formulate procedures for solving them through the use of electronic data processing equipment. Conducts studies to develop, design, and implement electronic data processing systems. Analyzes user requirements in order to design effective systems. Confers with persons concerned to determine their data processing problems and advises subject-matter personnel on the implications of new or revised systems of data processing operations. Users may be both within and outside the organization. Applies knowledge of computer equipment capabilities, subject matter to be programmed, information processing techniques, and symbolic logic. Develops a complete description of all specifications needed to enable programmers to prepare required digital computer programs. Requires the wide use and application of the principles and concepts of systems analysis and programming. Solves a wide range of difficult problems. May spend up to 40 percent of time performing programming duties that involve working from diagrams and charts which identify the nature of desired results, major processing steps to be accomplished, and the relationship between various steps in the problem-solving routine. Develops precise instructions in code language which, when entered into the computer system, causes a manipulation of data to achieve desired results.

Neither Harry nor Rosie receives any additional pay for the hours in excess of 40 that they work on their jobs each week. Both of them have talked about the 15 to 20 hours extra they work almost every week and have decided to talk to their boss, who is the Controller for Olympia, about receiving overtime pay.

ASSIGNMENT

Complete the forms following this module and answer the following questions:

1. Determine the exemption status of Mabel Jones, Harry Norman, and Rosie Hibbs.

2. Is Olympia required by law to pay Mabel, Harry, and/or Rosie overtime? Document reasons for your answer.

3. What can Olympia do to qualify Mabel, Harry, and Rosie as exempt employees?

OLYMPIA GUIDECHART[1/] FOR FAIR LABOR STANDARDS ACT QUALIFICATIONS FOR EXEMPTION FROM OVERTIME PAY

The four categories of employees that may qualify for exemption from overtime pay are Executive, Administrative, Professional, and Sales persons. It is very important to have a clear understanding, in general, of what differentiates Exempt and Non-Exempt positions so that any positions may be properly categorized and therefore maintained within the framework of the Fair Labor Standards Act. The following are general definitions:

An Exempt position is one which, by its unroutine nature and higher required compensation, demands skills and talents to make those decisions which substantially impact the management, technology, legality, or financial stature of an organization.

A Non-Exempt position is one which, by its more routine nature and lower required compensation, demands only a level of skill and talent necessary to carry out the more routine and less discretionary activities essential to supporting those functions which actively impact the management, technology, legality, or financial stature of an organization.

The following are specific definitions:

Executive

To be qualified as an "Exempt Executive" employee, all six of the following tests must be met:

(a) Has a primary duty consisting of the management of Olympia or of a department or subdivision thereof; and

(b) Customarily and regularly supervises the work of at least two other full-time employees or the equivalent thereof; and

(c) Has the authority to hire or fire other employees, or recommend hiring and firing or promotion, or other change of status of other employees; and

(d) Customarily and regularly exercises discretionary powers; and

(e) Does not devote more than 20 per cent (less than 40 per cent if he is employed by a retail or service establishment) of his hours of work to activities not directly and closely related to his managerial duties; and

(f) Receives payment on a salary basis at a rate of not less than $155/week ($8,060) exclusive of board, lodging, or other facilities.

1/ This Guidechart and the accompanying Determination Form were modeled from a program developed by Donald G. Winton, Corporate Compensation Manager, Reliance Electric Co., Cleveland, Ohio.

Streamlined Test for High-paid Executive:

Regardless of other considerations, an executive employee paid at least $250/week ($13,000), exclusive of board, lodging, or other facilities, may be "Exempt" if he meets tests (a) and (b) above.

Administrative

To be qualified as an "Exempt Administrative" employee, all five of the following tests must be met:

(a) Performs office or non-manual work directly related to management policies or general business operations of his employer or his employer's customers; and

(b) Customarily and regularly exercises discretion and independent judgment; and

(c) Regularly and directly assists a proprietor, executive, or administrator, or performs under only general supervision work along specialized or technical lines requiring special training, experience, or knowledge, or executes under only general supervision special assignments; and

(d) Does not devote more than 20 per cent of the hours worked in a workweek (40 per cent in a retail or service establishment) to activities which are not directly and closely related to those in (a), (b), and (c) above; and

(e) Receives payment on a salary or fee basis at a rate not less than $155/week ($8,060), exclusive of board, lodging, or other facilities.

Streamlined Test for Administrative Employee:

Regardless of other considerations, an administrative employee paid at least $250/week ($13,000), exclusive of board, lodging, or other facilities may be "Exempt" if he meets tests (a) and (b) above.

Professional

To be qualified as an "Exempt Professional" employee, all five of the following tests must be met:

(a) Primary duty consists of the performance of work requiring knowledge of an advanced type in a field of science or learning customarily obtained by a prolonged course of specialized instruction and study, or work that is original and creative in character in a recognized field of artistic endeavor and the result of which depends primarily on the invention, imagination, or talent of the employee; and

(b) Work requires the consistent exercise of discretion and judgment; and

(c) Work is predominately intellectual and varied in character and is such that the output produced or the result accomplished cannot be standardized in relation to a given period of time; and

(d) No more than 20 per cent of the hours worked in the workweek are devoted to activities other than those described in tests (a), (b), and (c) above; and

(e) Must be compensated at a rate not less than $170/week ($8,840), exclusive of board, lodging, or other facilities.

Streamlined Test for Professional Employee:

Regardless of other considerations, a professional employee paid at least $250/week ($13,000), exclusive of board, lodging, or other facilities, may be "Exempt" if he meets tests (a) and (b) above.

Outside Sales Person

To be qualified as an Exempt Outside Sales Person, both of the following tests must be met:

(a) Employed for the purpose of and is customarily and regularly engaged away from his employer's place or places of business in making sales or obtaining orders or contracts for services or for the use of facilities for which a consideration will be paid by the client or customer. Work performed incidental to and in conjunction with the employee's own outside sales or solicitations, including incidental deliveries and collections, shall also be regarded as Exempt work; and

(b) Hours of work of a nature other than described immediately above do not exceed 20 per cent of the hours worked in a workweek by Non-Exempt employees of the employer.

EXEMPT OR NON-EXEMPT STATUS DETERMINATION FORM

I. **EXEMPTION CATEGORY** (List most appropriate catagory under name of each employee)

Executive (E) **Administrative** (A) **Professional** (P) **Sales Person** (S)

II. **CLASSIFIERS**

	Mabel	Harry	Rosie
A. Functional (Answer each of the following questions with a Yes or No response for the jobs of Mabel, Harry, and Rosie)	NANCY		
• Does this position involve the incumbent in the Management of the enterprise?	NO		
• Does this position require the performance of office or non-manual work directly related to the management policies or general business operations of the employer or the employer's customers?	YES		
• Does this position demand the performance of work which requires knowledge of an advanced type in a field of science or learning customarily acquired by a prolonged study?	NO		
• Does this position involve work which is original and creative in character in a recognized field of artistic endeavor and the result of which depends primarily on the invention, imagination, or talent of the employee?	NO		
• Does this position require that the incumbent be engaged away from the employer's principal place of business for the purpose of making sales or obtaining orders?	NO		
B. Supervision Given			
• Does this position require the supervision of two or more full time employees.	YES		
C. Discretion/Latitude Involved			
• Does this position require that the incumbent exercise discretion and independent judgment in its performance? In other words, does the incumbent have a wide latitude for unreviewed action?	NO		
D. Nature of Work			
• Does this position require the incumbent to apply his/her mental processes to the solution, recommendation or execution of duties, problems, or processes which impact management, administrative, or technical decisions, are unroutine, and vary in nature?	NO		

	Mabel	Harry	Rosie

E. Level of Routine

This position involves 10% 20% 30% 40% 50% routine work in the execution of duties.* (List correct % for each employee) 50% ______ ______

F. Pay Level

Is the actual pay rate for this position in excess of $155/wk ($8,060) $170/wk ($8,840) $250/wk ($13,000) (List correct rate for each employee) UNK ______ ______

III. TO DETERMINE PROPER CATEGORY

Review your answers to make sure they truly reflect the contour of the position.

A. Check the category column (Exec, Adm, Prof, SalesPer) on the grid below.

B. If you have been able to determine that one of the functional classifiers in Section II Truly Represents the position, place an E opposite "Function" in the grid below. If none fit, place an N opposite "Function."

C. If your answer to "Supervision Given" is "Yes," place an E opposite "Supervision" in the grid below. If the answer is "No," place an N opposite "Supervision."

D. If your answer to Discretion/Latitude is "Yes," place an E opposite "Discretion/Latitude" in the grid below. If the answer is "no," place an N opposite "Discretion/Latitude."

E. If your answer to Nature of Work is "yes," place an E opposite "Nature of Work" in the grid below. If the answer is "No," place an N opposite "Nature of Work."

F. If your % selection under Level of Routine is 10% or 20% place an E opposite "Level of Routine" in the grid below. If your selection is 30%, 40%, or 50%, place an N opposite "Level of Routine."*

G. Place the Pay Level selection you have circled opposite "Pay Level" in the grid below.

*Recent rulings regarding routine work performed by exempt employees has limited strict interpretation of this tolerance allowance. An exempt employee supervising two or more employees may spend an unspecified amount of time doing routine work similar to or the same as subordinates if the main responsibility is management and the salary received with regard to hours worked is more than that received by subordinates who would be paid time-and-a-half for hours over 40 at their given base rate plus what they would have earned on overtime if they had worked a similar number of hours.

NON-EXEMPT

EXEMPTION CATEGORY	EXEC.			ADMIN.			PROF.			SALES		
EMPLOYEE	M	H	R	M	H	R	M	H	R	M	H	R
1. FUNCTION				E								
2. SUPERVISION GIVEN				E								
3. DISCRETION/LATITUDE				N								
4. NATURE OF WORK				N								
5. LEVEL OF ROUTINE				N								
6. PAY LEVEL EXCEEDS				—								

IV. ANALYSIS AND ASSIGNMENT OF CLASSIFICATION

If Items 1-4 are all E, item 5 is a maximum of 20%, and pay level is at least $155/wk ($170/wk in case of professional) then the job is Automatically Exempt.

However, if some items are indicated as Non-Exempt, the position may still be Exempt as follows:

Executive

If items 1 and 2 are "E" and the individual earns at least $250/wk, he/she is Exempt regardless of other items.

NOT SURE HOW MUCH NANCY MAKES. IF she makes at least $250/wk, she is exempt if not, non-exempt.

Administrative

If items 1 and 3 are "E" and the individual earns at least $250/wk, he/she is Exempt regardless of the other items.

Professional

If items 1 and 3 are "E" and the individual earns at least $250/wk, he/she is Exempt regardless of the other items.

Sales Persons

Because of pay variations due to sales incentive programs, no pay floor is set for sales persons. However, items 1 and 5 must be E and 20% or less respectively to qualify for exemption.

All Categories

- If you have been unable to represent the position with one of the functional classifiers (Section II), the position is Automatically Non-Exempt.
- If you have more than two "N's" under any given category (Exec. Adm. Prof. Sls Per.) and the pay is less than $250/wk, the position should be classified as Non-Exempt -- the reason being, that reasonable doubt exists and a risk would be taken in classifying the position as Exempt.

If major difficulties arise in properly classifying positions as Exempt or Non-Exempt, corporate compensation is available (through your employee relations manager) for assistance.

MODULE 3

IDENTIFYING JOB ANALYSIS METHODS

Complete the following form, identifying which method(s) of job analysis would be used to collect job content data for each of the 10 listed groups of employees.

FORM 1

DATA GATHERING METHODS

Select (x) the method you would use to collect job content data from each job group.

Job or Job Groups \ Job Analysis Methodology	Question-naire	Individual Interview	Group Interview	Obser-vation	Diary/ Log	If time permits, * COMBINATION Explanation
Management	X	X	X	X	X	X
Secretaries	X	X	X	X	X	X
Clerks	X	X	X	X	X	X
Assemblers	X	X	X	X	X	X
Equipment Operators	X	X	X	X	X	X
Inspectors	X	X	X	X	X	X
Mechanics	X	X	X	X	X	X
Warehouse Persons	X	X	X	X	X	X
Programmer-Analyst	X	X	X	X	X	X
Computer Operator	X	X	X	X	✓	X

KATHY - YOU SHOULD LOOK AT THE HANDOUT + CLASS NOTES FROM EVENING WE DISCUSSED THIS - NOT ALL METHODS ARE APPROPRIATE TO ALL SITUATIONS

MODULE 4

DETERMINING TIME REQUIREMENTS FOR A JOB ANALYSIS PROJECT

A division of Olympia has 5 secretaries at its regional office. Each secretary performs different assignments, although there is some similarity in assigned duties, e.g., answers phones, types correspondence, files records, completes forms, collects information to resolve problems, etc. Using your answer to secretary in the form in Module 3, complete the Time Analysis List. (Review job analysis time requirements in Chapter 5 of the text.)

JOB ANALYSIS TIME REQUIREMENTS

	Time Requirement	
<u>Incumbent's Time</u>		
Complete questionnaire (if using questionnaire)	______	
Prepare for interview (if using interview)	______	
Participate in interview (if using interview)	______	
Review and modify first draft of job definition-job responsibilities and duties	______	
Complete job specification questionnaire (if used)	______	
Review, modify, and approve job description	______	
Total Incumbent Time		_____
<u>Analyst's Time</u>		
Prepare job analysis questionnaire (if used)	______	
Prepare for interview (if used)	______	
Interview incumbent (if used)	______	
Review job analysis questionnaire (if used)	______	
Review interview data (if used)	______	
Prepare first draft job definition	______	
Review modified first draft job definition	______	
Review completed job specification questionnaire	______	
Write job description	______	
Total Analyst Time		_____
<u>Reviewer's Time</u> (e.g., Supervisor of Incumbent)		
Review incumbent completed job analysis questionnaire	______	
Review, modify, and approve first draft job definition	______	
Review, modify, and approve final draft of job description	______	
Total Reviewer Time		_____
Total		______

MODULE 5

ANALYZING NANCY HORN'S JOB

Mary Stewart, manager of the Olympia Electrical Supply and Service Center, had recently spoken to Sam Thomas, Wage and Salary Administrator, concerning a reclassification or regrading of the job of her secretary, Nancy Horn.

Over the past two years, Nancy has been assigned, and at times, has just assumed additional duties. The job Nancy now performs in no way resembles the one that existed when she entered the organization three years ago.

George Waters was asked to perform a desk audit of Nancy's job. George called Mary Stewart to get a little background information and to see if she preferred a specific time for him to conduct the interview. Mary mentioned that Nancy was taking her annual vacation the following week and asked George if he could interview Nancy this week. George had already scheduled some work at an Olympia PolySci Chemical manufacturing facility in Houston for the remainder of the week and told Mary he would be unable to work with Nancy before she went on vacation. Mary suggested that she switch the call to Nancy so that they could set their own schedule. After listening to each other's scheduling problems, George asked Nancy if she would be willing to write a detailed analysis of what she currently does on her job and mail it to him before leaving for vacation.

George has learned over the years that secretaries, as a group, write a more detailed and exhaustive description of their work than any other group. If problems occur when secretaries analyze their jobs, it is normally in the direction of verbosity -- seldom in lack of detail. George told Nancy to think of the major functions of her job -- the general activity areas in which specific results that are of value to the organization can be identified and measured. He then asked her to describe in detail the duties or tasks she performs relative to each function.

Nancy said that she would mail George a typed review or a general log of the work she does before leaving for vacation. George was happy to hear of Nancy's cooperation and told her that he would review and analyze her summary. From it, he would develop a list of responsibility and duty statements and mail them back to her office where they would be waiting for her when she returned. After she reviewed his interpretation of her job responsibilities and duties, they could schedule a personal interview and, at that time, George could conduct a desk audit of Nancy's job.

NANCY HORN'S DESCRIPTION OF HER WORK

My job is called office secretary. My immediate supervisor is Mary Stewart, Manager of an Olympia Electrical Supply & Service Center. Olympia Electrical Supply and Service Centers perform repairs and provide repair parts for major appliances (refrigerators, washers, dryers, ranges, etc.) manufactured by Olympia Electric Company (OEC). This center has 38 employees who perform functions from receiving and shipping repair and replacement parts to the servicing and repairing of OEC appliances in response to customer requests. Some repair work is done at the center; other repair work is performed at the homes of the customers. I spend part of my time as a personnel payroll clerk, some time as a secretary and assistant to Mrs. Stewart, and the remainder of the time supervising clerks and performing clerical activities.

I am responsible for maintaining accurate records of the time cards of 38 employees, preparing new time cards for the upcoming week and maintaining the old cards for future reference, tabulating time (weekly) worked by each employee from his or her time card to assure a full 40 hour week is worked and that any time over 40 hours is approved by that employee's immediate supervisor for overtime pay, maintaining a daily attendance log which indicates any absences of the 38 employees and whether those absences are taken from sick or annual leave or if pay is to be docked. I tabulate a bi-weekly regular payroll (for regular 40 hour work week) and a bi-weekly overtime payroll (for time worked over the regular 40 hours -- paid at a rate of time and a half). I tabulate a weekly payroll for any temporary employees, updating and correcting any errors on a monthly computer printout of each employee's leave accrual. The correcting and updating are based on records maintained from leave cards which are filled out upon an employee's absence, showing his or her name, Social Security number, number of hours of the absence, date of the absence, and whether or not it should be taken from sick or annual leave. These cards are sent to the Data Center where the information is logged into the computer for the next Employee Leave printout. I fill out a PR-1 (Personnel Request form) and a PA-1 (Personnel Action form) which indicate various actions taken for or against an employee or position, such as an appointment to a position, name and/or address change, rate change (6 month's pay increase, promotion, demotion, annual pay increase), leave without pay for unexcused absence or for insufficient sick or annual leave, termination, and a request form for a new employee to fill a vacant position. I file a Position Retention Justification form with the main personnel office for approval to retain and fill a vacant position at the Center.

I maintain the manager's appointment calendar, type memoranda and correspondence from the manager's or other center supervisor's handwritten rough drafts, correcting grammar, spelling and punctuation, and frequently rearranging sentence structure to create the best impression on the reader. I compose correspondence as needed or at the request of the manager or the three supervisors (shipping and receiving, in-house repair, and mobile repair) without direct dictation or a draft from which to work, and frequently compose response memoranda to the various units, organizations, or customers who request information.

I assist the manager in completing the Center's annual budget. This is done in a computer printed book which provides the various accounts the Center is allowed. It is necessary to determine how much each employee will cost the Center in salary and benefits, how much rent and utilities will cost in the next year, how much is needed to maintain the various phases of the Center's operation, any cost increases that might occur, and any requests for additional funds to improve the Center's services or just to maintain the status quo in the coming year. After all the annual figures are determined, they must be broken down into quarterly allotments and more money must be placed in the quarter that will require more funds. (The cost of heating is greater in the winter months, therefore more money must be allowed in those quarters to pay utility bills during that period.) This entire budget is submitted to the manager for any additions or deletions and approval and is then sent to the Budget Department at main headquarters for final approval. The budget book is done under the supervision of a Budget Analyst at main headquarters who provides brief instructions, is available to answer questions, and who also makes three to four personal calls a year to review our budgeting procedures and review our records. The nature of this project and the bulk of the other duties of this position require that much of the budget-related work be done on my own time, possibly at home after working hours.

I assist the manager in making the necessary purchases for the department through the Purchasing Department. After it is determined whether or not there are sufficient funds in the Department's budget (which is determined by checking the balance listed on a computer printed Expenditure Report issued by the Budget Department and maintained by this position along with a budget ledger showing the amount of each purchase), a Purchase Requisition is filled out which shows the suggested price of the item(s) to be purchased, from whom the Center wishes to buy, the description of the item(s), and the account from which the funds are to be taken. This form is signed by the manager and forwarded for approval to the Budget Department, Division of Accounts, and finally to Purchasing for approval, order, and delivery determination. Upon receipt of the item(s) from the vendor, I must notify the Purchasing Department of receipt of the goods by sending a copy of the Purchase Order which was issued by the Purchasing Department upon approval of the purchase. A file of all purchases is maintained in the Center's files for reference.

I take the manager's telephone calls and, whenever possible, screen out the unnecessary ones. I am responsible for the one WATS telephone line that is to be used only for business purposes. I am aware of the work the manager conducts so that in her absence I can relate information when it is appropriate or necessary to those persons asking specific questions. The manager is the Secretary-Treasurer of the Electrical Wholesale Distributor's Association and, therefore, as her secretary I am responsible for all the minutes from the monthly Association meetings; I type them and mail them to the membership. I am also responsible for Association correspondence, membership applications, membership cards (including issuing them to new members), membership dues, membership roster, which includes the names and addresses of all the members, the officers, and the Board of Directors. I keep the records and balance the checking account and the billing for the Association. I occasionally handle personal correspondence for the manager and I maintain files on all correspondence from the manager's office.

I make some decisions without supervision regarding department procedures in the absence of the department head or other supervisors.

I also supervise three clerical positions and have a working knowledge of their duties and the assumption of as many clerical duties as possible when a clerk is out of the office or when the workload is heavy. These duties include answering telephones, waiting on customers at the front desk (answering questions, giving directions, sending customers to the parts department, and talking with job applicants), accepting bills for services rendered to the Center by outside concerns or for purchases made by Center personnel. (If $50 or less, a log must be kept describing the service and the amount of the charges and must contain a bill or receipt. If the amount charged exceeds $50, a request must be filed and sent to the main office.) I also assist clerks in difficult situations with the public at the front desk and over the phone. I answer questions from clerks and advise them how to handle problems. I answer questions regarding Center policies and procedures. I make decisions without supervision regarding office procedures and assign work to clerks in the office. I route incoming mail to proper clerks for disposition. I also maintain a daily record of completed calls by each outside repair person, occasionally assisting outside repair supervisors to dispatch one of six mobile units to a specific problem location. I assist outside repair persons with particular problems, maintaining a log of all complaints and identifying the nature of the complaint and specific issues related to it. I summarize the complaints monthly and submit them to the Center manager.

I maintain and summarize records of all mileage entailed by Center personnel in their private vehicles while performing Center business. This requires that I total the number of miles each individual has driven from a daily speedometer reading (and a brief description of the activity involved in using the private vehicle) and compute the amount to be paid at 20¢ a mile. I fill out a payment request form at the end of each month with the name of the individual and the amount owed. I forward the request and a copy of the mileage reading to the finance officer at headquarters for payment.

I review and forward the outside Center vehicle mileage report each month (mileage for the trucks used by the repair people). The radio dispatcher totals the mileage of each truck monthly from speedometer readings taken daily and submits the figures to me for a grand total to be drawn and the total is sent to the safety officer on a memorandum. A report (including the speedometer reading from each truck on the last day of the month, the total miles each truck has driven in the month, and the grand total of miles for all six trucks for the month) is submitted to the Motor Maintenance Department and a copy retained in the files at the Center.

In addition, I maintain an ample supply of office supplies (typing paper, carbon paper, pens, pencils, machine ribbons, etc.) and order these supplies as needed from the main stockroom. I maintain a supply of office forms, draw up a format for new and more efficient forms, and, upon approval by the manager, order forms through proper channels. I also dispense with unnecessary forms and look for ways to offer better service through more efficient forms. I attempt to create better public relations by keeping office personnel morale up as much as possible and implement new procedures to ease work loads. I maintain a "coke fund," keeping balance sheets of funds on hand, counting money taken into the machine, ordering drinks and paying for drinks and machine rent from the balance in the fund. I keep the key to the machine.

ASSIGNMENT

1. Complete a job analysis questionnaire on Nancy Horn's job. Your instructor will assign one of the two job analysis questionnaires that follow this module.

2. In completing the analysis, identify areas where you would want clarification and further information from either Nancy or her boss, Mrs. Stewart. More details on budgeting; how involved does Nancy get? Ask both Nancy & Mrs. Stewart. From Nancy, percentage of time spent on all that she does.

3. Write a job definition for Nancy Horn's job; use the responsibility and duty information you just collected.

From Nancy, how often do you supervise the clerks? From Mrs. Stewart; out of everything Nancy does, which is most important & which does Nancy spend most time on? From Mrs. Stewart; does Nancy handle supplies on her own? What about purchasing?

1.0 Maintains records for payroll.
- computes employee weekly pay
- ~~checks employee absence & work hours~~
- calculates employee overtime pay.
- ~~calculates travel allowances.~~
- reconciles payroll errors & discrepancies.
- calculates temporary employees pay

2.0 Processes various forms & records for Dept.
- determines which forms to use.
- completes form using available data
- checks form for completeness & accuracy
- maintains files
- distributes forms to appropriate units, organizations

3.0 Acts as secretary & assistant to manager
- schedules managers appts.
- types correspondence
- corrects rough drafts
- composes correspondence for supervisors
- answers telephone calls for manager
- answers business questions during manager's absence
- orders supplies as needed for dept.

4.0 Supervise clerks
- observes clerks at work
- answers questions from clerks
- advises clerks

5.0 Maintain mileage records of repairmen in the dept.
- calculates total number of miles driven by repairmen
- compute amount to be paid
- compile payment request form

DRAWING YOUR JOB PICTURE

GENERAL - We plan to analyze all the component parts of your job and integrate all of the essential parts into an accurate description of your work. We are counting on your honest and correct accounts of what you do while performing your job. Be as objective and informative as you can in completing all pages of this questionnaire. Our first request is for you to complete this chart. The completed chart gives us an understanding of where your job fits in the organizational hierarchy.

YOUR IMMEDIATE SUPERVISOR

NAME: ______________________

JOB TITLE: ______________________

YOUR POSITION

NAME: ______________________

JOB TITLE: ______________________

YOUR SUBORDINATES

NAMES: ________ ________ ________ ________ ________

TITLES: ________ ________ ________ ________ ________

JOB ANALYSIS QUESTIONNAIRE

RESPONSIBILITIES AND DUTIES

Instructions: We want to find out exactly what you do in your job. What are all the activities you perform on your job? By completing this job analysis questionnaire, you will help us update or write a job description for your job. We will be using two terms to help describe your job: **RESPONSIBILITIES** and **Duties.**

RESPONSIBILITIES: **The major job activities you perform which make up your whole job.**

Duties: The specific, more detailed activities you perform when accomplishing each responsibility.

Look at the following EXAMPLES:

JOB:	Secretary I	
RESPONSIBILITY	1.0	Acts as a receptionist
Duties	1.1	Answers telephone, relaying information or transferring calls to appropriate individuals.
	1.2	Greets visitors, answering their questions and/or directing them to appropriate individual.
RESPONSIBILITY	2.0	Performs various administrative activities
Duties:	2.1	Schedules appointments
	2.2	Composes routine correspondence
	2.3	Makes travel arrangements
	2.4	Coordinates meetings by notifying participants of scheduled date and time, and by reserving meeting room

We would now like you to do the following:

1. On p. 1 of this questionnaire (Responsibility Identification Form), write the identifying information at the top of the page. Then write all the responsibilities of your job. (As a general rule, most jobs can be described with 3 to 7 responsibility statements.)

2. Beginning with p. 2 of the questionnaire, write the first responsibility you listed on page 1.

3. Now think of the more detailed activities you must perform to accomplish this responsibility. These are called duties. (Normally, 3 to 10 duties describe a Responsibility.)

4. On p. 3 of the questionnaire, write the second responsibility you listed on p. 1 and the duties related to it.

5. Continue writing one Responsibility and its associated duties on the remaining pages until you have covered all responsibilities listed on p. 1.

DEPARTMENT ____________ ORG. # ______ EMPLOYEE'S NAME ____________

JOB TITLE ____________ DATE ____________

RESPONSIBILITY IDENTIFICATION FORM

Rank Order	WHAT IS DONE? (Action Verb)	TO WHAT IS IT DONE? (Object)	WHY IS IT DONE? (Effect of the Action)
	RESPONSIBILITY #1		
	RESPONSIBILITY #2		
	RESPONSIBILITY #3		
	RESPONSIBILITY #4		
	RESPONSIBILITY #5		

JOB ANALYSIS QUESTIONNAIRE

Name of Employee ____

RESPONSIBILITY #1 ____

____

DUTIES:

1. ____

____

2. ____

____

3. ____

____

4. ____

____

5. ____

____

6. ____

____

7. ____

____

8. ____

____

9. ____

10. ____

____

(Continue on back of page if necessary)

RESPONSIBILITY #2 ____

____

DUTIES: ____

1. ____

2. ____

3. ____

4. ____

5. ____

6. ____

7. ____

8. ____

9. ____

10. ____

(Continue on back of page if necessary)

RESPONSIBILITY #3 ____

____

DUTIES:

1. ____

____

2. ____

____

3. ____

____

4. ____

____

5. ____

____

6. ____

____

7. ____

____

8. ____

____

9. ____

____

10. ____

____

(Continue on back of page if necessary)

RESPONSIBILITY #4 ____________________

____

DUTIES:

1. ____________________

____

2. ____________________

____

3. ____________________

____

4. ____________________

____

5. ____________________

____

6. ____________________

____

7. ____________________

____

8. ____________________

____

9. ____________________

____

10. ____________________

____

(Continue on back of page if necessary)

RESPONSIBILITY #5 ________________________________

____

DUTIES:

1. ________________________________

____

2. ________________________________

____

3. ________________________________

____

4. ________________________________

____

5. ________________________________

____

6. ________________________________

____

7. ________________________________

____

8. ________________________________

____

9. ________________________________

____

10. ________________________________

____

(Continue on back of page if necessary)

KNOWLEDGE AND ABILITIES

Instructions:

1. Please review the **RESPONSIBILITIES** you have just listed. Then think about the knowledge and abilities you must have to perform each **RESPONSIBILITY.** List below all the knowledge and abilities you can think of that relate to each **RESPONSIBILITY.** (Examples: Knowledge of laws and ordinances regarding building codes; knowledge of supervisory techniques; ability to direct the work of others; ability to communicate orally and in writing).

2. Review your knowledge list, thinking about how you acquired each one (that is, where you learned it). In the column labeled "How Knowledge Acquired," write a number using the code below which describes how you acquired each knowledge.

   1 = In grammar school
   2 = In high school
   3 = In junior (2 year) college
   4 = In college
   5 = In graduate school
   6 = In specialized training sessions
   7 = Through on-the-job experience
   8 = Other

3. After you have completed Instruction #2, write an asterisk (*) to the left of those knowledge and abilities that you think a person should have before being hired for your job.

RESPONSIBILITY #

	KNOWLEDGE	HOW KNOWLEDGE ACQUIRED	ABILITIES
1	______	______	______
	______	______	______
	______	______	______
	______	______	______
	______	______	______
2	______	______	______
	______	______	______
	______	______	______
	______	______	______
	______	______	______
3	______	______	______
	______	______	______
	______	______	______
	______	______	______

RESPONSIBILITY	KNOWLEDGE	HOW KNOWLEDGE ACQUIRED	ABILITIES
4			
5			
6			
7			

EDUCATION AND EXPERIENCE REQUIREMENTS/LICENSES/CERTIFICATION

1. If you were hiring someone to replace you in your present position, what is the lowest educational level you would require them to have? (check one)

   _______completion of a high school education
   _______graduation from a technical or junior (2 year) college
   _______graduation from a 4-year college or university
   _______possession of a master's degree or equivalent
   _______other (specify)

2. If you were hiring someone to replace you in your present position, how many years of experience would you require them to have? (i.e., minimum experience requirement)

3. What licenses or certificates **are legally required** to perform your job? (please list)

4. Are you required to either participate or attend any additional training in order to maintain your licensures or certifications? If yes, please list them below:

5. Are there any other jobs an applicant should have performed before entering this job? If yes, please list the job titles below:

MISCELLANEOUS

1. What specific laws or ordinances do you use or follow in your work? (Laws or ordinances that you must have knowledge of and use as a reference to perform your job)

2. Describe the physical demands of your job. (Example: work is generally sedentary; requires long periods of standing or walking; recurring bending or stooping)

3. Describe the normal and usual conditions of your work (Example: work is performed in an office; in a very noisy place; around much dust, dirt, grease, etc; around smoke, fumes, irritating chemicals or toxic conditions; outdoors; on call 24 hours/day)

JOB ANALYSIS QUESTIONNAIRE -- SUPERVISOR'S REVIEW SHEET

Name of Employee____ Date____________________

Job Title____ Department______________

Instructions:

Please review this employee's job analysis questionnaire to insure that it is accurate and complete. Then fill out the items below. Your certification in Item #5 below means that you accept responsibility for the accuracy and completeness with which the entire questionnaire describes the responsibilities and duties of the employee's job. If the employee's responses in the questionnaire do not express your idea of the responsibilities and duties that you have assigned to the employee, you should use this form to qualify and elaborate on the description. Two things are very important:

1. **PLEASE DO NOT CHANGE OR ALTER THE EMPLOYEE'S REPONSES.**

2. **DO NOT MAKE ANY STATEMENTS OR COMMENTS ABOUT THE INDIVIDUAL EMPLOYEE'S WORK PERFORMANCE, COMPETENCE, OR QUALIFICATIONS. This questionnaire will be used to evaluate the duties that constitute the position, not the performance or qualification of the employee.**

* *

1. Describe briefly the principal function of the unit you supervise.

2. Describe briefly the employee's position as you see it, explaining how it relates to the functions of the unit.

4. Describe any working conditions that cause you to feel stress when performing your job activities.

5. Please list below the number of the **most difficult** responsibility you perform. (The one that is hardest for you) Why is this responsibility difficult?

ADDITIONAL INFORMATION

1. Are there any job activities that you are not performing now that you should be? If so, please list them below.

2. Are there any job activities you are now performing that you should not be? If so, please list them below.

3. Is there any additional information that you would like to tell us about your job that you feel we should know?

IF YOU HAVE ANY PROBLEMS COMPLETING THIS FORM, PLEASE CONTACT:

CERTIFICATION

I certify that the above information is accurate and complete.

SIGNATURE OF EMPLOYEE________________________________DATE________________

OLYMPIA, INC.

JOB ANALYSIS QUESTIONNAIRE

GENERAL - Read the accompanying instructions carefully before completing this questionnaire. Your responses should be focused on the requirements of the job to which you are assigned, as opposed to your personal capabilities or background unless specifically relevant to what you do. Be as objective and as informative as you can. Concentrate detail on the most important aspects of what your job requires you to do. Should you feel that extra space is needed to properly answer a particular question, use the back of the page on which the question is asked and reference the question number along with your additional comments.

(Your answer need not be typed, but please print clearly)

Your Name: NANCY HORN Date: 29 MARCH 91

Official Job Title: Office Secretary Job Code: # ____

Division Olympia Electric Company Dept.: Olympia Electrical Supply + Service Center.

Your Work Location: ____ How Long On Present Job: 3 years

Immed. Supv's Name: Mary Stewart Title: Manager

1. Job Purpose: In one or two sentences, summarize the primary purpose(s) of your job -- what are the objectives which cause this particular job to exist? (You may wish to delay formulating this summary until you have answered the other questions. Also see sample Job Purpose for an Electronics Technician).

Sample: Electronics Technician - Assures the ongoing usefulness and accuracy of electronics instrumentation by performing necessary preventive maintenance, repair, and calibration of assigned equipment. Modifies existing equipment and assists higher classified personnel in the development, construction, testing, and installation of new equipment.

~~Performs secretarial duties for manager, by composing correspondence maintaining files + typing. Assists manager in composition of annual budget as well as performing payroll clerk duties. Also ensures communication between different offices within the company~~

Assists manager with budget + purchasing of the dept., as well as schedule appt.'s, ~~maintain payroll cards~~, types, and compiles correspondence to various units. Maintains payroll cards ensuring pay, leave, absences, overtime, are paid accordingly to each of employees. Supervise + assist clerks in day-day operations of the dept.

Job Analysis Questionnaire - continued

2. <u>Work Activities</u>: List the activities that you must perform in order to successfully complete your job assignments. Start each activity statement with an action verb that best describes a kind of thing you do. It may be helpful to think of the things you do beginning with the start of your work day and list in normal sequence each activity you perform during the day. If your job has no normal order or routine flow of work, first list the things you usually do each day; then list the things you do possibly once or twice a week or only once a week, once each two weeks, once a month, etc. Typical examples of action verbs are <u>operates</u>, <u>types</u>, <u>files</u>, <u>reviews</u>, <u>schedules</u>, <u>selects</u>, <u>joins</u>, <u>inserts</u>, <u>compiles</u>, <u>records</u>, <u>measures</u>, <u>analyzes</u>, <u>records</u>, <u>observes</u>, <u>enters</u>, <u>picks</u>, etc.

- Maintains records of time cards
  - prepares new time cards weekly
  - files old cards
  - tabulate time worked (weekly) for each of 38 employees
  - records absence log of each employee
  - tabulate bi-weekly payroll (regular + overtime)
  - calculate payrolls for temps.
    - reviews, corrects errors monthly
  - writes a PR-1 (personnel request form)
  - writes a PA-1 (personnel action form)
    - insert actions taken on employees
  - file Position Retention Justification form
- Schedules manager's appt. calendar
  - type
  - corrects rough drafts
  - compose correspondence for 4 people
- Assists compiling of annual budget
  - calculate cost of each employee (salary, benefits)
  - calculate rent, utilities for upcoming year
  - calculate $ to keep center in operation
  - analyze cost increases
  - analyze request for extra funds
  - calculate quarterly costs/allotments from annual budget
- assists in purchasing required items
- write + fill out Purchase requisitions
- files copy of Purchasing order
- answers telephone, screens calls
- operates/schedules the WATS line
- answers business questions when manager is gone
- Compiles/records/types minutes from assoc. mtgs.
  - distributes minutes to all members
  - answers correspondence
  - issues membership cards
  - reviews membership applications
  - records/maintains membership dues
  - records/compiles membership roster
  - compiles records
  - balances checking acct + billing of Assoc.
- At some times, changes dept. procedures with no supervision
- supervises 3 clerks
  - observes them at work
  - answers clerks questions
  - advise clerks
- Records calls by outdoor repairmen
  - assists in dispatching 1 of 6 mobile units, occasionally
  - records log of complaints.
  - review/summarize/analyze complaints monthly + pass them to manager
- records mileage of personnel in POV
  - calculates total number of miles driven daily be each employee
  - compute $ to be paid
  - compile payment request forms each month
- Review/analyze mileage of repairmen each month
  - calculate total mileage
- Operates supplies for office
  - orders supplies as needed
- Maintains file forms
- Develops new file forms
- Operates Coke fund
  - maintains money
  - orders drinks

Job Analysis Questionnaire - continued

3. Job Priorities: Are the activities you perform pre-scheduled or scheduled on a daily basis? Yes X ; No ___. If yes, how and by whom? If unscheduled, how do you determine the order in which you perform these activities? Both. My supervisor has me do certain things each day (put out weekly report, file forms, schedule appts.) that have to be done on a certain day. Most things I do, I set up my schedule to ensure it all gets done. There is a schedule set up for items that are required to be done by a certain time, and I also schedule daily to get what needs to be done accomplished.

4. Review and Approval of Work: (a) Other than your immediate supervisor, does anyone regularly provide guidance to you, review your work in progress or approve your completed work? Yes X ; No ___. If yes, give the name and title of each such person and indicate the type of guidance, review, or approval given. The 3 other supervisors (shipping + receiving, in-house repair, mobile repair) I type for them as well as compose correspondence when they request. After they've proofread + approved it, I send it off. Also, I assist the manager in compiling an annual budget. This is sent to the Budget Analyst for final approval. A budget analyst provides guidance to us as needed.

(b) Do you regularly provide guidance to anyone, assign, review, or approve work? Yes X ; No ___. If yes, give the name and title of each such person and briefly describe what you do. I provide guidance to clerks in difficult situations. Answer questions on policies/procedures. Assist outside repair supervisors by dispatching mobile units to sites. Assist outside repairmen with problems, keeping complaints + passing them to mgr.

5. Action/Decision Authority: What authority do you have to make decisions on your own or to take personal initiative in fulfilling the activities of your job? In describing, be sure to note any technical or organizational limits which affect the scope of your decisions or actions. I take personal initiative when I compose response memoranda to various organizations without direct dictation or a draft. Personal initiative on screening calls. Responsible for WATS line. Relate info. when mgr. is absent. Make some decisions based on dept. procedures with no supervision. Have responsibility of the clerks + make decisions for them. Keep supplies maintained and ordered. Keep the Coke fund going; drinks in the machine, money tabulated.

6. Inter-Departmental Work Flow: Is there any work which you complete in your department (division) which must go to another department before a significant work process can be completed or a major action taken? Yes X ; No ___. If yes, briefly describe and identify the other department(s). All of the weekly/bi-weekly payrolls. These are sent to Data Center where the info. is logged into a computer for next Employee Leave printout. Fill out PR-1 + PA-1 + Position Retention Justification describing various actions taken for/against an employee or position. These go to the main Personnel office for approval. Assisting with the annual budget. This goes to Budget dept. at main HDQTRS. Assist manager with purchases through Purchasing Dept. Look at Expenditure Report from Budget Dept. + fill out Purchase requisition showing suggested price of items to be purchased, where to buy, description of items, + account where funds are to be taken. This goes to Budget Dept., Division of Accts., + then to Purchasing. After receipt of these items I send the Purchase Order back to Purchasing Dept. I fill out a payment request form at end of each month + send it + a copy of mileage readings to finance office at HDQTRS, for payment. I send Safety Officer a memorandum →

Job Analysis Questionnaire - continued

7. Departmental/Outside Contacts: Indicate those persons in other departments (divisions) of Olympia or outside the Company with whom you are required to be in regular contact as a part of your job and for what purpose. Show "I" for inside the Company and "O" for outside

I/O Name, Title & Dept.	(Name of Co.) (If Outside) Purpose & Frequency of Contact
I - Data Center	personnel payrolls - weekly
I - Main Personnel Office	form requests to fill vacancies, increase salaries, promotions etc. - As Required
I - Budget Dept.	assist with budget - As required (about 3-4x a year)
I - Purchasing Dept.	Request on form, certain purchase - As required
O - Electrical Wholesale Distributors Association	minutes, membership roster, dues, acct. - Monthly
I - Outside Repair person	assist, pass info. to manager - Daily
I - Finance officer	Request payment for employees that use POV - Monthly
I - Safety officer	report on vehicle mileage - Monthly
I - Motor Mx. Dept.	report on mileage of trucks - Monthly
O - Coke Salesman - As required	

8. Job Mobility: Do you normally remain within your section area in performing your work? Yes X ; No ___ . If no, briefly describe your movements as to location, purpose, and approximate frequency. If work is done at a customer, prime contractor, or subcontractor location or "in the field," be sure to specify.

9. Equipment Used: List the tools or equipment you use in the performance of your job. Typewriter
Calculator
Computer
Telephone

→ with total readings of monthly truck mileage. Also submit a report to Motor Mx. Dept. on truck mileage, etc., monthly.

10. Work Aids: What kind of specific written guidelines, procedures, protocols, or other aids such as operating manuals, charts, code lists, catalogs, etc., are utilized in performing major aspects of your work? Comment, if appropriate, on their availability and usefulness.

Company policies + procedures are always available + useful.

11. Safety Equipment: What types of safety equipment are you required to have in doing your normal job? If you regularly leave your usual job area in doing your work, what additional safety equipment, if any, is necessary?

Fire extinguisher in office.

12. Physical Requirements of Job: In performing your regularly assigned activities, are there any requirements for you to exert significant physical effort, work in a cramped or awkward position, work from heights, etc.? Yes___; No___. If yes, describe what is required, how often, and what type of effort is involved.

Typing correspondence + working on word processor/computer for several hours a day. Is bad on back, causes fingers to cramp, + eye irritation.

13. Emotional and Psychological Demands: When performing your regularly assigned activities, are there any influences that cause you emotional or psychological concern? Yes___; No_X_. If yes, please describe these influences and their impact on your emotional and psychological well-being.

Job Analysis Questionnaire - continued

14. Job Requirements: If you were interviewing someone to fill the position you now hold:

(a) What kind of knowledge, specific skills and abilities, prior experience, formal training or certifications should that person possess at a minimum upon starting on the job?

Prior experience in typing, filing, working on a computer.
Skills - good writing & oral skills
Abilities - to work with other people
to work with numbers

(b) What kind of knowledge, skills and abilities would you expect the newly hired person to gain while on the job and how soon?

Better written & oral skills, a knowledge of budgets, setting them up & using them. Managing others, ability to distinguish what has priority. Better, smoother skills in writing reports, filling out forms. Knowledge/understanding of company's policies & procedures.

(c) What knowledge, skills, formal training or certifications would such a person have to gain in order to advance to the next higher position in his/her occupation?

Would have to be more skilled, knowledgeable & able to handle different problems/situations at the same time

15. Hardest Part of the Job: What do you consider to be the most demanding aspect of your job in terms of planning and completing your work? Give examples, if necessary.

Working the budget. It requires a lot of time and thought to put out an annual budget. You have to figure out what the company's needs are for the year, total up costs, add extra costs, cover everything. Nothing can be left out or it could very much affect the company. Other than that, it's just organization. If I don't plan, schedule, & organize, everything would not get done.

Job Analysis Questionnaire - continued

ADDITIONAL INFORMATION

16. What activities do you now perform that you believe should be performed by some other individual? Briefly explain why.

Dealing with the Electrical Wholesale Distributors Assoc. That takes up a lot of time & really is not specifically work-related. I do it as my boss is the Sec-Treas., not because the company requires me to. Also, if there was a payroll clerk, I could be a better secretary.

17. What activities do you now not perform that you believe you should perform? Briefly explain why.

NONE

18. Please comment on any aspect of your job that you feel requires further clarification.

Although it seems a lot of my job is filing, recording, typing, etc, the job is much more detailed. If I didn't do my job correctly, payrolls would either be late, wrong or not accomplished, and the same can be said for vacations. Supplies would dwindle, forms would be filled out improperly, & nothing would get done. My job touches a lot of aspects of the company that I help smooth & make contacts & ensure things are done properly.

If you did not answer Question 1, please return to page 1 and complete that question.

SUPERVISOR'S REVIEW
(Use Back of This Page If Necessary)

1. Has the employee omitted or inaccurately stated any significant aspect of the job? Yes____; No__X__. If yes, describe.

2. What are the most necessary qualifications for a person to have in order to be initially assigned to this job?

Ability to be able to work on several projects well and at the same time. To be able to type & compile correspondence, fill out forms properly, ensuring only the best paperwork leaves the office

3. If the job is part of an occupational family, describe what duties or responsibilities distinguish it from (a) the job immediately below and (b) the job immediately above. (Show lower & higher job titles)

(a) CLERK secretary

- no supervision in this job
- just basic skills are required (type, computer, dictation)
- many work with public, answering questions

(b) executive secretary

- work for only 1 person
- doesn't do payroll, supplies, budget, etc. for everyone
- works as asst. to 1 manager & aids him in accomplishing the job requirements.

________________ Date

________________ Immediate Supervisor's Signature

MODULE 6

DETERMINING NANCY HORN'S EXEMPTION STATUS AND WRITING A JOB DESCRIPTION

After performing a desk audit and completing a first-draft job definition, Nancy completed a job specification questionnaire for her job. The completed questionnaire follows this module.

ASSIGNMENT

1. Using the completed job definition and the information in the job specification questionnaire, determine the exemption status of Nancy Horn's job. (Use the exemption status forms included in Module 2.)

see page 25

2. Write a job description for Nancy Horn's job. Use the model of a job description that follows this module.

see pg 61

JOB SPECIFICATION QUESTIONNAIRE

Date 6/1/87

Incumbent Nancy Horn Job Title Office Secretary

1. KNOWLEDGE REQUIRED BY THE JOB.

Identify and briefly describe the knowledge required and used (that is essential) in doing acceptable work in your job. This includes:

. The nature or kind of knowledge needed, and

. How this knowledge is used in doing the work.

Knowledge may be further defined as information or facts, such as procedures, work practices, rules and regulations, policies, theories and concepts, principles, and processes, which you must know to be able to perform your work. Describe below what you have to know to do your job:

	KNOWLEDGE	HOW USED
1.	Knowledge of correct grammar, spelling, and word usage	for composition, editing, and typing activities
2.	Knowledge of clerical activities	to assist in filing, completion of forms, and teaching new clerks to perform their job assignments
3.		
4.	Knowledge of basic bookkeeping	to maintain various records
5.	Skill in operating typewriter	to type records, correspondence

List any tools, equipment, vehicles, and machines you use while performing your work:

Typewriter

Calculator Printer (output of computer)

Word-Processor (CRT)

Copying machine

List any licenses or certificates required for operation of your work assignment:

None

2. SUPERVISORY CONTROLS.

Supervisory Controls identifies and describes how your work assignments are made, the kinds of instructions given, the way priorities and deadlines are set, and how objectives and boundaries are defined. It also describes the amount of freedom you have in carrying out a work assignment. Do you develop your own work sequences or do you follow some kind of guidelines or instructions? Do you become involved in one-of-a-kind situations? If you do, whom do you contact or how do you make decisions concerning the situation? Finally, it describes the nature and extent of the review of work.

SUPERVISORY CONTROLS:

1. How is work assigned? By activities to be performed - same basic procedures followed in accomplishing assignments.

2. What guidelines or procedures are followed? Operates independently in performing well-defined activities; follows standing operating procedures.

3. How is work reviewed? By manager as work comes to her attention.

3. GUIDELINES.

Guidelines identify and describe the operating procedures and policies, traditional practices, or references such as manuals, dictionaries, handbooks, standing organizational instructions that are available, applicable, and specific as to how you perform your assignments. A second question to be answered is the amount of personal interpretation or adaptation permitted in relating your assignments to these guidelines.

1. Guides Follows Olympia procedures and general business practices.

2. Judgment Responding to customer problems and to some degree in directing efforts of clerks.

4. COMPLEXITY.

Complexity describes (1) the general nature and variety of assignments, methods, functions, projects, or programs performed in the job; (2) the facts or conditions the incumbent must consider in identifying what needs to be done. (This may include facts to be developed, checked, analyzed, interpreted, or evaluated by the employee before work progresses. Are these facts or conditions clearly identified and directly applicable to the activity or do they vary by situation or nature of the subject matter? Do work assignments involve unusual circumstances, incomplete, or conflicting data?) and (3) the level of difficulty and originality required in taking a course of action. (Must the employee consider differences in courses of action, refine methods, or develop new techniques?)

COMPLEXITY:

1. Complexity of Assignment Job fairly routine.

(Complexity continued)

2. Identifying what needs to be done Situation or job activities outline what needs to be done.

3. Difficulty and Originality Some originality required in composing correspondence.

5. SCOPE AND EFFECT.

Scope and effect concerns the end objective to be reached, such as service provided, results achieved, work performed, and the impact of the work product or service performed.

SCOPE AND EFFECT:

1. Purpose Maintain accurate records and receipts.

2. Impact Assist other employees perform assignments properly and receive payment for services they render.

6. PERSONAL CONTACTS.

Personal contacts describes the face-to-face, telephone, or radio contacts which the employee has in terms of the "work relationship" of the people contacted. (Do not describe contacts with supervisor as that was included in the Supervisory Controls section.) Indicate if contacts are with people outside your work organization. Identify the organization they represent (this could be "general public").

PERSONAL CONTACTS:

Individuals and Their Organizations Various members of organization and people external to the organization such as customers, suppliers, and others wishing to contact the manager; members of Electrical Wholesale Distributors Association.

7. PURPOSE OF CONTACTS.

Purpose of contacts describes purpose of personal contacts just identified. Purpose may be to exchange information, resolve problems, provide services, influence, question, or negotiate some issue. If contact includes special problems or behaviors, identify them. These may include "Contact is hostile, skeptical, uncooperative, or unreceptive."

PURPOSE OF CONTACTS: Give and exchange information about product and assist other members of organization in structured situations. Respond to requests from members of organization and from people outside organization.

8. PHYSICAL DEMANDS.

Physical demands describe the nature of physical demands placed on employees, such as climbing, lifting, pushing, balancing, stooping, kneeling, crouching, crawling, or reaching, etc. Indicate the frequency, intensity, and dimensions of the activity (by dimension, height climbed, amount of weight lifted, size of objects moved).

PHYSICAL DEMANDS: Usually perform work sitting, but must stand, stoop, and bend to file and operate certain office equipment.

9. WORK ENVIRONMENT.

Work environment describes physical surroundings in which the employee works. This includes temperature of work site, exposure to contagious diseases, discomfort, precautions that must be taken to avoid mishaps or discomfort. (It is not necessary to describe normal everyday safety precautions required of any and all employees.)

WORK ENVIRONMENT: Work in air-conditioned and heated office; typical office noise, but normally pleasant environment.

(This job specification questionnaire would be used in conjunction with the Factor Evaluation System (FES), a point-factor job evaluation method. The primary standards for FES follow in Module 7.)

#	TITLE OF POSITION OFFICE SECRETARY	1
NUMBER	TITLE	PAGE

RESPONSIBLE TO: TITLE OF IMMEDIATE SUPERVISOR MANAGER, Olympia Electrical Supply & Service Ctr.

RESPONSIBLE FOR: TITLE(S) OF REPORTING SUBORDINATES

EXEMPTION STATUS: NON-EXEMPT

TITLE OF IMMEDIATE SUPERVISOR MAN.

POSITION TITLE Office Secretary

TITLE OF IMMEDIATE SUBORDINATES Clerks

QUALIFICATIONS

KNOWLEDGE: correct grammar, spelling, word usage, clerical activities, basic bookkeeping
SKILL: operating typewriter, computer
EXPERIENCE: NONE
LICENSES: NONE

RESPONSIBILITIES AND DUTIES

Performs administrative assignments for the manager.

- schedules & maintains manager's appt. calendar.
- maintains business & personal files for manager
- receives & screens manager's calls, responding to questions in her absence
- calculate budgetary expenses, including salaries, benefits, rent, and utilities
- submits budget to manager for revision & approval.
- monitors budget throughout year to ensure availability of funds
- interacts with HDQTRS Budget Analyst to stay abreast of budgeting requirements.
- composes & corresponds for manager & 3 supervisors,
- coordinates activities of Elec'l. Wholesale Dist. Assoc taking & typing minutes, updating membership register, typing & mailing correspondence, taking applications, and performing accounting procedures.

Supervise 3 clerks

- establishes procedures for clerical assignments
- schedules work for clerical staff. →

MISSION

Assists manager with budget & purchasing of the dept., as well as schedule appts., type, & compile correspondence to various units. Maintains payroll cards ensuring pay, leave, absences, & overtime are paid accordingly to each of the employees. Supervise & assist clerks in day-day operations of the dept.

NUMBER	TITLE	PAGE

- counsels clerks on job-related performance + behaviors
- assists clerks in resolving difficult situations and answering questions regarding policies + procedures
- monitors clerical assignments.

Processes personnel records + other forms.

- prepares, tabulates, + maintains time cards.
- maintains attendance records for sick pay, vacation + personal holidays, correcting + updating monthly computer printout of each employee's records.
- completes + submits various personnel forms

Performs clerical assignments.

- completes purchase requisitions for approval by Budget Dept., Division of Accts., + Purchasing Dept.
- notifies Purchasing Dept. of receipt of goods by sending them a copy of the purchase order.
- Receives + distributes mail to appropriate clerks.
- Develops and summarizes complaint + repair reports.
- dispatches service calls.
- completes payment requests for services
- totals # of miles driven by each employee from daily speedometer readings.
- Computes amount to be paid for mileage at end of month
- maintains Coke fund + Coke machine.

APPROVAL OF INCUMBENT	APPROVAL OF SUPERVISOR	DATE

MODULE 7

EVALUATING NANCY HORN'S JOB

A committee was formed to determine the kind of job evaluation method to be used at Olympia. The assignment given to the committee was to review and analyze the strengths and weaknesses of various kinds of job evaluation methods.

After reviewing various methods, the committee focused their attention on 3 alternatives:

(1) market pricing;
(2) point-factor job evaluation; and
(3) multiple regression-based job evaluation using structured and scored questionnaires.

The committee decided not to recommend market pricing because it would not provide the kind of data needed for determining internally equitable relationships among the wide variety of jobs at Olympia. The committee also rejected the use of multiple regression because they felt that it would be difficult if not impossible to describe how the multiple regression method works in determining a hierarchical relationship among jobs and also because it would be difficult to communicate the mathematical process both to managers and to all employees in general.

After reviewing various point-factor job evaluation methods, the committee identified 2 possible options: the Factor Evaluation System (FES) developed by the U.S. Federal Government and the Hay Plan used by the Hay Consulting Group of Philadelphia, Pennsylvania.

ASSIGNMENT

1. Evaluate Nancy Horn's job using FES ~~and the Hay Plan~~. The Primary Standards of FES and detailed information on the Hay Plan and the 3 Hay Guide Charts follow this module.

2. From your evaluation, which method would you recommend Olympia use for job evaluation?

Hints for Evaluating Jobs:

When evaluating a job using a point-factor job evaluation plan, there are a few very basic practices or procedures that will simplify the process and dramatically improve its reliability. The first requirement is to become intimately familiar with the factors and the levels or degrees associated with each factor. Next, all members of the organization must spend some time and effort resolving misunderstandings and conflicts regarding the meaning and use of the words and terms used in the plan. One, if not the greatest, barrier to the effective use of any point-factor job evaluation plan is the failure to gain common understanding of the meaning of words and terms the old nemesis -- ambiguity, vagueness.

The next convention or accepted practice is that an evaluator evaluates each position/job under study as tightly or as strictly as possible. Tight interpretation or inference-making between job requirements/specifications and the levels/degrees of each factor will result in more common agreement and significantly less spread in differences of measurement of level/degree for the position/job under study. If all jobs are rated in the same manner, consistency and fair treatment will be the result.

When actually involved in evaluation, the rater may find that once he or she is familiar with the factor and its levels/degrees, a "bracketing" approach improves efficiency of operation. Bracketing simply means a very rapid move through the levels/degrees, quickly eliminating those levels/degrees that do not apply, then focusing on the levels/degrees that may apply, and finally settling on the appropriate level/degree.

The Hay Plan has a number of plan conventions that facilitate the reaching of common agreement as to worth of jobs both within and among organizations. The last pages of the descriptive material on the Hay Plan discuss the up-level-down profiling process. Very briefly, Hay has recognized that certain kinds of jobs require relatively higher levels of accountability than problem-solving, some typically require the same level, and others require less accountability than problem-solving. To determine up, down, or level, count the difference in points (if any) assigned to accountability and problem-solving on the STEPS table on the left-hand side of the PROFILE TABLE. In the first example provided on the page titled Evaluations, the points given to the factor accountability are located 2 steps higher than the points assigned to the factor problem-solving. Thus, accountability is 2 up from problem-solving and the job is a 2-up job. Certain kinds of jobs are not only level jobs, but 1-up, 2-down, etc., and if the job rated doesn't meet the basic portrait of a 1-up or 2-down job, it is quite likely that the job has been evaluated incorrectly. Organizations may also have their own conventions relative to interpretation and assignment of levels/degrees of factor to certain kinds of jobs or requirements made of a jobholder.

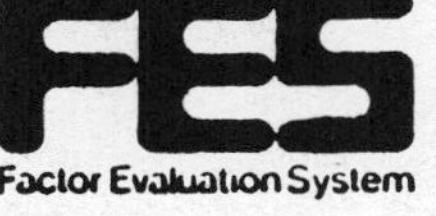

POSITION-CLASSIFICATION STANDARDS

General Introduction, Background, and Instructions
Section VII

Instructions for the Factor Evaluation System

PRIMARY STANDARD

The Primary Standard serves as a "standard-for-standards" for the Factor Evaluation System(FES). Factor-level descriptions for position classification standards are point-rated against the Primary Standard. Thus, it serves as a basic tool for maintaining alignment across occupations.

The Primary Standard has descriptions of each of the nine FES factors and the levels within each factor as well as the point values appropriate for each level. The nine factors are:

FACTOR 1, KNOWLEDGE REQUIRED BY THE POSITION

Factor 1 measures the nature and extent of information or facts which the workers must understand to do acceptable work (e.g., steps, procedures, practices, rules, policies, theories, principles, and concepts) and the nature and extent of the skills needed to apply those knowledges. To be used as a basis for selecting a level under this factor, a knowledge must be required and applied.

Level 1-1 *50 points*

Knowledge of simple, routine, or repetitive tasks or operations which typically includes following step-by-step instructions and requires little or no previous training or experience;

OR

Skill to operate simple equipment or equipment which operates repetitively, requiring little or no previous training or experience;

OR

Equivalent knowledge and skill.

Level 1-2 *200 points*

Knowledge of basic or commonly-used rules, procedures, or operations which typically requires some previous training or experience;

OR

Basic skill to operate equipment requiring some previous training or experience, such as keyboard equipment;

OR

Equivalent knowledge and skill.

Level 1-3 *350 points*

Knowledge of a body of standardized rules, procedures or operations requiring considerable training and experience to perform the full range of standard clerical assignments and resolve recurring problems;

OR

Skill, acquired through considerable training and experience, to operate and adjust varied equipment for purposes such as performing numerous standardized tests or operations;

Level 1-4 *550 points*

Knowledge of an extensive body of rules, procedures or operations requiring extended training and experience to perform a wide variety of interrelated or nonstandard procedural assignments and resolve a wide range of problems;

OR

Practical knowledge of standard procedures in a technical field, requiring extended training or experience, to perform such work as: adapting equipment when this requires considering the functioning characteristics of equipment; interpreting results of tests based on previous experience and observations (rather than directly reading instruments or other measures); or extracting information from various sources when this requires considering the applicability of information and the characteristics and quality of the sources;

OR

Equivalent knowledge and skill.

Level 1-5 *750 points*

Knowledge (such as would be acquired through a pertinent baccalaureate educational program or its equivalent in experience, training, or independent study) of basic principles, concepts, and methodology of a professional or administrative occupation, and skill in applying this knowledge in carrying out elementary assignments, operations, or procedures;

OR

In addition to the practical knowledge of standard procedures in Level 1-4, practical knowledge of technical methods to perform assignments such as carrying out limited projects which involves use of specialized, complicated techniques;

OR

Equivalent knowledge and skill.

Level 1-6 *950 points*

Knowledge of the principles, concepts, and methodology of a professional or administrative occupation as described at Level 1-5 which has been either: (a) supplemented by skill gained through job experience to permit independent performance of recurring assignments, or (b) supplemented by expanded professional or administrative knowledge gained through relevant graduate study or experience, which has provided skill in carrying out assignments, operations, and procedures in the occupation which are significantly more difficult and complex than those covered by Level 1-5;

OR

Practical knowledge of a wide range of technical methods, principles, and practices similar to a narrow area of a professional field, and skill in applying this knowledge to such assignments as the design and planning of difficult, but well-precedented projects;

OR

Equivalent knowledge and skill.

Level 1-7 *1250 points*

Knowledge of a wide range of concepts, principles, and practices in a professional or administrative occupation, such as would be gained through extended graduate study or experience, and skill in applying this knowledge to difficult and complex work assignments;

OR

A comprehensive, intensive, practical knowledge of a technical field and skill in applying this knowledge to the development of new methods, approaches, or procedures;

OR

Equivalent knowledge and skill.

Level 1-8 *1550 points*

Mastery of a professional or administrative field to:

—Apply experimental theories and new developments to problems not susceptible to treatment by accepted methods;

OR

—Make decisions or recommendations significantly changing, interpreting, or developing important public policies or programs;

OR

Equivalent skill and knowledge.

Level 1-9 *1850 points*

Mastery of a professional field to generate and develop new hypotheses and theories;

OR

Equivalent knowledge and skill.

FACTOR 2. SUPERVISORY CONTROLS

"Supervisory Controls" covers the nature and extent of direct or indirect controls exercised by the supervisor, the employee's responsibility, and the review of completed work. Controls are exercised by the supervisor in the way assignments are made, instructions are given to the employee, priorities and deadlines are set, and objectives and boundaries are defined. Responsibility of the employee depends upon the extent to which the employee is expected to develop the sequence and timing of various aspects of the work, to modify or recommend modification of instructions, and to participate in establishing priorities and defining objectives. The degree of review of completed work depends upon the nature and extent of the review, e.g., close and detailed review of each phase of the assignment; detailed review of the finished assignment; spot-check of finished work for accuracy; or review only for adherence to policy.

Level 2-1 — *25 points*

For both one-of-a-kind and repetitive tasks the supervisor makes specific assignments that are accompanied by clear, detailed, and specific instructions.

The employee works as instructed and consults with the supervisor as needed on all matters not specifically covered in the original instructions or guidelines.

For all positions the work is closely controlled. For some positions, the control is through the structured nature of the work itself; for others, it may be controlled by the circumstances in which it is performed. In some situations, the supervisor maintains control through review of the work which may include checking progress or reviewing completed work for accuracy, adequacy, and adherence to instructions and established procedures.

Level 2-2 — *125 points*

The supervisor provides continuing or individual assignments by indicating generally what is to be done, limitations, quality and quantity expected, deadlines, and priority of assignments. The supervisor provides additional, specific instructions for new, difficult, or unusual assignments including suggested work methods or advice on source material available.

The employee uses initiative in carrying out recurring assignments independently without specific instruction, but refers deviations, problems, and unfamiliar situations not covered by instructions to the supervisor for decision or help.

The supervisor assures that finished work and methods used are technically accurate and in compliance with instructions or established procedures. Review of the work increases with more difficult assignments if the employee has not previously performed similar assignments.

Level 2-3 — *275 points*

The supervisor makes assignments by defining objectives, priorities, and deadlines; and assists employee with unusual situations which do not have clear precedents.

The employee plans and carries out the successive steps and handles problems and deviations in the work assignment in accordance with instructions, policies, previous training, or accepted practices in the occupation.

Completed work is usually evaluated for technical soundness, appropriateness, and conformity to policy and requirements. The methods used in arriving at the end results are not usually reviewed in detail.

Level 2-4 — *450 points*

The supervisor sets the overall objectives and resources available. The employee and supervisor, in consultation, develop the deadlines, projects, and work to be done.

At this level, the employee, having developed expertise in the line of work, is responsible for planning and carrying out the assignment: resolving most of the conflicts which arise; coordinating the work with others as necessary; and interpreting policy on own initiative in terms of established objectives. In some assignments, the employee also determines the approach to be taken and the methodology to be used. The employee keeps the supervisor informed of progress, potentially controversial matters, or far-reaching implications.

Completed work is reviewed only from an overall standpoint in terms of feasibility, compatibility with other work, or effectiveness in meeting requirements or expected results.

Level 2-5 — *650 points*

The supervisor provides administrative direction with assignments in terms of broadly defined missions or functions.

The employee has responsibility for planning, designing, and carrying out programs, projects, studies, or other work independently.

Results of the work are considered as technically authoritative and are normally accepted without significant change. If the work should be reviewed, the review concerns such matters as fulfillment of program objectives, effect of advice and influence of the overall program, or the contribution to the advancement of technology. Recommendations for new projects and alteration of objectives are usually evaluated for such considerations as availability of funds and other resources, broad program goals or national priorities.

FACTOR 3. GUIDELINES

This factor covers the nature of guidelines and the judgment needed to apply them. Guides used in General Schedule occupations include, for example: desk manuals, established procedures and policies, traditional practices, and reference materials such as dictionaries, style manuals, engineering handbooks, the pharmacopoeia, and the Federal Personnel Manual.

Individual jobs in different occupations vary in the specificity, applicability and availability of the guidelines for performance of assignments. Consequently, the constraints and judgmental demands placed upon employees also vary. For example, the existence of specific instructions, procedures, and policies may limit the opportunity of the employee to make or recommend decisions or actions. However, in the absence of procedures or under broadly stated objectives, employees in some occupations may use considerable judgment in researching literature and developing new methods.

Guidelines should not be confused with the knowledges described under Factor 1, Knowledge Required by the Position. Guidelines either provide reference data or impose certain constraints on the use of knowledges. For example, in the field of medical technology, for a particular diagnosis there may be three or four standardized tests set forth in a technical manual. A medical technologist is expected to know these diagnostic tests. However, in a given laboratory the policy may be to use only one of the tests; or the policy may state specifically under what conditions one or the other of these tests may be used.

Level 3-1 *25 points*

Specific, detailed guidelines covering all important aspects of the assignment are provided to the employee.

The employee works in strict adherence to the guidelines; deviations must be authorized by the supervisor.

Level 3-2 *125 points*

Procedures for doing the work have been established and a number of specific guidelines are available.

The number and similarity of guidelines and work situations requires the employee to use judgment in locating and selecting the most appropriate guidelines, references, and procedures for application and in making minor deviations to adapt the guidelines in specific cases. At this level, the employee may also determine which of several established alternatives to use. Situations to which the existing guidelines cannot be applied or significant proposed deviations from the guidelines are referred to the supervisor.

Level 3-3 *275 points*

Guidelines are available, but are not completely applicable to the work or have gaps in specificity.

The employee uses judgment in interpreting and adapting guidelines such as agency policies, regulations, precedents, and work directions for application to specific cases or problems. The employee analyzes results and recommends changes.

Level 3-4 *450 points*

Administrative policies and precedents are applicable but are stated in general terms. Guidelines for performing the work are scarce or of limited use.

The employee uses initiative and resourcefulness in deviating from traditional methods or researching trends and patterns to develop new methods, criteria, or proposed new policies.

Level 3-5 *650 points*

Guidelines are broadly stated and nonspecific, e.g., broad policy statements and basic legislation which require extensive interpretation.

The employee must use judgment and ingenuity in interpreting the intent of the guides that do exist and in developing applications to specific areas of work. Frequently, the employee is recognized as a technical authority in the development and interpretation of guidelines.

FACTOR 4, COMPLEXITY

This factor covers the nature, number, variety, and intricacy of tasks, steps, processes, or methods in the work performed; the difficulty in identifying what needs to be done; and the difficulty and originality involved in performing the work.

Level 4-1 *25 points*

The work consists of tasks that are clear-cut and directly related.

There is little or no choice to be made in deciding what needs to be done.

Actions to be taken or responses to be made are readily discernible. The work is quickly mastered.

Level 4-2 *75 points*

The work consists of duties that involve related steps, processes, or methods.

The decision regarding what needs to be done involves various choices requiring the employee to recognize the existence of and differences among a few easily recognizable situations.

Actions to be taken or responses to be made differ in such things as the source of information, the kind of transactions or entries, or other differences of a factual nature.

Level 4-3 *150 points*

The work includes various duties involving different and unrelated processes and methods.

The decision regarding what needs to be done depends upon the analysis of the subject, phase, or issues involved in each assignment, and the chosen course of action may have to be selected from many alternatives.

The work involves conditions and elements that must be identified and analyzed to discern interrelationships.

Level 4-4 *225 points*

The work typically includes varied duties requiring many different and unrelated processes and methods such as those relating to well-established aspects of an administrative or professional field.

Decisions regarding what needs to be done include the assessment of unusual circumstances, variations in approach, and incomplete or conflicting data.

The work requires making many decisions concerning such things as the interpreting of considerable data, planning of the work, or refining the methods and techniques to be used.

Level 4-5 *325 points*

The work includes varied duties requiring many different and unrelated processes and methods applied to a broad range of activities or substantial depth of analysis, typically for an administrative or professional field.

Decisions regarding what needs to be done include major areas of uncertainty in approach, methodology, or interpretation and evaluation processes resulting from such elements as continuing changes in program, technological developments, unknown phenomena, or conflicting requirements.

The work requires originating new techniques, establishing criteria, or developing new information.

Level 4-6 *450 points*

The work consists of broad functions and processes of an administrative or professional field. Assignments are characterized by breadth and intensity of effort and involve several phases being pursued concurrently or sequentially with the support of others within or outside of the organization.

Decisions regarding what needs to be done include largely undefined issues and elements, requiring extensive probing and analysis to determine the nature and scope of the problems.

The work requires continuing efforts to establish concepts, theories, or programs, or to resolve unyielding problems.

FACTOR 5, SCOPE AND EFFECT

Scope and Effect covers the relationship between the nature of the work, i.e., the purpose, breadth, and depth of the assignment, and the effect of work products or services both within and outside the organization.

In General Schedule occupations, effect measures such things as whether the work output facilitates the work of others, provides timely services of a personal nature, or impacts on the adequacy of research conclusions. The concept of effect alone does not provide sufficient information to properly understand and evaluate the impact of the position. The scope of the work completes the picture, allowing consistent evaluations. Only the effect of properly performed work is to be considered.

Level 5-1 *25 points*

The work involves the performance of specific, routine operations that include a few separate tasks or procedures.

The work product or service is required to facilitate the work of others; however, it has little impact beyond the immediate organizational unit or beyond the timely provision of limited services to others.

Level 5-2 *75 points*

The work involves the execution of specific rules, regulations, or procedures and typically comprises a complete segment of an assignment or project of broader scope.

The work product or service affects the accuracy, reliability, or acceptability of further processes or services.

Level 5-3 *150 points*

The work involves treating a variety of conventional problems, questions, or situations in conformance with established criteria.

The work product or service affects the design or operation of systems, programs, or equipment; the adequacy of such activities as field investigations, testing operations, or research conclusions; or the social, physical, and economic well being of persons.

Level 5-4 ***225 points***

The work involves establishing criteria; formulating projects; assessing program effectiveness; or investigating or analyzing a variety of unusual conditions, problems, or questions.

The work product or service affects a wide range of agency activities, major activities of industrial concerns, or the operation of other agencies.

Level 5-5 ***325 points***

The work involves isolating and defining unknown conditions, resolving critical problems, or developing new theories.

The work product or service affects the work of other experts, the development of major aspects of administrative or scientific programs or missions, or the well-being of substantial numbers of people.

Level 5-6 ***450 points***

The work involves planning, developing, and carrying out vital administrative or scientific programs.

The programs are essential to the missions of the agency or affect large numbers of people on a long-term or continuing basis.

FACTOR 6. PERSONAL CONTACTS

This factor includes face-to-face contacts and telephone and radio dialogue with persons not in the supervisory chain. (NOTE: Personal contacts with supervisors are covered under Factor 2, Supervisory Controls.) Levels described under this factor are based on what is required to make the initial contact, the difficulty of communicating with those contacted, and the setting in which the contact takes place (e.g., the degree to which the employee and those contacted recognize their relative roles and authorities).

Above the lowest level, points should be credited under this factor only for contacts which are essential for successful performance of the work and which have a demonstrable impact on the difficulty and responsibility of the work performed.

The relationship of Factors 6 and 7 presumes that the same contacts will be evaluated for both factors. Therefore, use the personal contacts which serve as the basis for the level selected for Factor 7 as the basis for selecting a level for Factor 6.

Level 6-1 — ***10 points***

The personal contacts are with employees within the immediate organization, office, project, or work unit, and in related or support units;

AND/OR

The contacts are with members of the general public in very highly structured situations (e.g., the purpose of the contact and the question of with whom to deal are relatively clear). Typical of contacts at this level are purchases of admission tickets at a ticket window.

Level 6-2 — ***25 points***

The personal contacts are with employees in the same agency, but outside the immediate organization. People contacted generally are engaged in different functions, missions, and kinds of work, e.g., representatives from various levels within the agency such as headquarters, regional, district, or field offices or other operating offices in the immediate installations;

AND/OR

The contacts are with members of the general public, as individuals or groups, in a moderately structured setting (e.g., the contacts are generally established on a routine basis, usually at the employee's work place; the exact purpose of the contact may be unclear at first to one or more of the parties; and one or more of the parties may be uninformed concerning the role and authority of other participants). Typical of contacts at this level are those with persons seeking airline reservations or with job applicants at a job information center.

Level 6-3 — ***60 points***

The personal contacts are with individuals or groups from outside the employing agency in a moderately unstructured setting (e.g., the contacts are not established on routine basis; the purpose and extent of each contact is different and the role and authority of each party is identified and developed during the course of the contact). Typical of contacts at this level are those with persons in their capacities as attorneys; contractors; or representatives of professional organizations, the news media, or public action groups.

Level 6-4 — ***110 points***

The personal contacts are with high-ranking officials from outside the employing agency at national or international levels in highly unstructured settings (e.g., contacts are characterized by problems such as: the officials may be relatively inaccessible; arrangements may have to be made for accompanying staff members; appointments may have to be made well in advance; each party may be very unclear as to the role and authority of the other; and each contact may be conducted under different ground rules). Typical of contacts at this level are those with members of Congress, leading representatives of foreign governments, presidents of large national or international firms, nationally recognized representatives of the news media, presidents of national unions, state governors, or mayors of large cities.

FACTOR 7. PURPOSE OF CONTACTS

In General Schedule occupations, purpose of personal contacts ranges from factual exchanges of information to situations involving significant or controversial issues and differing viewpoints, goals, or objectives. The personal contacts which serve as the basis for the level selected for this factor must be the same as the contacts which are the basis for the level selected for Factor 6.

Level 7-1 — *20 points*

The purpose is to obtain, clarify, or give facts or information regardless of the nature of those facts, i.e., the facts or information may range from easily understood to highly technical.

Level 7-2 — *50 points*

The purpose is to plan, coordinate, or advise on work efforts or to resolve operating problems by influencing or motivating individuals or groups who are working toward mutual goals and who have basically cooperative attitudes.

Level 7-3 — *120 points*

The purpose is to influence, motivate, interrogate, or control persons or groups. At this level the persons contacted may be fearful, skeptical, uncooperative, or dangerous. Therefore, the employee must be skillful in approaching the individual or group in order to obtain the desired effect, such as, gaining compliance with established policies and regulations by persuasion or negotiation, or gaining information by establishing rapport with a suspicious informant.

Level 7-4 — *220 points*

The purpose is to justify, defend, negotiate, or settle matters involving significant or controversial issues. Work at this level usually involves active participation in conferences, meetings, hearings, or presentations involving problems or issues of considerable consequence or importance. The persons contacted typically have diverse viewpoints, goals, or objectives requiring the employee to achieve a common understanding of the problem and a satisfactory solution by convincing them, arriving at a compromise, or developing suitable alternatives.

FACTOR 8, PHYSICAL DEMANDS

The "Physical Demands" factor covers the requirements and physical demands placed on the employee by the work assignment. This includes physical characteristics and abilities (e.g., specific agility and dexterity requirements) and the physical exertion involved in the work (e.g., climbing, lifting, pushing, balancing, stooping, kneeling, crouching, crawling, or reaching). To some extent the frequency or intensity of physical exertion must also be considered, e.g., a job requiring prolonged standing involves more physical exertion than a job requiring intermittent standing.

NOTE: Regulations governing pay for irregular or intermittent duty involving unusual physical hardship or hazard are in Chapter 550, Federal Personnel Manual.

Level 8-1 — *5 points*

The work is sedentary. Typically, the employee may sit comfortably to do the work. However, there may be some walking; standing; bending; carrying of light items such as papers, books, small parts; driving an automobile, etc. No special physical demands are required to perform the work.

Level 8-2 — *20 points*

The work requires some physical exertion such as long periods of standing; walking over rough, uneven, or rocky surfaces; recurring bending, crouching, stooping, stretching, reaching, or similar activities; recurring lifting of moderately heavy items such as typewriters and record boxes. The work may require specific, but common, physical characteristics and abilities such as above-average agility and dexterity.

Level 8-3 — *50 points*

The work requires considerable and strenuous physical exertion such as frequent climbing of tall ladders, lifting heavy objects over 50 pounds, crouching or crawling in restricted areas, and defending oneself or others against physical attack.

FACTOR 9, WORK ENVIRONMENT

The "Work Environment" factor considers the risks and discomforts in the employee's physical surroundings or the nature of the work assigned and the safety regulations required. Although the use of safety precautions can practically eliminate a certain danger or discomfort, such situations typically place additional demands upon the employee in carrying out safety regulations and techniques.

NOTE: Regulations governing pay for irregular or intermittent duty involving unusual physical hardship or hazard are in Chapter 550, Federal Personnel Manual.

Level 9-1 — *5 points*

The work environment involves everyday risks or discomforts which require normal safety precautions typical of such places as offices, meeting and training rooms, libraries, and residences or commercial vehicles, e.g., use of safe work practices with office equipment, avoidance of trips and falls, observance of fire regulations and traffic signals, etc. The work area is adequately lighted, heated, and ventilated.

Level 9-2 — *20 points*

The work involves moderate risks or discomforts which require special safety precautions, e.g., working around moving parts, carts, or machines; with contagious diseases or irritant chemicals; etc. Employees may be required to use protective clothing or gear such as masks, gowns, coats, boots, goggles, gloves, or shields.

Level 9-3 — *50 points*

The work environment involves high risks with exposure to potentially dangerous situations or unusual environmental stress which require a range of safety and other precautions, e.g., working at great heights under extreme outdoor weather conditions, subject to possible physical attack or mob conditions, or similar situations where conditions cannot be controlled.

FACTOR EVALUATION SYSTEM

POSITION EVALUATION STATEMENT

TITLE: Office Secretary

DEPARTMENT: Olympia Electrical Supply + Service Ctr.

EVALUATION FACTORS	POINTS ASSIGNED	COMMENTS*
1. Knowledge Required by the Position	350 / 1850 (1-3)	FACTOR + SUB-FACTOR
2. Supervisory Controls	450 / 650 (2-4)	
3. Guidelines	125 / 650 (3-5)	
4. Complexity	150 / 450 (4-6)	
5. Scope and Effect	150 / 450	
6. Personal Contacts	60 / 110	
7. Purpose of Contacts	120 / 220	
8. Physical Demands	5 / 50	
9. Work Environment	5 / 50	
SUMMARY: TOTAL POINTS	1415 / 4480	

YOU DID THE BASIC PROCESS OK, BUT I THINK YOU EVALUATED THE JOB A BIT HIGH

The Three Fundamental Aspects of Jobs (As Reflected in the Guide Charts):

KNOW-HOW

This is the sum total of every kind of skill, however acquired, required for acceptable performance. It has both breadth (comprehensiveness) and depth (thoroughness). Thus, a job may require some knowledge about a lot of things, or a lot of knowledge about a few things. The total Know-How is the product of breadth times depth.

This concept makes it practical to weigh and compare the total Know-How content of different jobs in terms of "how much knowledge about how many things." Know-How specifically is comprised of:

1. Specialized and Technical Know-How: By this we mean an understanding of the technical aspects of the job assignments -- whether this be such things as mechanical engineering, actuarial science, accounting or marketing -- or the less tangibly defined Know-How derived from experience, such as sales "savvy", knowledge-in-depth about a product line, understanding of general manufacturing techniques and/or specific factory methods. Some of this "Know-How depth" can be obtained only formally (a Ph.D. in Physics), some can be obtained either by formal education or by practice (a lending officer) and some can be obtained only by experience (salesmanship). NOTE: An important concept is the "equivalency" of work experience and formal education. Many exempt assignments can be and are handled extremely well by noncollege graduates who have the fundamental intelligence and personal characteristics on which to build a sound structure of specific work experience.

2. Breadth of Managerial and Consultative Skills: The only kind of Know-How considered here is management skill, either as directly practiced (line manager), as transmitted by consulting activities (staff specialist) or both (manager of appropriate staff operation). Management has to do with the following:

    Organization
    - Structure
    - Staffing
    - Development of people
    - Appraisal and Recognition

    Policy Making and Long-Range Planning (Strategic)

    Administration
    - Planning (Tactical)
    - Execution
    - Review and Control

    Integration of Functions

Requirements for breadth of managerial skills needed in a job assignment relate closely to the size and complexity of the group or groups managed. The group leader of a few people generally has little to do in the above listed management activities. On the other hand, the manager of a large organizational unit has a very large management responsibility, and is personally involved with problems of organization, policy and review to such an extent that execution must be almost totally delegated to subordinates.

3. Human Relations

This dimension has three degrees:

- Basic - where ordinary courtesy is sufficient for position accomplishment.

- Important - handling people in situations where human repercussions are to be anticipated but are not critical considerations in the overall position content.

- Critical - where motivating others to do something is a critical requirement of the position and the position cannot function without this emphasis on the Human Relations skills.

PROBLEM SOLVING

This is the amount of original, self-starting thinking required by the job for analyzing, evaluating, creating, reasoning, arriving at and making conclusions. It has two aspects or dimensions, the Environment in which thinking takes place, and Thinking Challenge.

Problem Solving utilizes Know-How: "You think with what you know." This is true of even the most creative work. . . The raw material of anything is knowledge of facts, principles and means; ideas are put together from something already there. Therefore, problem-solving is treated as a percentage utilization of know-how, and is determined by the problem-solving environment and by the type of thinking.

To the extent that thinking is circumscribed by standards, covered by precedents or referred to others, the requirement for problem solving is diminished, and the emphasis of the assignment correspondingly is on Know-How.

ACCOUNTABILITY

This is the measured effect of the job on end results. It has three interrelated dimensions:

The Freedom to Act

The job's Impact on end results

The Magnitude of the end result which the job most clearly affects.

Freedom to Act is measured by the existence or absence of personal or procedural control and guidance (supervision or direction). The degrees of freedom in increasing order of importance are defined in the left-hand vertical Guide Chart column. Limitations on Freedom to Act are largely organizational and can differ between seemingly equivalent jobs in different departments. As with Problem Solving Environment, Freedom to Act here is circumscribed by (1) the boss-subordinate relationships, (2) Company, departmental or functional group policies and (3) budgets. Authority to act, to approve, to make decisions lies at the heart of this concept. Freedom to Act also expresses the accountability built into the job. The controls over action may be supervisory or procedural or both.

The second dimension of Accountability, Impact of jobs on end results, is measured in four degrees of increasing effect. They are:

Remote: Informational, recording, or incidental services for use by others in relation to some important end results--when a task is performed as a task with little recognition of the use to which it will be put.

Contributory: Interpretive, advisory, or facilitating services for use by others in taking action. This category applies to instances where decisions are made and action is taken by others as a result of information, data or counsel provided by the incumbent.

Shared: Participating with others (except own subordinates and superiors), within or outside the organizational unit, in taking action. Here results accrue on the basis of joint actions.

Primary: Controlling impact on end results, where shared accountability of others is subordinate--i.e., the results produced are directed and controlled by a single individual.

The third and final dimension, Magnitude, relates to the portion of the total organization most affected by the job. It is usually expressed in terms of dollars (e.g. size of budget controlled by job).

(AMI Equivalent - Accountability Magnitude Index - To maintain real-dollar consistency in the magnitude dimension of the Accountability factor, the AMI recognizes changes in economic conditions -- basically a recognition of inflation or possibly deflation. This index would vary for each organization with the primary variation being the year the plan was initially implemented within the organization.)

EVALUATING KNOW-HOW

I. Technical Depth Levels: Levels A through D are considered trained skills levels, E, F, G, and H slots represent the specialized, technical and professional skills constituting the functional knowledge which is a basic qualification for management jobs. In other words, the first four categories relate to knowledge of "what" and "how" something is done, whereas E through H level jobs, in addition to the "what" and "how", require knowing which techniques are appropriate to a situation and why.

A. Primary: Elementary plus some secondary (or equivalent) education; plus work indoctrination.

Jobs falling into this slot are extremely simple in nature, and can be learned within a matter of several days. Little formal education is required.

B. Elementary Vocational: Familiarization in uninvolved, standardized work routines and/or use of simple equipment and machines.

Covered by this slot are jobs with highly repetitive and basically simple assignments, often requiring operating knowledge of such equipment like Typewriters, Duplicating Machines, Adding Machines, and Keypunch Machines.

C. Vocational: Procedural or systematic proficiency, which may involve a facility in the use of specialized equipment.

The type of proficiency referred to includes among others, shorthand, and bookkeeping. By specialized equipment we mean tabulating machines and related peripheral data processing as well as offset duplicating machines.

D. Advanced Vocational: Some specialized (generally nontechnical) skills, however acquired, giving additional breadth or depth to a generally single functional element.

The specialized skills referred to may be in the fields of advanced bookkeeping, computer operations, design drafting. It also covers supervision over these and lesser skill levels.

E. Basic Technical-Specialized: Sufficiency in a technique which requires a grasp either of involved practices and precedents; or of scientific theory and principles; or both.

This slot is generally represented by basic college education or advanced vocational skills strengthened by years of on-the-job experience.

F. Seasoned Technical Specialized: Proficiency, gained through wide exposure of experiences in a specialized or technical field, in a technique which combines a broad grasp either of involved practices and precedents; or of scientific theory and principles; or both.

This slot encompasses jobs requiring basic college education supplemented by substantial, very pertinent work experience in a field of expertise. Conversely, it may also include jobs necessitating advanced degrees where formal knowledge permits almost immediate performance competent in an F Level position.

G. Technical Specialized Mastery: Determinative mastery of techniques, practices and theories gained through wide seasoning and/or special development.

This category covers jobs requiring expertise supplemented by additional depth to the point of being an authoritative source of knowledge within a company. It also represents positions which call for expertise in several or more specialized fields.

H. Professional Mastery: Exceptional and unique mastery in scientific or other learned disciplines.

This level is intended for a recognized scientific or learned discipline of such technical depth as to merit recognition of authority beyond the confines of a company.

2. Managerial Breadth Categories: There is a strong tendency to overslot here, particularly with respect to the use of II and III. We make a clear distinction between management and supervision. Managing involves planning, integration and coordination of activities, whereas supervising is only the accomplishment of assigned tasks by individuals. Below are more specific explanations of the individual slot definitions. It is important to note that the size of a company very much influences the number of managerial breadth categories found on a Guide Chart. The diagram on the facing page illustrates the concept of managerial breadth.

I. Minimal

Covered by this category are all nonmanagerial positions, i.e. both individual performers and supervisors.

II. Related

Included here are single function department managers. Actual supervision of various activities is largely delegated. Typical managerial responsibilities include the integration of supportive activities, hiring and firing of personnel, and external coordination with other managers in planning and executing for end results.

III. Diverse

This category covers multi-functional managers. By multifunctional we mean at least two functional areas of an important nature and size.

IV. Broad

This slot pertains to positions who integrate all of the major functions of an operating complex (normally have profit and loss accountability for such operations) or coordinate a major function across several operating complexes.

3. Human Relation Skills: This third aspect of Know-How is measured, along with Managerial Know-How, on the Guide Chart's horizontal axis. Below the meaning of the three HR skills is explained briefly. It is important that an HR judgment is not made on the basis of the three HR Titles (Basic, Important, Critical) but rather on the basis of their definitions.

Facing this page is a chart illustrating the concepts of technical/specialized expertise in conjunction with managerial breadth or scope.

1. Basic

   Here the human relations skill is entirely subordinate to technical or procedural skills. Jobs included are those of an individual nature, where there is no need to influence others in carrying out assignments. Most nonexempt jobs fall into this category.

2. Important

   Again, the HR skills are subordinate to the success of an assignment. However, normal courtesy and effectiveness with people is just not enough to carry the job. #2 HR skills involve interplay with subordinates and superiors of a more critical nature. This slot is awarded to positions that have to do some coordinating outside the incumbent's unit or company organization.

3. Critical

   In this HR skill level, the position requires an ability to motivate, convince or sell people to successfully attain end results. The majority of supervisory and management positions fall into this slot.

EVALUATING PROBLEM SOLVING

I. Thinking Environment Levels are circumscribed by: company, departmental or functional policies, practices, procedures, and instructions. In general, policies describe the "what" of a subject matter, procedures detail the steps necessary to follow through on a policy (how, where, by whom), and instructions outline the specific hows, such as the operation of a machine, or the typing of a letter. We strongly caution against the mechanical application of organization echelons to determine levels, which mostly results in heavy evaluation concentrations of either routine thinkers or geniuses.

A. Strict Routine: Simple rules and detailed instructions. Rules are very basic and instructions quite specific (mostly oral orders). Ex: "File only red copies;" dispatch mail on hand at 3 and 7 P. M.; mail according to class and weight rate schedule; sweep hallway and return for further work assignments.

B. Routine: Established routines and standing instructions. This slot covers a number of the positions in the clerical hierarchy. Thinking restrictions are less severe than in Slot A; positions carry out specific assignments until instructed to do otherwise.

C. Semi-routine: Somewhat diversified procedures and precedents. There is a definite crossover between B and C. Now the thinking environment has the somewhat less limiting aspects of procedures, rather than instructions. Approximately half of the clerical and nonexempt jobs are covered by this slot.

D. Standardized: Substantially diversified procedures and specialized standards. Positions are instructed what to do both by supervisors and by diversified, yet explicit, well established procedures. There is some leeway as to how an assignment can be carried out to assure timely completion ofa project.

E. Clearly Defined: Clearly defined policies and principles. This is a definite crossover from the preceding slot. Policies, even though clearly defined, are now the limiting factor; i.e., the "what" is distinctly stated. The "how" is largely determined by the incumbent's own judgment. By principles we mean principles of disciplines such as engineering, law, accounting, and lending.

F. Broadly Defined: Broad policies and specific objectives. The determination of the "what to do" in achieving objectives is largely left up to the incumbent. However, the objectives themselves would tend to be stated specifically.

G. Generally Defined: General policies and ultimate goals. This slot covers positions in which the "what" is specified in only very general terms, such as "steady increase in sales." The specific objectives must be determined for achieving goals.

H. Abstractly Defined: General laws of nature or science, business philosophy and cultural standards. Positions at this level ponder about the nature, size and growth rate of the business.

2. Thinking Challenge: On the horizontal axis of the PS Guide Chart we measure the complexity inherent in the problems of a job assignment. Whereas slots I and 2 cover nearly all nonexempt jobs, 3 and 4 encompass the majority of exempt positions.

   1. Repetitive

      This type of thinking challenge involves the recall of specific learned things in simple, stable and repetitive situations. An example might be a person sorting out black and white balls.

   2. Patterned

      Here we are confronted with a mix and match situation. The majority of nonexempt jobs are covered by this slot.

   3. Interpolative

      Interpolative implies being confronted with a number of different questions, each having several different answers to it. It is in other words, a pick and choose situation. Decisions can still be made rather rapidly.

   4. Adaptive

      Adaptive means innovative imitation requiring constructive thinking where the response often involves study or contemplation.

   5. Uncharted

      This applies to truly creative thinking about something never done before.

EVALUATING ACCOUNTABILITY (continued)

I. Freedom to Act: This is quantitatively the most important aspect of Accountability. In most companies more organizational echelons exist than there are Freedom to Act Levels. Beware of mechanical slotting according to organization levels. The controls over actions may be supervisory or procedural or both. Therefore, each slot states both procedural and supervisory controls. Such controls do not necessarily have to be present in combination, as indicated by the definition clauses of "the job is subject wholly or in part" to....

A. Prescribed: These jobs are subject to Direct and detailed instructions and close supervision.

Done exactly as told; no variations permitted unless specifically authorized. Supervision on a continuing or hour-to-hour basis.

B. Controlled: These jobs are subject to Instructions and established work routines and close supervision.

Work routines permit some rearrangement of work sequence, and supervision is somewhat less stringent.

C. Standarized: These jobs are subject, wholly or in part to Standardized practices and procedures, general work instructions, and supervision of progress and results.

Practices and procedures permit variations in work routine; supervision in periodic.

D. Generally Regulated: These jobs are subject, wholly or in part to practices and procedures covered by precedents or well-defined policy, supervisory review (after the fact).

Some latitude in modifying practices and procedures to accomplish assignment. Review may be at the end of a day or a week. Assignments specify the "what" and "by when."

E. Directed: These jobs are subject to broad practices and procedures covered by functional precedents and policies, achievement of a circumscribed operational activity, managerial direction.

Free to decide how to achieve the predetermined end results. Check on results on a monthly basis.

F. Oriented Direction: These jobs are broadly subject to functional policies and goals and general managerial direction.

Free to determine the general results. It is up to the incumbent to draw on available resources to accomplish end results. (Review: 6 months-12 months)

G. Broad Guidance: These jobs are inherently subject only to broad policy and general management guidance.

Determines the "what" or end results to be accomplished. (Review: End of year).

H. Strategic Guidance: These jobs be reason of their size, independent complexity and high degree of effect on company results, are subject only to general guidance from top-most management.

Determines overall goals.

I. Generally Unguided: Determines overall direction of business.

2. Impact of Job on End Results and Magnitude: These two aspects must be considered together, as our earlier water-ripple example demonstrates. Catching the impact where it is most appropriate for individual positions is the important part.

The four Impact definitions are quite self explanatory and need little further explanation. We consider Remote and Contributory as indirect and Shared and Primary as direct Impacts.

Remote impact applies mostly to nonexempt clerical positions whose activities have no measurable impact on certain end results.

Contributory impact is seen in most staff positions, who may analyze or advise on a subject matter, but leave the decision-making to those they advise.

Shared-A basic rule of this impact is that accountability cannot be shared with subordinates or superiors, but only with equals. Typical examples include bank loan committees or the shared accountability between Engineering and Manufacturing for a successful product.

Primary impact fits most line management positions. Examples are a Foreman's accountabilities for his unit's value added, and a Sales Manager's accountability for his department's sales.

Magnitude: The dollar magnitudes on the Accountability Guide Charts are very broad and are basically used to simply indicate a position's influence over a small, medium or large part of company dollars. It is quite important to note that regardless of the Magnitude and Impact selected for a certain position, the Freedom to Act judgment is not influenced by it.

A question arises as to what kind of dollars we are talking about. We are talking about either dynamic dollars that reflect the position's overall impact such as goals (market quotas for example) or stewardship (operating budgets for examples) or static dollars which in some institutions such as banks, most clearly reflect the nature of the position's financial impact. It is important to note that preferably dynamic dollars should be used. In general then we consider those dollars entrusted to or affected by the positions under examination. Typical examples may include a Purchasing Agent's impact on purchasing dollars, a Peronnel Manager's impact on payroll dollars, and a Salesman's impact on his sales dollars. Definitely not to be used are profit dollars. They are performance considerations dealt with in a manner beyond the scope of this seminar. In determining magnitude. Accountability dollar values should be added only if the incumbent has the same impact on them. Duplication of dollar values such as adding production and sales dollars must be avoided since the latter already includes manufacturing dollars.

Hay
Management
Consultants

DEFINITION: Know-How is the sum total of every kind of skill, however acquired, needed for acceptable job performance. This sum total which comprises the overall fund of knowledge has three dimensions, the requirements for:

- • Depth and breadth of knowledge, ranging from basic knowledge of the most simple work routines, to unique and authoritative knowledge within learned disciplines.
- •• Know-How of integrating and harmonizing the diversified functions involved in managerial situations (operating, supporting and administrative). This Know-How may be exercised consultatively as well as executively and involves in some combination the areas of organizing, planning, executing, controlling and evaluating.
- ••• Active, practicing skills in the area of human relationships.

MARCH 1988

KNOW-HOW

GUIDE CHART

MEASURING KNOW-HOW: Know-How has both scope (variety) and depth (thoroughness). Thus, a job may require some knowledge about a lot of things, or a lot of knowledge about a few things. The total Know-How is the combination of scope and depth. This concept makes practical the comparison and weighing of the total Know-How content of different jobs in terms of: "HOW MUCH KNOWLEDGE ABOUT HOW MANY THINGS."

• LEARNED DISCIPLINES / PRACTICAL PROCEDURES / SPECIALIZED TECHNIQUES	T. Performance of a task or tasks highly specific as to objective and content with limited awareness of surrounding circumstances and events.			•• MANAGERIAL KNOW-HOW: I. Performance or supervision of an activity or activities specific as to objective and content, with appropriate awareness of related activities.			II. Operational or conceptual integration or coordination of activities which are relatively homogeneous in nature and objective.			III. Operational or conceptual integration of activities which are diverse in nature and objectives.			IV. Integration of all major functions in the nation.			
••• Human Relations Skills →	1	2	3	1	2	3	1	2	3	1	2	3	1	2	3	
L. LIMITED Basic instructions and simple work routines to carry out manual tasks.	29	33	38	38	43	50	50	57	66	66	76	87	87	100	115	
	33	38	43	43	50	57	57	66	76	76	87	100	100	115	132	L.
	38	43	50	50	57	66	66	76	87	87	100	115	115	132	152	
A. PRIMARY Basic literacy and/or ciphering skills plus work indoctrination for performance of repetitive operational or clerical routines which may involve use of common tools and standard single purpose machines.	38	43	50	50	57	66	66	76	87	87	100	115	115	132	152	
	43	50	57	57	66	76	76	87	100	100	115	132	132	152	175	A.
	50	57	66	66	76	87	87	100	115	115	132	152	152	175	200	
B. ELEMENTARY VOCATIONAL Familiarization with uninvolved, standardized work routines, and/or use of equipment and machines.	50	57	66	66	76	87	87	100	115	115	132	152	152	175	200	
	57	66	76	76	87	100	100	115	132	132	152	175	175	200	230	B.
	66	76	87	87	100	115	115	132	152	152	175	200	200	230	264	
C. VOCATIONAL Procedural or systematic proficiency, which may involve a facility in the use of specialized equipment.	66	76	87	87	100	115	115	132	152	152	175	200	200	230	264	
	76	87	100	100	115	132	132	152	175	175	200	230	230	264	304	C.
	87	100	115	115	132	152	152	175	200	200	230	264	264	304	350	
D. ADVANCED VOCATIONAL Some specialized (generally non-theoretical) skill(s), acquired on or off the job, giving additional breadth or depth to a generally single function.	87	100	115	115	132	152	152	175	200	200	230	264	264	304	350	
	100	115	132	132	152	175	175	200	230	230	264	304	304	350	400	D.
	115	132	152	152	175	200	200	230	264	264	304	350	350	400	460	
E. BASIC SPECIALIZED Sufficiency in a technique which requires a grasp either of involved practices and precedents, or of scientific theory and principles, or both.	115	132	152	152	175	200	200	230	264	264	304	350	350	400	460	
	132	152	175	175	200	230	230	264	304	304	350	400	400	460	528	E.
	152	175	200	200	230	264	264	304	350	350	400	460	460	528	608	
F. SEASONED SPECIALIZED Proficiency, gained through wide exposure, in a technique which combines a broad understanding either of involved practices and precedents, or of scientific theory and principles, or both.	152	175	200	200	230	264	264	304	350	350	400	460	460	528	608	
	175	200	230	230	264	304	304	350	400	400	460	528	528	608	700	F.
	200	230	264	264	304	350	350	400	460	460	528	608	608	700	800	
G. SPECIALIZED MASTERY Determinative mastery of techniques, practices and theories gained through wide seasoning and/or special development.	200	230	264	264	304	350	350	400	460	460	528	608	608	700	800	
	230	264	304	304	350	400	400	460	528	528	608	700	700	800	920	G.
	264	304	350	350	400	460	460	528	608	608	700	800	800	920	1056	

••• HUMAN RELATIONS SKILLS		
1. **BASIC:** Courtesy, tact and effectiveness in dealing with others in every day working relationships, including contacts to request or provide information.	2. **IMPORTANT:** Alternative or combined skills in understanding and/or influencing people are important in achieving job objectives, causing action or understanding in others.	3. **CRITICAL:** Alternative or combined skills in understanding, selecting, developing and motivating people are important in the highest degree.

Hay
Management
Consultants

MARCH 1988

PROBLEM SOLVING

GUIDE CHART

DEFINITION: Problem Solving is the original "self-starting" thinking required by the job for analyzing, evaluating, creating, reasoning, arriving at and making conclusions. To the extent that thinking is circumscribed by standards, covered by precedents, or referred to others, Problem Solving is diminished and the emphasis correspondingly is on Know-How.

Problem Solving has two dimensions:

- • The environment in which the thinking takes place.
- • • The challenge presented by the thinking to be done.

MEASURING PROBLEM SOLVING: Problem Solving measures the intensity of the mental process which employs Know-How to: (1) identify, (2) define, and (3) resolve a problem. "You think with what you know." This is true of even the most creative work . . . The raw material of any thinking is knowledge of facts, principles, and means; ideas are put together from something already there. Therefore, Problem Solving is treated as a percentage utilization of Know-How.

• THINKING ENVIRONMENT — Thinking guided or circumscribed by:	• • THINKING CHALLENGE: 1. REPETITIVE — Identical situations requiring solution by simple choice of learned things.	2. PATTERNED — Similar situations requiring solution by discriminating choice of learned things which generally follow a well defined pattern.	3. INTERPOLATIVE — Differing situations requiring a search for solutions or new applications within area of learned things.	4. ADAPTIVE — Variable situations requiring analytical, interpretive, evaluative, and/or constructive thinking.	
A. STRICT ROUTINE Simple rules and detailed instructions.	10% / 12%	14% / 16%	19% / 22%	25% / 29%	A.
B. ROUTINE Established routines and standing instructions.	12% / 14%	16% / 19%	22% / 25%	29% / 33%	B.
C. SEMI-ROUTINE Somewhat diversified procedures and precedents.	14% / 16%	19% / 22%	25% / 29%	33% / 38%	C.
D. STANDARDIZED Substantially diversified procedures and specialized standards.	16% / 19%	22% / 25%	29% / 33%	38% / 43%	D.
E. CLEARLY DEFINED Clearly defined policies and principles.	19% / 22%	25% / 29%	33% / 38%	43% / 50%	E.
F. BROADLY DEFINED Broad policies and specific objectives.	22% / 25%	29% / 33%	38% / 43%	50% / 57%	F.
G. GENERALLY DEFINED General policies and ultimate goals.	25% / 29%	33% / 38%	43% / 50%	57% / 66%	G.

■ITION: Accountability is the answerability for an action and for the consequences thereof. It is the measured effect of the job on end results. It has three dimensions in the following order of importance:

- • **Freedom to Act** — the degree of personal or procedural control and guidance as defined in the left-hand column below.
- •• **Job Impact on End Results** — as defined at upper right.
- ••• **Magnitude** — Magnitude measurement gauges how much of the organization is affected by the jobholder's accomplishment of the job's primary purpose. It may be indicated in quantitative terms such as annualized dollars, or by other descriptions such as large, medium, small, or minimal.

MARCH 1988

ACCOUNTABILITY

GUIDE CHART

JOB IMPACT

A. Indirect support services which do not have a clearly measurable effect on work flow or persons served.	A. **ANCILLARY:** Informational, recording, or incidental services for use by others in relation to some important end result.
C. Direct support services or production tasks for use or completion by others.	C. **CONTRIBUTORY:** Interpretive, advisory, or facilitating services for use by others in taking action.
S. Nonstandard services or production tasks which noticeably affect the work results.	S. **SHARED:** Participating with others (except own subordinates and superiors), within or outside the organizational unit, in taking action.
P. Leadership role in services provided or production tasks performed.	P. **PRIMARY:** Controlling impact on end results, where shared accountability of others is secondary.

AMI for use with 1987 dollars is 3.30.

• FREEDOM TO ACT / ••• MAGNITUDE →	(0) Under $10M Minimal				(1) $10M - $100M Very Small				(2) $100M - $1MM Small				(3) $1MM - $10MM Medium				(4) $10MM - $100MM Medium Large				
AMI EQUIVALENT →																					
•• IMPACT →	A	C	S	P	A	C	S	P	A	C	S	P	A	C	S	P	A	C	S	P	
L. LIMITED These jobs are subject to: Explicit instructions covering simple tasks.	5	7	9	12	7	9	12	16	9	12	16	22	12	16	22	29	16	22	29	38	
	6	8	10	14	8	10	14	19	10	14	19	25	14	19	25	33	19	25	33	43	L.
	7	9	12	16	9	12	16	22	12	16	22	29	16	22	29	38	22	29	38	50	
A. PRESCRIBED These jobs are subject to: Prescribed instructions covering assigned tasks and/or immediate supervision.	8	10	14	19	10	14	19	25	14	19	25	33	19	25	33	43	25	33	43	57	
	9	12	16	22	12	16	22	29	16	22	29	38	22	29	38	50	29	38	50	66	A.
	10	14	19	25	14	19	25	33	19	25	33	43	25	33	43	57	33	43	57	76	
B. CONTROLLED These jobs are subject to: Instructions and established work routines and/or close supervision.	12	16	22	29	16	22	29	38	22	29	38	50	29	38	50	66	38	50	66	87	
	14	19	25	33	19	25	33	43	25	33	43	57	33	43	57	76	43	57	76	100	B.
	16	22	29	38	22	29	38	50	29	38	50	66	38	50	66	87	50	66	87	115	
C. STANDARDIZED These jobs are subject, wholly or in part, to: Standardized practices and procedures and/or general work instructions and/or supervision of progress and results.	19	25	33	43	25	33	43	57	33	43	57	76	43	57	76	100	57	76	100	132	
	22	29	38	50	29	38	50	66	38	50	66	87	50	66	87	115	66	87	115	152	C.
	25	33	43	57	33	43	57	76	43	57	76	100	57	76	100	132	76	100	132	175	
D. GENERALLY REGULATED These jobs are subject, wholly or in part, to: Practices and procedures covered by precedents or well-defined policy and/or supervisory review.	29	38	50	66	38	50	66	87	50	66	87	115	66	87	115	152	87	115	152	200	
	33	43	57	76	43	57	76	100	57	76	100	132	76	100	132	175	100	132	175	230	D.
	38	50	66	87	50	66	87	115	66	87	115	152	87	115	152	200	115	152	200	264	
E. DIRECTED These jobs, by their nature or size, are subject to: Broad practice and procedures covered by functional precedents and policies and/or achievement of a circumscribed operational activity, and/or managerial direction.	43	57	76	100	57	76	100	132	76	100	132	175	100	132	175	230	132	175	230	304	
	50	66	87	115	66	87	115	152	87	115	152	200	115	152	200	264	152	200	264	350	E.
	57	76	100	132	76	100	132	175	100	132	175	230	132	175	230	304	175	230	304	400	
F. ORIENTED DIRECTION These jobs, by their nature or size, are broadly subject to: Functional policies and goals and/or general managerial direction.	66	87	115	152	87	115	152	200	115	152	200	264	152	200	264	350	200	264	350	460	
	76	100	132	175	100	132	175	230	132	175	230	304	175	230	304	400	230	304	400	528	F.
	87	115	152	200	115	152	200	264	152	200	264	350	200	264	350	460	264	350	460	608	
G. GUIDED These jobs are inherently subject only to broad policy and general management guidance.	100	132	175	230	132	175	230	304	175	230	304	400	230	304	400	528	304	400	528	700	
	115	152	200	264	152	200	264	350	200	264	350	460	264	350	460	608	350	460	608	800	G.
	132	175	230	304	175	230	304	400	230	304	400	528	304	400	528	700	400	528	700	920	

AIDS IN USING THE GUIDE CHARTS

In assessing KH levels for positions in the same structure, as a "rule of thumb," a:

One-step KH difference would be a normal promotion

Two-step KH difference would be a healthy promotion

Three-step KH difference would be a gigantic, if not unlikely, promotion and a job level may or may not be missing in the structure

Four-step KH difference would be a virtually impossible promotion and a job level is no doubt missing in the structure

---

The Most Typical KH/PS Relationships for Exempt Positions

KH Points	Problem Solving %							
152	25	29	33					
175		29	33	38				
200		29	33	38				
230			33	38	43			
264			33	38	43			
304				38	43	50		
350				38	43	50		
400					43	50	57	
460					43	50	57	
528						50	57	66
608						50	57	66
700						50	57	66
	C3	C3	D3	D4	D4	E4	F4	F5
	D2	D3	E3	E3	E4	F4	G4	G4

In balancing PS and AC points, consider the type job being evaluated.

AC + 3	Clearly a line job
AC + 2	About half line and staff
AC + 1	Staff job with a little "umph" in the "do"
PS = AC	Level staff position
AC - 1	Staff job with a little "umph" in the "think"
AC - 2	Job in which the "think" far outweighs the "do"
AC - 3	Almost pure research

In evaluating positions of F level or below in Freedom to Act (AC), generally:

PS letter should be the same or one less than KH letter

AC letter should be the same or one less than PS letter

Evaluations

	Know-How	Problem Solving	Accountability	Total Points	Profile
1.	GIV3 800	G4 (57%) 460	G4S 608	1868	2 Up
2.	GI2 350	E5 (57%) 200	D4C 132	682	3 Down
3.	GII3 608	G4 (66%) 400	G4C 400	1408	level

To determine the percentage profile of an evaluation, we need to know the Problem Solving percentage and the Up, Down or Level characteristic of this evaluation. Evaluation example I above has 57% PS and is 2 Up. Referring to our table on the **next page**, we look for the intersect point of 57% and 2 Up and arrive at a percentage profile of: 43-25-32, -Example 2 has 57% PS and is 3 Down. The intersect point on our table tells us that this evaluation has a 51-30-19 percentage profile. - Our third example, which is level and has 66% PS, indicates a percentage profile of 44-28-28.

Finally, we come to the meaning of Up, Level and Down profiles:

Up profiles: Generally up profiles describe action oriented jobs, as performed by line supervisors or managers. The real emphasis is on achieving certain end results, with Problem Solving taking a secondary position. Most all top management line jobs tend to have three and four up profiles. Such profiles are also common for foreman and supervisory positions in the production area, and salesmen. Two Up profiles on the other hand are found among supervisors' or managerial jobs with responsibility for service functions.

Level profiles: Jobs considered as having level profiles include those with equal AC and PS points. Jobs with I Up or I Down profiles can also be considered as level in terms of job concept. Typical examples are most all staff oriented positions, and managers or supervisors of problem solving oriented functions.

Down profiles: Two, three and four down profiles are considered in this category. The emphasis here is on problem solving, accountability being of secondary importance. Individual, i.e. none managerial or none supervisory positions engaged in research or engineering are known to be of a typical down profile nature. Four Down profiles go with real deep thinking jobs, such as scientists or personnel engaged in basic research. Hardly any supervisory or managerial positions have Down profiles. An exception could be a research supervisor of a very small departmental unit.

STEP VALUES	STEPS BELOW 100%
7360	
6400	
5600	
4864	
4224	
3680	
3200	
2800	
2432	
2112	
1840	
1600	
1400	
1216	
1056	
920	
800	
700	
608	
528	
460	
400	
350	
304	
264	
230	
200	
175	
152	
132	
115	
100	
87	1
76	2
66	3
57	4
50	5
43	6
38	7
33	8
29	9
25	10
22	11
19	12
16	13
14	14
12	15
10	16
9	17
8	18

TO FIND PROBLEM SOLVING POINTS: IN COLUMN BELOW THAT CORRESPONDS TO KH POINTS, READ PS POINTS OPPOSITE % PS/KH

% PS/KH	KH Pts. 29	33	38	43	50	57	66	76	87	100	115	132	152	175	200	230	264	304	350	400	460	528	608	700	800	920	1056	1216	1400
87%	25	29	33	38	43	50	57	66	76	87	100	115	132	152	175	200	230	264	304	350	400	460	528	608	700	800	920	1056	1216
76%	22	25	29	33	38	43	50	57	66	76	87	100	115	132	152	175	200	230	264	304	350	400	460	528	608	700	800	920	1056
66%	19	22	25	29	33	38	43	50	57	66	76	87	100	115	132	152	175	200	230	264	304	350	400	460	528	608	700	800	920
57%	16	19	22	25	29	33	38	43	50	57	66	76	87	100	115	132	152	175	200	230	264	304	350	400	460	528	608	700	800
50%	14	16	19	22	25	29	33	38	43	50	57	66	76	87	100	115	132	152	175	200	230	264	304	350	400	460	528	608	700
43%	12	14	16	19	22	25	29	33	38	43	50	57	66	76	87	100	115	132	152	175	200	230	264	304	350	400	460	528	608
38%	10	12	14	16	19	22	25	29	33	38	43	50	57	66	76	87	100	115	132	152	175	200	230	264	304	350	400	460	528
33%	9	10	12	14	16	19	22	25	29	33	38	43	50	57	66	76	87	100	115	132	152	175	200	230	264	304	350	400	460
29%	8	9	10	12	14	16	19	22	25	29	33	38	43	50	57	66	76	87	100	115	132	152	175	200	230	264	304	350	400
25%	7	8	9	10	12	14	16	19	22	25	29	33	38	43	50	57	66	76	87	100	115	132	152	175	200	230	264	304	350
22%	6	7	8	9	10	12	14	16	19	22	25	29	33	38	43	50	57	66	76	87	100	115	132	152	175	200	230	264	304
19%	5	6	7	8	9	10	12	14	16	19	22	25	29	33	38	43	50	57	66	76	87	100	115	132	152	175	200	230	264
16%	5	5	6	7	8	9	10	12	14	16	19	22	25	29	33	38	43	50	57	66	76	87	100	115	132	152	175	200	230
14%	4	4	5	6	7	8	9	10	12	14	16	19	22	25	29	33	38	43	50	57	66	76	87	100	115	132	152	175	200
12%	3	4	5	5	6	7	8	9	10	12	14	16	19	22	25	29	33	38	43	50	57	66	76	87	100	115	132	152	175
10%	3	3	4	4	5	6	7	8	9	10	12	14	16	19	22	25	29	33	38	43	50	57	66	76	87	100	115	132	152

CHARACTERISTIC HAY PROFILES (Percentage of KH-PS-AC)

TO FIND PROFILE, IN COLUMN BELOW THAT CORRESPONDS TO STEP DIFFERENCE BETWEEN AC & PS POINTS, READ PROFILE OPPOSITE % PS/KH

% PS/KH	ACCOUNTABILITY HIGHER THAN PROBLEM SOLVING				AC = PS	ACCOUNTABILITY LOWER THAN PROBLEM SOLVING			
	4 UP	3 UP	2 UP	1 UP	LEVEL	1 DOWN	2 DOWN	3 DOWN	4 DOWN
87%	29 26 45	32 27 41	33 29 38	35 30 35	36 32 32	38 33 29	40 34 26	41 36 23	42 37 21
76%	32 25 43	34 26 40	36 28 36	38 29 33	40 30 30	42 31 27	43 32 25	44 34 22	45 35 20
66%	36 23 41	38 24 38	40 26 34	42 27 31	44 28 28	45 29 26	46 31 23	47 32 21	49 32 19
57%	39 22 39	41 23 36	43 25 32	45 26 29	46 27 27	48 28 24	49 29 22	51 30 19	53 30 17
50%	42 21 37	44 22 34	46 23 31	48 24 28	50 25 25	52 26 22	53 27 20	55 27 18	56 28 16
43%	45 20 35	47 21 32	49 22 29	52 22 26	54 23 23	55 24 21	56 25 19	58 25 17	59 26 15
38%	49 19 32	51 19 30	53 20 27	55 21 24	56 22 22	59 22 19	60 23 17	62 23 15	62 24 14
33%	53 17 30	55 18 27	56 19 25	59 19 22	60 20 20	62 20 18	63 21 16	65 21 14	66 22 12
29%	56 16 28	58 17 25	60 17 23	62 18 20	64 18 18	65 19 16	66 19 15	68 19 13	69 20 11
25%	59 15 26	62 15 23	63 16 21	65 16 19	66 17 17	68 17 15	70 17 13	70 18 12	72 18 10
22%	62 14 24	65 14 21	66 15 19	68 15 17	70 15 15	72 15 13	72 16 12	74 16 10	75 16 9
19%	66 12 22	68 13 19	70 13 17	72 13 15	72 14 14	74 14 12	75 14 11	76 15 9	77 15 8
16%	69 11 20	70 12 18	72 12 16	74 12 14	76 12 12	76 13 11	77 13 10	79 13 8	80 13 7
14%	72 10 18	74 10 16	76 10 14	76 11 13	78 11 11	79 11 10	80 11 9	81 12 7	82 12 6
12%	75 9 16	76 9 15	77 10 13	79 10 11	80 10 10	81 10 9	82 10 8	83 11 6	84 11 5
10%	77 8 15	79 8 13	80 9 11	81 9 10	82 9 9	83 9 8	84 9 7	85 10 5	86 9 5

PROFILES CHECK EVALUATION JUDGEMENT

POINTS — **PERCENTAGES**

KH	PS	AC	TOTAL
B11 76	B2(16) 12	BOC 16	104
DATA ENTRY OPERATOR A			

KH 72, PS 12, AC 16

KH	PS	AC
72	12	16

72–12–16

=100%

KH	PS	AC	TOTAL
E12 230	D4(38) 87	D2C 76	393
SYSTEMS ANALYST			

KH 59, PS 22, AC 19

59–22–19

=100%

KH	PS	AC	TOTAL
E13 264	E3(38) 100	D2P 132	496
MANAGER, COMPUTER OPERATIONS			

KH 53, PS 20, AC 27

53–20–27

= 100%

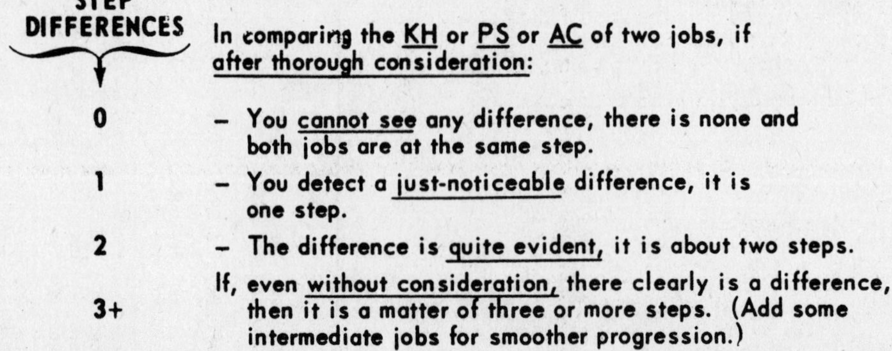

STEP DIFFERENCES

In comparing the KH or PS or AC of two jobs, if after thorough consideration:

0 – You cannot see any difference, there is none and both jobs are at the same step.

1 – You detect a just-noticeable difference, it is one step.

2 – The difference is quite evident, it is about two steps.

3+ If, even without consideration, there clearly is a difference, then it is a matter of three or more steps. (Add some intermediate jobs for smoother progression.)

HAY

POSITION EVALUATION STATEMENT

TITLE: ____________________

DEPARTMENT: ____________________

EVALUATION FACTORS	LEVEL	POINTS ASSIGNED	COMMENTS
1. KNOW HOW: Training Skills Managerial Know How Human Relations Skill			
2. PROBLEM SOLVING: Thinking Environment Thinking Challenge			
3. ACCOUNTABILITY: Freedom to Act Magnitude Impact			
4. WORKING CONDITIONS: Physical Effort Environments Risk of Accident			

SUMMARY		
	TOTAL POINTS	

Nancy Horn's Job Specifications: HAY

KNOW-HOW:

The employee must have knowledge of correct grammar, spelling, and word usage for composing, editing, and typing activities; knowledge of clerical activities to assist in filing, completing forms, and teaching new clerks to perform their job assignments; knowledge of basic bookkeeping to maintain various records and skill in operating a typewriter to type records and correspondence.

PROBLEM-SOLVING:

In carrying out assigned duties, the employee follows Olympia procedures and general business practices. The job is fairly routine, and the options are limited.

ACCOUNTABILITY:

The employee operates independently in performing well-defined activities. The same basic procedures are followed in accomplishing assignments, but employees must use some judgment in responding to customer problems and, to some degree, in directing the efforts of clerks.

The employee's work is reviewed by the manager as the work comes to the manager's attention. The situation or job activities outline what needs to be done.

The employee assigns work to clerks, answers clerks' questions, and trains clerks. The employee is responsible for assisting other employees in performing their assignments properly.

The impact of the job is on the receipt of payment for services rendered, customer relations, clerk effectiveness, and administrative procedures.

MODULE 8

DETERMINING WHETHER TO MAKE OR BUY A SURVEY

In the past, Olympia participated in a regional survey that provided useful data on market practices for a large number of service-related jobs including clerks and secretaries; professionals in accounting, finance, and data processing; and managerial positions. The organization that sponsored the survey was acquired by a foreign company and the compensation professional who directed the survey was transferred to the West Coast. At this time, no one has been willing to accept responsibility for continuing the survey.

Elaine Grentner of Olympia Data Design is seriously considering accepting the job of directing the Community Survey. However, before making a final decision, she has been conducting an in-depth analysis regarding the costs involved with the Community Survey, money available both from her company and other participating organizations, and the possibility of either purchasing existing surveys or commissioning a professional compensation consulting firm to develop and implement the survey.

Elaine thought that possibly Pat Fox at main headquarters could provide her with some good ideas that would assist her in making a decision on the course of action she should take. Following a conversation with Pat, Elaine received a letter listing questions that she should answer and other helpful data. Pat told Elaine that if she would answer the questions and carefully review the survey availability and cost data he provided, the best course of action would become apparent. A summary of Pat's questions and Elaine's answers follow.

Q.1.0: What use do you make of compensation survey data?

A.1.1: Review relationships among pay grade midpoints and median and mean rates of pay of survey benchmark jobs that are assigned to the specific pay grades.

A.1.2: See if any significant differences have occurred among median or mean rates of pay for survey benchmark jobs and comparable jobs in Olympia.

A.1.3: Check the maximum and minimum of each Olympia pay grade. The 25th and 75th percentile data provided in the previous survey have helped me identify changes that should be made in the ranges of the pay grade.

A.1.4: Develop percentage change in pay since last survey of surveyed benchmark jobs. This gives me a first approximation of what I may need or should request for pay structure adjustments or for merit budget money.

A.1.5: In summary, the previous survey has been outstanding in allowing me to assess the competitive position of both jobs and the entire pay structure. It has been useful in tracking year to year changes. This tracking data, along with other local and national economic data, have permitted me to project future pay movements with considerable accuracy.

Q.2.0: What kind of data do you want a survey to provide?

A.2.1: Pay data on benchmark jobs in such major occupation groups as secretaries; clerks; data processing jobs; maintenance jobs; professionals in such functional areas as accounting, finance, sales, engineering, and data processing; and managers at various levels.

A.2.2: The kinds of firms or organizations that provide inputs to the survey. By kind, I mean product (output) and size (both by some kind of revenue generation and number of employees).

A.2.3: The date the survey was conducted.

A.2.4: Must feel confident that survey will be one that is long-lasting. (Since projections are an important part of my analysis, I must know that the survey data have a consistent base for tracking purposes.)

Q.3.0: What size survey are you talking about, i.e., (1) How many organizations do you want to participate? (2) What kinds of organizations do you want to participate? (3) How many jobs do you want the survey to cover? (4) What kind of data do you want to capture, i.e., actual pay data or average pay data?

A.3.1: To develop the kind of data I want, pay data on approximately 50 jobs will be required, which probably means that at least 25 organizations should participate. I would like to be able to produce decile and quartile data and maximum and minimum data, e.g., actual high and low, average high and low. I would like at least 25 rates of pay on each job and data from at least 5 and possibly as many as 10 firms on each job.

A.3.2: I will also need pay data on at least one job in every pay grade. In the most heavily populated pay grades, I would like to have at least 4 benchmark jobs surveyed.

In his letter, Pat also sent Elaine the following data to review:

1. Survey opportunities -- Elaine, you should have at least four options. They are (1) connect yourself with another major survey conducted by a credible organization in your area -- possibly some association, government jurisdiction, educational institution, or other private sector business is now conducting a survey; (2) develop your own survey -- we will discuss this in more detail later; (3) purchase one or more surveys that are conducted annually and cover the jobs for which you require data; (4) commission a professional organization that is in the business of conducting compensation surveys to do one for you -- possibly you could contact the organizations that participated in the previous survey and even some that currently do not participate, and you all could share in the cost.

If you have any thought of conducting your own survey, here are some additional pieces of information you should consider:

1. I consider a major survey to be any survey that collects pay data on 50 or more jobs and requires data from 30 or more organizations.

2. If you are considering conducting your own survey, you need:

.1 A survey manager -- requires 5 to 6 months of work per year (annual salary of $30,000 to $45,000)

.2 2 data entry operators full time for 2 months (must be competent - there is room for significant error) ($1,200 per month per operator)

.3 Data collectors -- good salespersons. Must be good at job matching and must understand survey requirements. Each visit requires 2 - 3 hours ($1,800 - $2,000 per month in base pay)

.4 Data editor -- checks incoming data for easily identifiable logical or "face" related mistakes. Reviews data entry data for recognizable mistakes; checks grade level differences of job by participating organization; identifies anticipated results to assist in identifying errors (probably some individual who does data collection - 80 to 100 hours ($1,500 to $1,800 per month in base pay)

.5 Systems analyst -- designs software program that will analyze pay data and provide desired summary outputs. Takes from 30 to 60 hours - 50 hours is a good average. (Hourly rate - $40 to $60; average, $50/hour)

.6 Programmer -- codes and documents software program. 60 to 120 hours -- 100 hours average. ($25 to $35 per hour; average, $30/hour)

Program may include use of some "canned" statistical package. Will also include such components as (1) data entry; (2) data analysis and editing; (3) data manipulation; (4) data summaries.

Other costs are:

1. Design and printing of data collection instrument (approx. $500)
2. Survey Data Summary Manuals for participants -- each manual may cost from $15 to $25 to produce.

If you contact a major professional organization that produces a tailor-made survey, you can expect a charge of anywhere between $20,000 and $50,000 for the survey. Here is a list of professional organizations that provide surveys and some representative costs of their commercially available surveys:

Firm Executive and Managerial	Location	Approx. Cost of Survey
ECS, Inc.	Ft. Lee, NJ	$360 to $600 per survey
The Hay Group	Philadelphia, PA	$350 to $1,075 (must be a client)
Hewitt Associates	Lincolnshire, IL	$900 (must be a client/ participant)
Management Compensation Service	Scottsdale, AZ	$1,000 - $1,500
Sibson & Co., Inc.	Princeton, NJ	$500 - $550 (must be a participant)
Towers Perrin, Forster & Crosby	New York, NY	$950 - $1,300

Middle & Lower Level Mgrs. Administrators & Professionals	Location	Approx. Cost of Survey
Abbott, Langer & Associates	Crete, IL	$75 - $350
Administrative Management Society	Willow Grove, PA	$115 for nonmembers
Bureau of Labor Statistics - U.S. Government	Washington, DC	Extremely modest charge
ECS, Inc.	Ft. Lee, NJ	$360 to $600 per survey
Management Compensation Services	Scottsdale, AZ	$1,000 - $1,500
Mercer-Meidinger-Hansen	Deerfield, IL	$100 - $600
Organization Resources Counselors, Inc.	New York, NY	Approx. $2,100 (participants only)
Towers, Perrin, Forster & Crosby	New York, NY	$950 - $1,300 (participants only)

Nonexempt Work Force		
Abbott, Langer & Associates	Crete, IL	$75 - $250
Administrative Management Society	Willow Grove, PA	$115 for nonmembers

Bureau of Labor Statistics	Washington, DC	Extremely modest charge
ECS, Inc.	Ft. Lee, NJ	$360 to $600 per survey
Mercer-Meidinger-Hansen	Deerfield, IL	$100 - $650

This is a very brief list of firms/organizations that provide survey data. I'm giving you this list just to give you some idea of the kinds of firms and possible costs of data. In the Richard I. Henderson book, Compensation Management: Rewarding Performance, 5th Edition, there is an extensive list of organizations and the kind of survey data they provide.

ASSIGNMENT

Please review the following three courses of action Elaine has selected as the best options available to her. Review each selection and identify the strengths and weaknesses of each option.

A. Purchase a group of available surveys that are produced annually by reputable firms.

B. Organize a survey group to replace the one previously used and continue the same survey.

C. Contact other previous participants in the survey and inform them that the compensation consulting organization of Surveys, Inc. is willing to replicate the previous survey at a cost of $35,000 per year. If only 14 companies participate, the cost will be over $2,500 for each participant. It is possible that as many as 50 companies could participate, but it is not known whether or not they would be willing to spend $700 annually to obtain the survey data.

1. What choice should Elaine make?

2. Would it be possible for Elaine to start up a survey with $7,500? Describe the kind of survey Elaine could develop with $7,500. (Use the cost data provided in the module to help develop this response.)

OLYMPIA SURVEY DESIGN ANALYSIS CHECKLIST

1. Establishing market rate for job to be surveyed:

   a. Identify relevant geographic area.

   b. Identify competitive organizations, businesses, etc.

   c. Identify size of participant (number of employees in jobs being surveyed).

2. Existing sources of information:

   a. Bureau of Labor Statistics or other government agencies.

   b. Societies and associations.

   c. Private businesses specializing in compensation/pay surveys.

   d. Criteria used for selecting outside surveys.

3. Performing own survey:

   a. Jobs to be surveyed.

   b. Information desired.

   c. Processing limitations (number of jobs, number of participants it is feasible to accommodate).

   d. Method(s) used for collecting data.

e. Design of information collection instruments.

f. Use of collected data.

g. Design of data summaries and reporting papers.

4. Jobs to be surveyed:

a. Visibility of occurrence of job.

b. Job content similarity/standardization.

c. Levels of jobs in job family/occupation.

5. Data to be collected:

a. Actual base pay.

b. Pay ranges for jobs.

c. Typical overtime earnings.

d. Bonus/cash profit sharing.

e. Normal/typical hiring rate (if not minimum).

f. If multi-incumbent position, number of incumbents.

f. Incumbent information (sex, age, time in job).

g. Specific other compensation information (money and in-kind payments, i.e., thrift/savings plan, profit sharing, pension, insurances (all kinds), parking cafeteria, etc.)

6. Using survey data:

a. Proper job match.

b. Select appropriate pay statistics (median, mean, 1Q, 3Q, etc.)

c. Identify statistics to represent "competitive" midpoint.

d. Relate midpoint to Olympia pay administration considerations.

7. Using content for job matching:

a. Focus on content rather than titles.

b. Identify job family or occupation.

c. Identify levels within family (differences in responsibility, knowledge, skill).

d. Identify highest level at which incumbent operates for significant portion of time.

MODULE 9

DEVELOPING AND IMPLEMENTING A PAY SURVEY

Olympia Data Design provides a wide variety of information services for all other Olympia divisions and also for outside organizations. Compensation for all kinds of jobs within Olympia has always been and continues to be an extremely sensitive issue. From systems analysis and programming professionals to computer operators and data entry employees, turnover becomes a critical issue when pay is not competitive. Of all of the jobs throughout Olympia, data processing/information systems jobs require the closest of attention to technological changes (both computer-related software and hardware) and market changes in rates of pay.

Over the years, compensation professionals of Olympia have relied on third-party surveys from a variety of sources for establishing market rates of pay for data processing jobs. Because of the wide variety of activities performed by Olympia data processing personnel and the way the activities are grouped together, it becomes difficult at times to identify comparability in jobs for determining market rates of pay.

Olympia is seriously considering developing its own survey. To ensure a rational, logical, and systematic approach in the design, the compensation department developed the Olympia Survey Design Analysis Checklist. The Checklist follows this module.

ASSIGNMENT

1. Focusing on data processing/information systems related jobs, develop a form for gathering compensation/pay information.

2. How will the data be collected?

3. How will the data be summarized and reported? Develop a summary sheet for presenting the survey data.

4. What should be the time frame covered from the initial implementation of the survey to the sending of summaries to the participants? Complete the time analysis form following this module to assist in developing your answer.

SURVEY DESIGN AND IMPLEMENTATION TIME ANALYSIS

		Time
1.	Identifying benchmark jobs.	____
2.	Writing job summaries.	____
3.	Developing data collection form.	____
4.	Identifying desired participating organizations.	____
5.	Collecting data.	____
6.	Validating data.	____
7.	Transcribing, summarizing, and analyzing data.	____
8.	Developing a summary.	____
9.	Mailing summary to participants.	____
	Total Time Required	____

MODULE 10

PAY STRUCTURE DESIGN: RECOGNIZING PAY STRUCTURE ARCHITECTURE

Olympia Data Design (ODD) has been using a market pricing approach for establishing and adjusting rates of pay for its jobs. However, as ODD has increased in size, now having almost 1,000 employees on its payroll, it has become more difficult to maintain proper and equitable pay relationships among its many different jobs through market pricing.

Sylvia Chandler has just completed a rating of all jobs (the FES Factor Comparison Work Sheet following this module lists the FES ratings for the 22 benchmark jobs included within Olympia's Community Survey). Sylvia has also received some recommendations from Pat Fox at Corporate Headquarters concerning pay structure architectural features that she should consider. These recommendations follow this module.

Sylvia developed two forms -- (1) a Third-Party Survey Summary Analysis Form and (2) a Pay Structure Minimum and Maximum Analysis Form to assist her in making the best possible use of data from the recently completed Olympia Community Survey and from the following seven surveys:

ECS	-	Office Personnel Report
ECS	-	Supervisory Management Report
ECS	-	Professional and Scientific Personnel Report
ECS	-	Middle Management Report
ECS	-	Top Management Report
Bureau of Labor Statistics	-	Professional, Administrative, Technical and Clerical Pay Survey (PATC)
Bureau of Labor Statistics	-	Atlanta, GA, Area Wage Survey

ASSIGNMENT

Design a pay structure for ODD following the pay structure design architecture criteria and using the data provided in the two analysis forms and the job evaluation rating scores of the 22 benchmark jobs. (Graph paper is included with this module.)

PAY STRUCTURE ARCHITECTURAL FEATURES

1. The pay policy line should parallel the identified "market" as closely as possible.

2. The minimum rate of pay any employee should receive is $5.00 per hour or $10,400 per year.

3. Midpoint-to-midpoint differences between adjacent pay grades may vary from 5 to 10 percent. - Midpoint-to-midpoint differences may increase in a consistent and rational manner between pay grades or among groups of pay grades, or there may be an identical difference between pay grades.*

4. Spread of the range for pay grades may vary from 20 to 50 percent (vertical axis dimension) - Spread of the range may increase in a consistent and rational manner between pay grades or among groups of pay grades, or there may be an identical spread for all pay grades.

5. The point range for the horizontal dimension of the pay grades must relate to the number of grades required in the pay structure and the number of points in the job evaluation plan. - ODD uses the FES job evaluation method which provides a minimum of 190 points and a maximum of 4480 points. The horizontal width of the pay grade may increase in a logical and systematic manner or be identical for all pay grades.

THIRD-PARTY SURVEY SUMMARY ANALYSIS FORM

Olympia Benchmark Job Titles	Olympia Community Survey		ECS Survey			BLS PATC Survey			BLS Atlanta Area Wage Survey			Established "Market" Rate of Pay
	Pay Stat.	Kind of Pay Stat.	Matching Job Title/Survey	Pay Stat.	Kind of Pay Stat.	Matching Job Title	Pay Stat.	Kind of Pay Stat.	Matching Job Title	Pay Stat.	Kind of Pay Stat.	
105 MAIL CLERK	256	wk	Mail Clerk	247	wk	Messenger	233	wk	Messenger	240	wkly	256
155 GENERAL CLERK C	248		Clerk-Jr.	233		File Clerk I	212		File Clerk I	221.5		248
160 GENERAL CLERK B	316		Clerk-Int.	274		II	246		File Clerk II	212		316
165 GENERAL CLERK A	336		Clerk-Sr.	329		III			File Clerk III	255		336
175 SECRETARY	336		Secretary-Jr.	281		Sec. Level I	315		Sec. Level II	341.5		336
180 EXECUTIVE SECRETARY	411		Executive Secretary	394		V	558		V	620		490
405 DATA ENTRY OP B	251		Data Entry Operator Jr	260		Keyboard Entry Op. I	258		Keyboard Entry Op. I	279.5		260
410 DATA ENTRY OP A	290		Data Entry Operator Sr.	323		II	325		II	332		320
420 TAPE LIBRARIAN	321		—	—	—	—	—		Comp. Data Libr.	378		340
425 COMPUTER OPERATOR	339		Comp. Op.-Int	334	wk	Comp. Op II	343		Comp. Op II	342.5		339
430 SR COMPUTER OPERATOR	409		Comp. Op-Sr.	403		IV	450		IV	450		480
435 COMPUTER RM SUPV	503		—	—	—	—	—	—	—	—		520
445 MANAGER - OP	815		D.P. Mgr	967	wk	—	—	—	—	—		900
500 COMP PROGRAMMER B	381		—	—	—	Comp. Prog. III	449		Comp. Prog. III	448.5		520
505 COMP PROGRAMMER A	452		—	—	—	IV	473		IV	472.5		610
510 SR COMP PROGRAMMER	642		—	—	—	V	642		V	642		680
515 SYSTEMS ANALYST I	545		Sys. Anal. II	573	wk	Comp. Sys. An. II	694		Comp. Sys. Ana. II	698.5		700
520 SYSTEMS ANALYST II	635		III	669		III	838		III	510.5		725
525 SYSTEMS ANALYST III	724		IV	760		IV	990		IV	684		770
526 SR SYSTEMS ANALYST	830		V	831		V	1187		V	757.5		830
530 MGR - DATA SYSTEMS	896		Elec. D.P. Man.	1229	wk	—	—	—	—	—	—	896
535 ASST VP DATA SYST	1121		—		—	—	—	—	—	—	—	1121

+407

PAY STRUCTURE MINIMUM AND MAXIMUM ANALYSIS FORM

Olympia Benchmark Job Titles	Olympia Community Survey				ECS Surveys				BLS PATC Survey				BLS Atlanta Area Wage Survey				"Market"	
	Selected				Selected				Selected				Selected				Selected	
	Minimum Stat.	Minimum Kind	Maximum Stat.	Maximum Kind	Minimum Stat.	Minimum Kind	Maximum Stat.	Maximum Kind	Minimum Stat.	Minimum Kind	Maximum Stat.	Maximum Kind	Minimum Stat.	Minimum Kind	Maximum Stat.	Maximum Kind	Minimum Stat.	Maximum Stat.
105 MAIL CLERK	199	WK	268	WK	214	WK	303	WK					198.5	WK	268	WK	200	264.5
155 GENERAL CLERK C	208		339		212		297						195.		237.5		200	264.5
160 GENERAL CLERK B	244		389		238		343						195.		223.		240	317
165 GENERAL CLERK A	259		391		278		409						225		267		270	342
175 SECRETARY	256		461		245		352						300		350		300	397
180 EXECUTIVE SECRETARY	350		534		321		470						566.5		673		400	529
405 DATA ENTRY OP B	208		315		228		319						240		293		200	265
410 DATA ENTRY OP A	227		316		265		380						270.5		377		250	331
420 TAPE LIBRARIAN	255		405										293.5		404.5		260	344
425 COMPUTER OPERATOR	285		479		290		417						286		367		300	397
430 SR COMPUTER OPERATOR	360		602		333		490						401		527.5		475	628
435 COMPUTER RM SUPV	434		808		—	—	—	—					—	—	—	—	510	674
445 MANAGER - OP	642		1094		790	WK	1194	WK					—	—	—	—	800	1058
500 COMP PROGRAMMER B	328		457		—	—	—	—					468		614.5		510	674
505 COMP PROGRAMMER A	393		582		—	—	—	—					422.5		505.		610	807
510 SR COMP PROGRAMMER	538		732		—	—	—	—					595		668.5		675	893
515 SYSTEMS ANALYST I	479		638		475	WK	727	WK					631		761.5		700	926
520 SYSTEMS ANALYST II	542		729		537		815						481		538.5		725	959
525 SYSTEMS ANALYST III	602		821		608		923						633.5		753.5		770	1018
526 SR SYSTEMS ANALYST	696		926		633		977						714		808		800	1058
530 MGR - DATA SYSTEMS	694		1117		—	—	—	—					—	—	—	—	800	1058
535 ASST VP DATA SYST	912		1346		—	—	—	—					—	—	—	—	850	1075

JOB DESCRIPTION TITLE	FACTOR 1	FACTOR 2	FACTOR 3	FACTOR 4	FACTOR 5	FACTOR 6	FACTOR 7	FACTOR 8	FACTOR 9	TOTAL POINTS
Asst. VP Data Systems	8 / 1550	5 / 650	4 / 450	4 / 225	4 / 225	3 / 60	4 / 220	1 / 5	1 / 5	3390
Mgr - Data Systems	7 / 1250	4 / 450	4 / 450	4 / 225	4 / 225	3 / 60	3 / 120	1 / 5	1 / 5	2790
Sr. Systems Analyst	7 / 1250	4 / 450	4 / 450	4 / 225	4 / 225	3 / 60	2 / 50	1 / 5	1 / 5	2720
Systems Analyst III	7 / 1250	4 / 450	3 / 275	4 / 225	3 / 150	3 / 60	2 / 50	1 / 5	1 / 5	2470
Systems Analyst II	6 / 950	4 / 450	3 / 275	4 / 225	3 / 150	3 / 60	2 / 50	1 / 5	1 / 5	2170
Systems Analyst I	6 / 950	3 / 275	3 / 275	4 / 225	3 / 150	2 / 25	2 / 50	1 / 5	1 / 5	1960
Sr. Comp Programmer	6 / 950	3 / 275	3 / 275	3 / 150	3 / 150	2 / 25	1 / 20	1 / 5	1 / 5	1855
Comp Programmer A	6 / 950	2 / 125	3 / 275	3 / 150	2 / 75	2 / 25	1 / 20	1 / 5	1 / 5	1630
Comp Programmer B	5 / 750	2 / 125	2 / 125	2 / 75	2 / 75	1 / 10	1 / 20	1 / 5	1 / 5	1190
Manager - DP	7 / 1250	4 / 450	4 / 450	4 / 225	4 / 225	2 / 25	2 / 50	1 / 5	1 / 5	2685
Computer Rm Supervisor	5 / 750	3 / 275	2 / 125	3 / 150	3 / 150	2 / 25	2 / 50	1 / 5	1 / 5	1535
Sr. Computer Operator	4 / 550	2 / 125	2 / 125	2 / 75	3 / 150	2 / 25	1 / 20	2 / 20	2 / 20	1110
Computer Operator	3 / 350	2 / 125	2 / 125	2 / 75	2 / 75	2 / 25	1 / 20	2 / 20	2 / 20	835
Tape Librarian	2 / 200	2 / 125	1 / 25	2 / 75	2 / 75	2 / 25	1 / 20	1 / 5	1 / 5	555
Data Entry Operator A	2 / 200	2 / 125	1 / 25	2 / 75	1 / 25	1 / 10	1 / 20	1 / 5	1 / 5	490
Data Entry Operator B	2 / 200	1 / 25	1 / 25	1 / 25	1 / 25	1 / 10	1 / 20	1 / 5	1 / 5	340
Executive Secretary	3 / 350	3 / 275	2 / 125	2 / 75	2 / 75	2 / 25	2 / 50	1 / 5	1 / 5	985
Secretary	3 / 350	2 / 125	2 / 125	2 / 75	2 / 75	2 / 25	1 / 20	1 / 5	1 / 5	805
General Clerk A	2 / 200	2 / 125	2 / 125	2 / 75	1 / 25	1 / 10	2 / 50	1 / 5	1 / 5	620
General Clerk B	2 / 200	2 / 125	1 / 25	1 / 25	1 / 25	1 / 10	1 / 20	1 / 5	1 / 5	440
General Clerk C	2 / 200	1 / 25	1 / 25	1 / 25	1 / 25	1 / 10	1 / 20	1 / 5	1 / 5	340
Mail Clerk	2 / 200	1 / 25	1 / 25	1 / 25	1 / 25	1 / 10	1 / 20	1 / 5	1 / 5	340

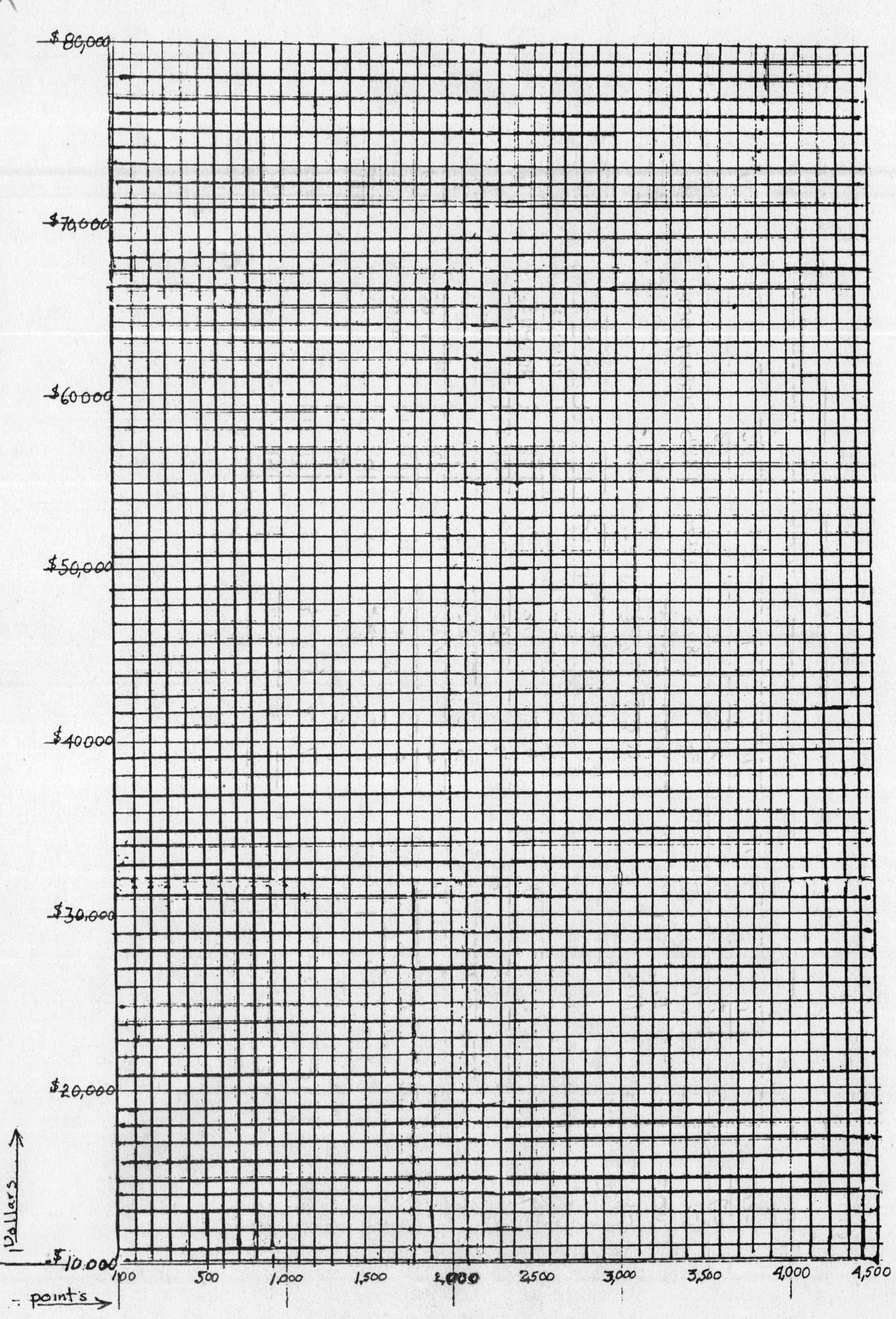
$80,000
$70,000
$60000
$50,000
$40000
$30,000
$20,000
$10,000
Dollars
100
500
1,000
1,500
2,000
2,500
3,000
3,500
4,000
4,500
points

JOBS INCLUDED IN OLYMPIA COMMUNITY SURVEY

(Summary of Survey Data - In Weekly Rates)

JOB CODE	TITLE	# of Incumbents Reported Rates	Lowest Reported Rate	10th Percentile (10%)	First Quartile (25%)	Median (50%)	Average $\bar{x}$ (mean)	Third Quartile (75%)	90th Percentile (90%)	Highest Reported Rate
105	MAIL CLERK	151	156	199	215	243	256	287	368	449
155	GENERAL CLERK C	1075	178	208	208	251	248	266	339	429
160	GENERAL CLERK B	1594	188	244	244	316	300	349	389	684
165	GENERAL CLERK A	1292	239	259	277	336	317	365	396	484
175	SECRETARY	1725	240	256	280	336	335	367	461	526
180	EXECUTIVE SECRETARY	1209	305	350	371	411	445	534	534	703
405	DATA ENTRY OPERATOR B	1223	154	208	208	251	220	260	315	421
410	DATA ENTRY OPERATOR A	729	163	227	227	290	274	264	316	479
420	TAPE LIBRARIAN	41	232	255	255	321	313	337	405	534
425	COMPUTER OPERATOR	320	255	285	316	329	370	445	479	528
430	SENIOR COMPUTER OPERATOR	353	308	360	393	409	477	594	602	602
435	COMPUTER ROOM SUPERVISOR	162	365	434	491	503	650	808	808	808
445	MANAGER--DATA PROCESSING	33	598	642	692	815	882	949	1094	1615
500	COMPUTER PROGRAMMER B	107	320	328	358	381	409	448	457	575
505	COMPUTER PROGRAMMER A	311	360	393	407	452	479	519	582	679
510	SENIOR COMPUTER PROGRAMMER	992	410	538	546	642	678	732	732	814
515	SYSTEMS ANALYST I	201	410	479	506	545	554	590	638	757
520	SYSTEMS ANALYST II	255	404	542	624	635	634	650	729	856
525	SYSTEMS ANALYST III	325	388	602	660	724	714	769	821	968
526	SENIOR SYSTEMS ANALYST	182	575	696	750	830	823	903	926	1067
530	MANAGER--DATA SYSTEMS	64	647	694	819	896	912	996	1117	1306
535	ASSISTANT VICE PRESIDENT DATA SYSTEMS	25	844	912	957	1121	1132	1269	1346	1692

POSITION DESCRIPTIONS

SECTION I

CLERICAL

MAIL CLERK — JOB CODE 105

Under immediate supervision, assists with the sorting of ordinary and registered incoming mail and processing of outgoing mail. Makes scheduled internal deliveries and pickups of routings among departments. This is an entry level position.

GENERAL CLERK C — JOB CODE 155

Under immediate supervision, performs simple repetitive activities covered by standard specific instructions. May maintain files of correspondence, file material, proofread, check computations, operate simple office machines, type and photocopy. This is an entry level position.

GENERAL CLERK B — JOB CODE 160

Under immediate supervision, performs routine but somewhat varied clerical duties in accordance with standard procedures. Work may occasionally require some independent judgment and knowledge of related operations. May maintain files of correspondence, file material, perform simple arithmetic calculations, perform simple posting of accounts, operate office machines and type.

GENERAL CLERK A — JOB CODE 165

Under general supervision, performs complex and diverse duties involving the application of standard procedures to a variety of details requiring independent analysis. Work usually requires some independent judgment and a thorough knowledge of department policies and procedures. May maintain files of correspondence, file materials, perform arithmetic calculations, post accounts, operate office machines, and type.

SECRETARY — JOB CODE 175

Under immediate supervision, performs stenographic and clerical duties with a moderately high degree of speed and accuracy. May take dictation in shorthand or transcribe from a dictaphone. May take and transcribe materials which are highly technical or which are not specifically dictated for transcription (i.e., meetings or conferences). May be required to use word processing equipment. Sets up and maintains office files and performs other clerical duties.

EXECUTIVE SECRETARY JOB CODE 180

Under general supervision, performs secretarial duties for a mid-level company executive. Takes and transcribes dictation of both confidential and routine nature and types letters, reports and memoranda. May be required to use word processing equipment. Composes correspondence of a semi-routine nature. Maintains complex and confidential files. Requires a high level of secretarial skills.

DATA ENTRY OPERATOR B JOB CODE 405

Under immediate supervision, operates data entry devices, including keypunch machine, key-to-disc and/or key-to-tape machines. Records various types of transactions and verifies data. This is an entry level position.

DATA ENTRY OPERATOR A JOB CODE 410

Under immediate supervision, operates data entry devices including keypunch machine, key-to-disc and/or key-to-tape machines to record various types of transactions; verifies data; keys more complex data than data entry Operator B. May assist in training new employees.

TAPE LIBRARIAN JOB CODE 420

Under general supervision, assists in classifying, cataloging and maintaining library of magnetic tape reels, punched cards and systems reference publications used for electronic data processing purposes.

COMPUTER OPERATOR JOB CODE 425

Under general supervision, controls and operates the main components of a third generation computer system, including both primary and peripheral electronic equipment. Coordinates with Data Processing Supervisor all computer runs in accordance with the daily schedule. Analyzes procedural and technical hardware problems and takes necessary corrective action. Maintains various operation and production records.

SENIOR COMPUTER OPERATOR JOB CODE 430

Under general supervision, monitors and controls third generation computer equipment to maximize throughput and efficiency and minimize operational problems. Maintains familiarity with all pre-established run instructions to facilitate proper equipment set-up and job handling. Has basic working knowledge of internal software package to help provide assistance in solving program halt situations.

COMPUTER ROOM SUPERVISOR JOB CODE 435

Under the general supervision of Assistant Manager--Data Processing, directly supervises non-exempt employees who operate computers and peripheral data processing equipment on an assigned shift. Coordinates and assists in scheduling jobs performed by the unit. Occasionally may operate the machines. Trains, assigns and evaluates the employees under his/her supervision. This is a first-line supervisor.

MANAGER--DATA PROCESSING JOB CODE 445

Under the direction of Assistant Vice President--Data Processing, manages the computer operations function of the organization which includes the automated processing and input functions. May coordinate corporate initiatives and regular operations with branch or division offices to a centralized data processing system. Responsible for a staff of 30.

Assignments are received in objective-oriented terms. Reviews the progress of work objectives and schedules. Advises subordinates on problems. Errors can cause critical delays and considerable reallocation of resources. Exercises supervision through subordinate supervisors.

COMPUTER PROGRAMMER B JOB CODE 500

Under general supervision, learns programming and flow charting. May function as the junior programmer in a project team headed by a Systems Analyst or Senior Programmer. Prepares relatively simple, new and revised computer programs. Prepares detailed flow charts and writes, tests and corrects programs. Prepares simple documentation.

Requires limited use and application of the basic principles and concepts of programming. Program specifications are outlined and work is performed according to specific instructions. This is the first position in a three-level hierarchy.

COMPUTER PROGRAMMER A JOB CODE 505

Under general supervision, frequently as a member of a project team headed by a Systems Analyst or Senior Programmer, prepares new and revised computer programs. Prepares detailed flow charts. Writes, tests and corrects programs. Prepares documentation to facilitate operational use and later modification. May assist Systems Analysts and Senior Programmers with the study, design, development and implementation of computer systems. Makes changes in existing programs.

Requires limited use and application of the basic principles and concepts of programming. Program specifications are outlined, but work is performed without detailed instructions and is expected to proceed without direction. Errors have a moderate impact on the organization. This is the second position in a three-level hierarchy.

SENIOR COMPUTER PROGRAMMER JOB CODE 510

Under general supervision, prepares relatively complex, new and revised computer programs. Prepares detailed flow charts. Writes, tests and corrects programs. Prepares documentation to facilitate operational use and later modification. May assist Systems Analysts with the study, design, development and implementation of computer systems. Makes changes in computer programs. May assist in the training of new programmers.

Acts as a team leader on projects and as working supervisor for less proficient programmers. Requires the full use and application of the principles and concepts of programming with more limited use of the principles and concepts of systems design. Solves a variety of problems. Work is assigned by incumbent's supervisor but work is completed thereafter with minimal direction. Incumbent may exercise some decision making or variation of methods to accomplish assigned goals. Errors may have a significant impact on the organization. This is the senior position in a three-level hierarchy.

SYSTEMS ANALYST I JOB CODE 515

Under general supervision of Manager--Data Systems, designs and develops programs and implements electronic data processing systems. May attend meetings to determine and analyze user requirements. Applies knowledge of computer capabilities, subject matter to be programmed and information processing techniques. Writes, tests and corrects the computer program application.

Requires full use and application of the principles and concepts of programming, with more limited use and application of principles and concepts of systems design. Solves a variety of problems. May exercise decision making responsibility; however, all decisions are reviewed and approved by supervisor. May act as project leader on projects of moderate scope or on a portion of a major project. Errors have a moderate impact on the organization. This is the junior position in a four-level hierarchy.

SYSTEMS ANALYST II JOB CODE 520

Under the general supervision of Manager-Data Systems, conducts studies to develop, design and implement electronic data processing systems. Attends meetings to analyze user requirements in order to design effective systems. Applies knowledge of computer equipment capabilities, subject matter to be programmed and information processing techniques. May establish cost and scheduling estimates. Coordinates with appropriate parties within and outside the organization.

Requires the wide use and application of the principles and concepts of systems analysis and programming. Solves a wide range of difficult problems. May assume lead work responsibilities on project of moderate scope or on a portion of a major project. Instructs junior personnel. Exercises decision making responsibility in selecting an optimum system design to fulfill the user's needs. Errors have a serious impact on the organization. This is the second position in a three-level hierarchy

SYSTEMS ANALYST III JOB CODE 525

Under the general supervision of Manager--Data Systems, conducts studies to develop, design and implement electronic data processing systems. Attends meetings to analyze user requirements in order to design effective systems. Applies knowledge of computer equipment capabilities, subject matter to be programmed and information processing techniques. Establishes cost and scheduling estimates. Coordinates projects with appropriate parties within and outside the organization. Acts in a lead capacity.

Requires the extensive use and application of the principles and concepts of systems analysis and programming. May require knowledge of data base management, telecommunications equipment and project management. Solves complex problems requiring ingenuity and innovation. Serves as project leader on projects of moderate complexity and scope or on a significant portion of a major project. This is the third position in a four-level hierarchy.

SENIOR SYSTEMS ANALYST JOB CODE 526

Under the general supervision of Manager--Data Systems, conducts studies to develop, design and implement electronic data processing systems. Conducts or attends meetings to analyze user requirements in order to design effective systems. Applies knowledge of computer equipment capabilities, subject matter to be programmed and information processing techniques. Establishes cost and scheduling estimates and is responsible for meeting those estimates. Coordinates projects with appropriate parties within and outside the organization. Acts as a project leader.

Requires the extensive use and application of the principles and concepts of systems analysis, programming, project management, computer hardware and computer operations in order to develop software systems and coordinate the work of others. May require knowledge of telecommunications equipment and design or data base management. Solves complex problems requiring ingenuity and innovation. Serves as project leader on major projects and responsible for the efficient operations of project teams and subordinate analysts and programmers in meeting deadlines, goals and objectives. This is the senior position in a four-level hierarchy.

MANAGER--DATA SYSTEMS JOB CODE 530

Under the direction of Assistant Vice President--Data Systems, provides managerial direction to the operations and administrative activities of a department whose function is to design, develop and implement electronic data processing systems. Monitors departmental effectiveness, works with management of other departments to resolve problems and makes recommendations on automation policy. Coordinates corporate initiatives in support of a centralized computer operation, which may include several branch or division offices. Directly and indirectly supervises a staff of 20-40.

Assignments are received in objective/task-oriented terms. Requires knowledge of systems analysis, design and programming, computer hardware, project management and software applications. May require knowledge of telecommunications equipment and design or data base management. Advises subordinates and reviews completed work. Errors can cause serious delays and considerable reallocation of resources.

ASSISTANT VICE PRESIDENT--DATA SYSTEMS JOB CODE 535

Under the direction of a Vice President, provides managerial direction to the operations and activities of a department whose function is to design, develop and implement electronic data processing systems. Insures procedural compliance in the development, implementation and support of application systems. Contributes to development of automation policy and establishment of performance standards. Coordinates corporate initiatives. Directly and indirectly manages a staff of 50-70, usually through subordinate managers.

Assignments are received in objective-oriented terms. Requires knowledge of systems analysis, design and programming, software applications, computer hardware and project management. May require knowledge of telecommunications equipment and design or data base management. Establishes priorities. Allocates resources. Errors can cause serious delays and serious reallocation of resources.

ECS

Two Executive Drive
Fort Lee, New Jersey 07024
(201) 585 - 9808

a subsidiary of THE Wyatt COMPANY

Office Personnel Report

Seventeenth edition **1987/88**

Data in Effect: May 1, 1987
Publication Date: September, 1987

Position Descriptions

ACCOUNTING CLERK-JUNIOR - Under immediate supervision performs simple, repetitive tasks within the general accounting, accounts payable and auditing departments. Posts journal entries, processes payments, verifies information, files and assists in preparation of reports. Includes trainees.

ACCOUNTING CLERK-INTERMEDIATE - Under general supervision performs a variety of routine bookkeeping functions in accordance with standard procedures. Reconciles bank accounts, posts to and balances general or subsidiary ledgers, processes payments and compiles segments of monthly closings, annual reports, etc. May contact other departments and/or outside agencies to resolve common problems.

ACCOUNTING CLERK-SENIOR (GROUP LEADER) - Under general supervision handles a wide variety of advanced accounting work including maintenance of, and preparing reports on, complex budget or income and expenditure records, exercising considerable initiative in arranging details to obtain job objectives. May direct and check work of Junior and Intermediate Clerks.

BOOKKEEPER-SENIOR - Maintains a complete and systematic set of records of business transactions. Balances books and prepares reports to show receipts, expenditures, accounts receivable and payable, and various other items pertinent to the operation of a business. May perform other related duties.

CHAUFFEUR-EXECUTIVE - Principal duty is chauffeuring top level executives in company limousine. Often on call beyond normal working hours to transport executives to and from corporate facilities, meetings and special events. Responsible for the appearance, operation, maintenance and service of the vehicle.

CHAUFFEUR-MESSENGER - Drives a motor vehicle used for transporting office personnel, visitors, and/or mail, and for running miscellaneous errands. Responsible for the maintenance of the vehicle, and may make minor repairs or adjustments.

CLERK-JUNIOR - Under immediate supervision, performs basic clerical duties such as copying data, compiling records, filing, tabulating, posting, distributing mail, and other incidental clerical duties. Includes trainees.

CLERK-INTERMEDIATE - Performs routine but somewhat varied clerical duties in accordance with standard procedures under general supervision. Work requires some independent judgment and knowledge within department as well as a general understanding of other departments' functions. Duties include maintaining records, preparing various forms, verifying information and resolving common problems. May do limited typing and/or operate a terminal console.

CLERK-SENIOR (GROUP LEADER) - Performs complex and diverse duties involving the application of standard procedures to a variety of details requiring independent analysis. Work requires judgment in the selection and interpretation of data, and a thorough knowledge of department and company policies and procedures dealing with the area of responsibility. May direct and check work of Junior and Intermediate Clerks.

CLERK-TYPIST - Performs clerical work of routine but varied nature in conjunction with moderate but proficient typing. Types reports, business correspondence, forms, and other matter. May file records and reports. Posts information to records, may sort and distribute mail. Answers telephones and performs similar duties.

COMPUTER OPERATOR-JUNIOR - Under direct supervision performs routine duties to operate a computer and peripheral equipment, such as printers, tape and disk drives. Follows detailed instructions, assists higher level operators and routes error messages to appropriate personnel. (In many companies this is considered a training position.)

COMPUTER OPERATOR-INTERMEDIATE - Under immediate supervision sets up computer programs of intermediate difficulty according to standard procedures. Monitors computer and peripheral equipment and researches simple error messages. Capable of completing general phases of sophisticated computer operations under guidance of higher level operator.

COMPUTER OPERATOR-SENIOR - Under general supervision operates a computer handling a wide range of tasks of varying complexity. May direct the training and productivity of subordinate operators, and assist the operations supervisor in scheduling and in the maintenance of records on machine operation and production. In some installations this position may require a fundamental knowledge of programming.

CORRESPONDENT - Composes and writes or dictates letters to customers or other business establishments seeking information, or in reply to communications received. Examines incoming correspondence, and gathers necessary data in order to formulate a reply. Handles correspondence relating to a variety of subjects such as requests for merchandise, claims for lost or damaged goods, incorrect billing, and unsatisfactory service rendered.

CREDIT AND COLLECTION CLERK - Contacts various credit sources, insures credit packages or customer applications are complete and notifies customers of delinquent payments. Calls for information or sends standard forms to credit companies, banks, and loan associations. Maintains files on incomplete packages. Reviews lists for delinquent accounts and prepares routine follow-up letters. May operate terminal console to input or update computerized accounts.

CUSTOMER SERVICE CLERK - Assures that customers receive efficient and courteous service through processing of orders by mail, telephone, or in person. Provides pricing and delivery information. Receives and answers, within established guidelines, customer questions and complaints. Acts as a liaison between customer and various company departments. Maintains appropriate records and prepares required reports. May operate terminal console, perform typing assignments and related clerical duties.

DATA CONTROL CLERK - Receives and reviews source documents for data input. Checks accuracy and relevance of input and output data by visual examination, by correcting codes and by batching for computer processing. Verifies output against control totals, reviews format of printout and if reports are satisfactory, distributes information to proper departments.

DATA ENTRY OPERATOR-JUNIOR - Enters data through an electronic keyboard to record and verify a variety of routine source data under supervision. This position may include trainees.

DATA ENTRY OPERATOR-INTERMEDIATE - Enters data through an electronic keyboard to process a variety of business and statistical source data. Follows standard procedures, with allowance for some level of independent judgment and verifies input. Performs with moderate speed and accuracy.

DATA ENTRY OPERATOR-SENIOR - Enters data through an electronic keyboard to record or verify a variety of complex or uncoded data with a high level of speed and accuracy. Works with some latitude for independence of action when necessary in the selection and interpretation of data, and scheduling of work.

DATA ENTRY OPERATOR (GROUP LEADER) - Performs as Senior Operator, and in addition, is responsible for work distribution and review of a group of operators engaged in entering data from a variety of accounting, statistical and other sources.

DUPLICATING MACHINE OPERATOR-JUNIOR - Operates a small duplicating offset machine producing non-complex single color forms, reading material, etc. Responsible for proper maintenance of equipment and supplies.

DUPLICATING MACHINE OPERATOR-SENIOR - Operates a duplicating offset machine performing reproduction work of some complexity in either single or multi-color. Handles all phases of equipment set-up, operation and maintenance. May prepare own plates, inks and maintains own supplies.

EMPLOYEE BENEFITS CLAIM CLERK - Reviews for accuracy and completeness, and processes employee claims under the organization's various benefit plans including but not limited to group insurance, basic and major medical and pension. Maintains employee benefits records and prepares required reports. May counsel employees regarding eligibility and coverage. Transmits correct claim benefit checks to employees.

FILE CLERK-JUNIOR - Maintains correspondence, cards, invoices, or other classified or indexed records arranged systematically in a file according to an established system. Following general instructions, inserts and removes material upon request and notes its disposition. May perform related routine clerical duties.

FILE CLERK-SENIOR - In addition to duties stipulated for Junior File Clerk, may perform considerable clerical work in searching and investigating the information contained in the files, inserting additional data, preparing reports, and supplying written information on request. May assign and review work of Juniors.

IMPORT/EXPORT CLERK - Computes duties, tariffs, price conversions, weight and volume of merchandise that is imported or exported to foreign countries. Examines invoices, bills of lading and shipping statements. Verifies conversion of merchandise weights or volumes based on country's method of weight and measure. May convert foreign currency into U.S. equivalent using rate charts. May correspond with foreign companies on routine matters.

INPUT/OUTPUT CLERK - Inspects and controls data processing work received from and distributed to user departments. Serves as liaison with users on matters concerning the timely execution of scheduled production. Inspects documents received for processing to assure compliance with input standards. Dispatches and follows up work delivered to operations staff to assure conformance to overall schedules and operation flow. Inspects completed production to assure completeness and conformance to output standards. May analyze run failures to determine cause and initiate necessary corrective action.

INVENTORY CONTROL CLERK - Maintains records of materials in inventory and on order. Provides data as required, to forecast estimates and schedule of goods in process and needs for future orders. May notify appropriate supervision when stock reaches designated order point. May operate terminal console.

MAIL CLERK - Prepares incoming mail for distribution, and processes outgoing mail. Duties include mail distribution and collection, determining and affixing postage, and maintaining records on postage, registered mail and packages.

MESSENGER/OFFICE PERSON - Sorts and delivers letters, packages, records, etc., to offices or departments within a company, or to and from outside establishments. May perform a variety of other miscellaneous clerical or minor duties.

NOTE: *THE FOLLOWING FOUR POSITIONS indicate levels of secretarial skill and experience. Employees in these positions report to individuals whose rank or title is below that of a senior executive. Senior management, for the purpose of this survey, are assisted by secretary to Vice President/Division Manager, secretary to Executive Vice President, and secretary to Chief Executive Officer. Summary position descriptions for secretaries to senior management are shown separately, as indicated below.*

SECRETARY-JUNIOR - Under direct supervision, performs standard secretarial and minor administrative duties. Types letters, memorandums and reports. May take and transcribe dictation. May work for one or more individuals. Usually requires one year of specialized secretarial training. Entry level position. May use word processing equipment or PC in performing assigned tasks.

SECRETARY-INTERMEDIATE - Under general supervision, performs standard and some advanced secretarial duties. Position requires knowledge of practices and procedures of the function. Receives visitors; reads and routes incoming mail. May take and transcribe dictation. May make travel arrangements and reservations. Schedules appointments for superior. Normally requires one to three years experience. May use word processing equipment or PC in performing assigned tasks.

SECRETARY-SENIOR - Under limited supervision and on own initiative, performs standard and advanced secretarial duties. Position requires superior skills in taking and transcribing dictation and a thorough knowledge of practices and procedures of the function and company policy and procedures. May generate and maintain confidential files and reports. Normally requires a minimum of three years secretarial experience. May use word processing equipment or PC in performing assigned tasks.

EXECUTIVE SECRETARY - Under limited direction, performs standard and advanced secretarial duties for an executive of the company. Disposes of matters of a routine nature to conserve superior's time. Maintains regular and follow-up files and confidential data. Collects information needed by superior for conferences and reports. Arranges meetings as directed. May direct and review work of secretarial staff. Normally requires three to five years experience. May use word processing equipment or PC in performing assigned tasks.

SECRETARY-LEGAL - Prepares papers and correspondence of a legal nature, such as contracts, briefs, summonses, complaints and motions. Requires several years secretarial experience and knowledge of legal terminology. May use word processing equipment or PC in performing assigned tasks.

SECRETARY-BILINGUAL - Performs secretarial duties mentioned above with the additional ability of speaking and writing in a foreign language. May also take and transcribe dictation in a foreign language. May use word processing equipment or PC in performing assigned tasks.

SECRETARY TO STAFF VICE PRESIDENT OR DIVISION MANAGER OR EXECUTIVE - Performs diversified secretarial duties for company executive at Vice President level or equivalent, who is responsible for a major function such as operations, manufacturing, finance or sales. May take and transcribe dictation of a complex and confidential nature and assists in designated administrative details using initiative and judgment. Requires knowledge of company policy, organization, and a high level of technical skill. May use word processing equipment or PC in performing assigned tasks.

SECRETARY TO EXECUTIVE VICE PRESIDENT - Performs secretarial and related service for Executive or Senior Vice President. Composes letters and memoranda from dictation, verbal direction, or from knowledge of company policy or procedures. Assists Vice President in some administrative details, usually of a confidential nature. Requires a high degree of knowledge, competence and secretarial skills, and operates with considerable independence. May use word processing equipment or PC in performing assigned tasks.

SECRETARY TO CHIEF EXECUTIVE OFFICER - Performs secretarial and related service for Chief Executive Officer. Handles details of a confidential nature, and performs some administrative functions. Requires broad knowledge of corporate operations and policy, and a high level of experience, discretion and technical skill. Usually operates with great latitude for independent judgment and initiative. May use word processing equipment or PC in performing assigned tasks.

TELEPHONE OPERATOR-PBX - Operates a switchboard receiving incoming calls and places outgoing local and long distance calls. Does not include those performing clerical or receptionist duties.

TELEPHONE OPERATOR-CHIEF - Directs the activities of telephone operators and usually operates a switchboard. Maintains records relevant to the telephone service. Receives complaints of poor or inadequate service and determines action to be taken. May contact telephone company for repair or service of malfunctioning equipment.

TERMINAL OPERATOR - Using an electronic keyboard, inputs or accesses data and retrieves required information on visual display in response to specific requests. May cross reference data to assure accuracy and completeness of information. May activate printer if required.

TRAVEL CLERK - Coordinates business travel arrangements for all personnel within a company. Contacts airlines, car rentals, hotels, etc., and schedules travel arrangements for employees according to their itinerary. Insures appropriate transportation used at most economic cost. Notifies employees of arrangements, verifies agency documents for accuracy and proper billing and forwards information to employees. May perform light typing and maintain records.

TYPIST-JUNIOR - Types routine letters and standardized reports that require little or no planning for set up or arrangement. Works under specific detailed instructions and may perform related routine clerical duties. Includes trainees.

TYPIST-SENIOR - Types letters, reports, tabulations, and other material of average difficulty from either clear copy or rough draft with a high degree of speed and accuracy. Work involves planning for arrangement of material, correction of errors in spelling and grammar, and for self-checking of finished copy. May also perform simple clerical duties. Does not include stenographers or dictating machine operators.

WORD PROCESSING OPERATOR-JUNIOR - Under direct supervision, operates automated word processing equipment. Requires typing skills, knowledge of grammar, punctuation, spelling, and ability to use reference materials. Prepares typewritten documents from various sources of written or dictated input. Enters corrections, updates, or revision of copy on tape, card, disc or other storage material. Edits and proofreads material for accuracy and completeness. Entry level position.

WORD PROCESSING OPERATOR-INTERMEDIATE - Under general supervision, operates automated word processing equipment. Prepares more complex documents, is familiar with department terminology and company practices. Limited latitude for interpreting instructions. Usually requires at least one year of experience.

WORD PROCESSING OPERATOR-SENIOR - Possesses a comprehensive knowledge and high degree of skill in computerized word processing equipment. Exercises independent judgment in interpreting instructions to prepare complex and detailed documents. Is familiar with department terminology and company practices. May plan, distribute and check work. May assist in training of lower level operators. Usually requires three years of experience.

Subregion: Lower Southeast States

	NO OF FIRMS	NO IN POS	WTD AVG SALARY	AVG SALARY	SALARY 1ST QRTL	SALARY MEDIAN	SALARY 3RD QRTL	MEDIAN HRLY RATE	RATIO OF MEDIAN SALARY TO U.S. MEDIAN	AVG SAL RANGE MIN	AVG SAL RANGE MAX	NO OF HIRES
Accounting Clerk-Junior.	51	292	267	263	235	266	286	6.66	98.2	232	335	40
Accounting Clerk-Intermediate.	87	636	313	311	272	311	342	7.85	100.3	261	378	64
Accounting Clerk-Senior (Group Leader) . .	60	316	349	367	317	360	403	9.04	98.4	299	438	30
Bookkeeper-Senior.	16	106	334	349	300	350	376	8.93	92.1	285	417	7
Chauffeur-Executive.	4	5	379	350	274	314	460	8.14	77.2	268	378	
Chauffeur-Messenger.	8	27	251	258	222	256	292	6.61	88.9	213	305	10
Clerk-Junior	49	578	223	233	208	234	260	5.87	97.9	212	297	127
Clerk-Intermediate	72	1,218	268	274	243	272	297	7.10	98.0	238	343	199
Clerk-Senior (Group Leader).	45	650	319	329	291	338	358	8.65	100.9	278	409	20
Clerk-Typist	51	559	256	254	230	250	268	6.37	97.7	219	312	96
Computer Operator-Junior	23	93	296	296	266	292	325	7.30	97.3	260	372	13
Computer Operator-Intermediate	66	304	327	334	300	328	362	8.39	93.7	290	417	47
Computer Operator-Senior	55	186	403	403	364	392	438	9.92	94.7	333	490	10
Correspondent.	9	275	281	309	297	323	330	8.07	99.4	269	401	–
Credit & Collection Clerk.	27	175	280	299	268	295	326	7.37	96.1	256	376	17
Customer Service Clerk	33	469	320	359	274	318	354	7.95	100.0	–	–	–
Data Control Clerk	21	68	313	305	269	306	349	7.65	99.4	251	364	13
Data Entry Operator-Junior	21	152	232	260	223	260	296	6.50	104.0	228	319	93
Data Entry Operator-Intermediate	64	543	246	274	249	270	300	6.85	96.3	237	345	–
Data Entry Operator-Senior	40	190	317	323	281	315	369	8.07	96.6	265	380	10
Data Entry Operator (Group Leader)	23	38	353	363	309	342	448	8.75	90.7	291	436	2
Duplicating Machine Operator-Junior. . . .	24	56	297	271	229	246	306	6.31	87.1	234	334	11
Duplicating Machine Operator-Senior. . . .	19	76	374	361	307	356	396	9.18	104.9	289	418	3
Employee Benefits Claim Clerk.	37	43	328	327	284	328	362	8.20	95.9	276	406	3
File Clerk-Junior.	26	193	220	225	194	221	240	5.74	98.2	198	281	64
File Clerk-Senior.	16	60	243	267	209	251	322	6.43	92.8	225	316	10
Import/Export Clerk.	4	9	294	294	251	293	337	7.32	83.7	275	401	–
Input/Output Clerk	12	23	326	327	279	319	352	7.96	99.8	243	347	2
Inventory Control Clerk.	31	114	291	285	254	274	310	6.95	88.4	241	343	9
Mail Clerk	61	174	249	247	213	238	267	6.02	96.4	214	303	40
Messenger/Office Person.	18	61	237	230	206	227	257	5.87	92.8	201	284	12
Secretary-Junior	35	319	265	281	245	286	300	7.32	98.3	245	352	29
Secretary-Intermediate	103	1,178	307	313	286	319	337	8.16	97.6	265	384	123
Secretary-Senior	79	938	364	355	325	353	385	9.00	96.7	293	427	69
Executive Secretary.	55	611	382	394	343	395	443	10.15	95.1	321	470	30
Secretary-Legal.	19	87	384	380	321	376	426	10.02	94.1	312	468	4

All salaries shown are weekly salary rates, with the exception of the median hourly rate.

Subregion: Lower Southeast States

	NO OF FIRMS	NO IN POS	WTD AVG SALARY	AVG SALARY	SALARY 1ST QRTL	SALARY MEDIAN	SALARY 3RD QRTL	MEDIAN HRLY RATE	RATIO OF MEDIAN SALARY TO U.S. MEDIAN	AVG SAL RANGE MIN	AVG SAL RANGE MAX	NO OF HIRES
Secretary-Bilingual.												
Secretary to Staff VP or Div Mgr or Exec .	63	369	404	407	359	395	462	10.30	92.9	324	477	29
Secretary to Executive Vice President. . .	36	109	458	448	385	425	511	11.08	90.4	360	531	6
Secretary to Chief Executive Officer . . .	48	55	497	493	402	484	580	12.27	91.7	382	565	2
Telephone Operator-PBX	33	158	264	268	234	258	300	6.85	91.7	219	315	15
Telephone Operator-Chief	17	18	333	335	308	337	366	8.42	94.4	270	399	1
Terminal Operator.	6	38	261	262	232	256	292	6.66	91.9	205	290	
Travel Clerk	8	94	281	345	291	346	393	8.64	98.4	275	410	3
Typist-Junior.	11	55	225	241	198	241	262	6.02	99.6	200	278	17
Typist-Senior.	10	49	257	270	231	270	285	6.74	98.4	217	319	8
Word Processing Operator-Junior.	24	66	273	271	248	274	290	7.00	99.5	235	344	27
Word Processing Operator-Intermediate. . .	46	227	299	302	276	302	333	7.60	97.0	260	379	31
Word Processing Operator-Senior.	35	142	363	362	329	356	399	9.12	95.7	293	435	5

SUPPLEMENTAL DATA 164 PARTICIPANTS

INDUSTRY AND EMPLOYMENT CLASSIFICATION

INDUSTRY GROUP	NO.	PCT.	TOTAL NUMBER OF EMPLOYEES	NO.	PCT.
Manufacturing	62	37.8	UNDER 200	82	50.0
Energy	2	1.2	200 - 499	27	16.5
Trade	10	6.1	500 - 999	18	11.0
Utilities	6	3.7	1,000 - 1,999	16	9.8
Services	39	23.8	2,000 - 4,999	14	8.5
Banking & Finance	13	7.9	5,000 - 9,999	3	1.8
Insurance	17	10.4	10,000 - 19,999	4	2.4
Non-Profit	15	9.1	20,000 - Over	-	-
TOTAL	164	100.0	TOTAL	164	100.0

(Percentages may not add to 100% due to rounding.)

NONEXEMPT POLICIES AND PRACTICES

OFFICE WORKWEEK

	PERCENT		PERCENT
35 hrs.	7.3	38 3/4 hrs.	3.7
36 1/4 hrs.	3.7	40 hrs.	71.3
37 1/2 hrs.	14.0	Other	-

SHIFT DIFFERENTIAL

Reporting 107
Paying 65

	AVERAGE SHIFT DIFFERENTIAL PERCENT	$/HOUR
Second Shift	8.7	.35
Third Shift	10.4	.43

AVERAGE PERCENT INCREASE

	1986 ACTUAL	1987 PLANNED	1988 PROJECTED
Merit	5.8	5.4	5.3
General (C.O.L)	4.5	3.8	3.5
Total Increase	5.8	5.5	5.4
Salary Ranges	4.9	4.4	4.1

Metropolitan Area: Atlanta, GA

	NO OF FIRMS	NO IN POS	WTD AVG SALARY	AVG SALARY	SALARY 1ST QRTL	SALARY MEDIAN	SALARY 3RD QRTL	MEDIAN HRLY RATE	RATIO OF MEDIAN SALARY TO U.S. MEDIAN	AVG SAL RANGE MIN	AVG SAL RANGE MAX	NO OF HIRES
Accounting Clerk-Junior.	11	33	266	261	242	268	282	6.77	98.9	245	358	10
Accounting Clerk-Intermediate.	22	233	307	316	290	315	343	7.98	101.4	269	382	42
Accounting Clerk-Senior (Group Leader) . .	17	145	377	374	328	383	410	9.72	104.8	319	463	22
Bookkeeper-Senior.	5	17	295	314	274	288	368	7.20	75.8	287	414	4
Chauffeur-Executive.												
Chauffeur-Messenger.												
Clerk-Junior	13	108	233	236	216	241	251	6.02	100.8	220	310	43
Clerk-Intermediate	22	349	300	273	255	273	288	7.14	98.6	245	361	60
Clerk-Senior (Group Leader).	15	122	356	342	324	349	368	9.00	104.2	290	427	9
Clerk-Typist	14	126	261	259	240	253	285	6.64	98.6	234	326	36
Computer Operator-Junior	6	30	284	301	266	314	327	8.10	104.7	283	397	7
Computer Operator-Intermediate	18	85	354	355	332	353	384	9.15	100.7	314	452	13
Computer Operator-Senior	13	59	414	440	369	440	462	11.00	106.3	389	568	1
Correspondent.												
Credit & Collection Clerk.	6	15	292	298	265	310	327	7.93	101.0	248	354	4
Customer Service Clerk	13	74	337	434	289	339	418	8.72	106.6	377	556	25
Data Control Clerk	5	14	287	298	269	277	339	7.14	90.0	277	383	6
Data Entry Operator-Junior	7	84	225	277	244	260	323	6.93	104.0	235	339	69
Data Entry Operator-Intermediate	16	143	251	265	240	263	277	6.88	93.9	247	353	46
Data Entry Operator-Senior	6	49	335	326	281	308	386	7.83	94.3	286	396	3
Data Entry Operator (Group Leader)	5	11	380	394	322	361	483	9.31	95.8	327	485	
Duplicating Machine Operator-Junior. . . .	5	11	301	299	232	309	361	7.97	109.6	265	362	3
Duplicating Machine Operator-Senior. . . .	5	12	422	382	315	359	460	9.57	105.7	333	462	
Employee Benefits Claim Clerk.	7	7	324	324	270	297	389	7.42	86.9	293	416	
File Clerk-Junior.	8	63	220	240	204	225	283	5.93	100.2	213	298	28
File Clerk-Senior.	5	14	262	283	212	274	358	7.07	101.3	255	351	3
Import/Export Clerk.												
Input/Output Clerk												
Inventory Control Clerk.	10	20	277	286	252	280	313	7.22	90.2	257	352	4
Mail Clerk	19	64	276	261	233	244	285	6.42	98.8	233	324	10
Messenger/Office Person.												
Secretary-Junior	7	19	328	306	270	286	361	8.05	98.3	263	379	1
Secretary-Intermediate	36	331	331	319	298	322	345	8.30	98.5	278	406	63
Secretary-Senior	28	333	394	371	345	369	387	9.54	101.1	314	457	42
Executive Secretary.	20	166	453	423	382	415	472	10.75	99.8	340	498	14
Secretary-Legal.	4	32	422	395	333	408	444	10.99	102.0	338	500	1

All salaries shown are weekly salary rates, with the exception of the median hourly rate.

Metropolitan Area: Atlanta, GA

	NO OF FIRMS	NO IN POS	WTD AVG SALARY	AVG SALARY	SALARY 1ST QRTL	SALARY MEDIAN	SALARY 3RD QRTL	MEDIAN HRLY RATE	RATIO OF MEDIAN SALARY TO U.S. MEDIAN	AVG SAL RANGE MIN	AVG SAL RANGE MAX	NO OF HIRES
Secretary-Bilingual												
Secretary to Staff VP or Div Mgr or Exec	13	134	437	460	401	422	530	11.25	99.3	361	537	7
Secretary to Executive Vice President	10	50	475	503	427	475	601	11.87	101.1	399	582	3
Secretary to Chief Executive Officer	12	14	536	540	448	508	649	13.50	96.1	430	636	
Telephone Operator-PBX	6	10	265	264	233	279	291	7.19	98.9	237	324	4
Telephone Operator-Chief												
Terminal Operator												
Travel Clerk												
Typist-Junior												
Typist-Senior												
Word Processing Operator-Junior	6	13	293	292	272	299	312	7.80	108.7	250	361	3
Word Processing Operator-Intermediate	16	55	319	323	293	327	346	8.57	105.0	283	412	17
Word Processing Operator-Senior	11	66	387	394	363	370	399	9.78	99.5	321	476	4

SUPPLEMENTAL DATA 55 PARTICIPANTS

INDUSTRY AND EMPLOYMENT CLASSIFICATION

INDUSTRY GROUP	NO.	PCT.	TOTAL NUMBER OF EMPLOYEES	NO.	PCT.
Manufacturing	22	40.0	UNDER 200	33	60.0
Energy	–	–	200 – 499	10	18.2
Trade	1	1.8	500 – 999	4	7.3
Utilities	2	3.6	1,000 – 1,999	3	5.5
Services	14	25.5	2,000 – 4,999	5	9.1
Banking & Finance	5	9.1	5,000 – 9,999	–	–
Insurance	8	14.5	10,000 – 19,999	–	–
Non-Profit	3	5.5	20,000 – Over	–	–
TOTAL	55	100.0	TOTAL	55	100.0

(Percentages may not add to 100% due to rounding.)

NONEXEMPT POLICIES AND PRACTICES

OFFICE WORKWEEK

	PERCENT		PERCENT
35 hrs.	10.9	38 3/4 hrs.	5.5
36 1/4 hrs.	5.5	40 hrs.	50.9
37 1/2 hrs.	27.3	Other	–

SHIFT DIFFERENTIAL

Reporting 39
Paying 21

	AVERAGE SHIFT DIFFERENTIAL PERCENT	$/HOUR
Second Shift	8.8	.45
Third Shift	10.2	.67

AVERAGE PERCENT INCREASE

	1986 ACTUAL	1987 PLANNED	1988 PROJECTED
Merit	5.9	5.9	5.5
General (C.O.L)	4.8	4.3	–
Total Increase	5.9	5.8	5.5
Salary Ranges	4.5	4.7	4.1

ECS

Two Executive Drive
Fort Lee, New Jersey 07024
(201) 585 - 9808

a subsidiary of THE Wyatt COMPANY

Supervisory Management Report

Thirty-second edition 1987/88

Data in Effect: January 1, 1987
Publication Date: June, 1987

GENERAL DUTIES AND RESPONSIBILITIES OF SUPERVISORS

The functions of individual office, plant, and general supervisors vary widely throughout industry. However, there are a number of duties and responsibilities which are common to most of these supervisors. Some of the more common ones are listed below:

1. Plan and schedule the work of a section, department or organization for maximum effective utilization of employees, equipment and material within budgetary, cost and quality standards.

2. Estimate manpower requirements. Requisition and select qualified employees necessary to perform work.

3. Assign employees to jobs. Instruct them in proper performance of work and familiarize them with company rules and regulations.

4. Maintain discipline of employees under their supervision in accordance with established rules and regulations. Initiate appropriate disciplinary action.

5. Assume responsibility for the proper application of established employee relations, wage and salary administration policies, safety and health regulations, and union agreements.

6. Initiate action and approve, or recommend approval of promotions, merit increases, transfers, leaves of absence and other personnel changes.

7. Coordinate the functions performed under their supervision with those performed under other supervision.

8. Arrange for proper maintenance of machines, equipment, and facilities for which they are responsible.

9. Prepare reports concerning departmental activities.

CLASSIFICATION GUIDE FOR FIRST-LINE OFFICE SUPERVISORY POSITIONS

LEVEL	DEFINITION OF CHARACTERISTICS OF SUPERVISORY LEVEL
1	Lowest discernible level of office supervisory responsibility. *Supervision exercised is usually partial or part-time*, being restricted largely to assigning work and directing efforts, with *little or no responsibility for initiating action* on hiring, firing, lay-offs, promotions, salary increases or other personnel activities normally associated with true supervisory status. *Much of supervisor's working time may be spent performing work of the type supervised, which may result in classification of employee as nonexempt.* Indicative of this semi-supervisory status, typical titles for positions in this level are: Group or Section Leader, Senior or Chief Clerk and Coordinator.
2	Positions in this level usually involve responsibility for supervising, directly or through group leaders and assistants, employees with generally similar occupational skills, or employees with relatively limited variety of skills. One or more exempt employees may be supervised. Other responsibilities of this level involve assignment of work in accordance with schedules fixed by higher supervision and subject to higher approval. *This level is classified as exempt*. Typical position titles are: Section Supervisor/Chief and Assistant Supervisor.
3	*This is the highest level below that of a major department head.* It usually involves responsibility for supervising employees with considerable variation in skills and pay, also employees with more complex skills. One or more exempt employees may be supervised. Other responsibilities frequently found on this level involve day-to-day planning of departmental operations, developing methods, authorizing overtime and controlling costs. Typical position title is Supervisor.

OFFICE SUPERVISORS: • **Data Processing Supervisors**

30 **APPLICATIONS PROGRAMMING SUPERVISOR:** Developing, maintaining and modifying applications programs used to process commercial or scientific data. May involve instructions for operations personnel and verifying the maintenance of programming quality standards.

31 **EQUIPMENT OPERATIONS SUPERVISOR:** Monitoring and controlling of computer equipment by operating a central console or on-line terminal. Selecting and loading input and output. Observing the operation of equipment and control panel for error lights, verification printouts, error messages and faulty output. May assist in maintaining operating records.

32 **SOFTWARE SYSTEMS SUPERVISOR:** Designing, debugging, documenting and installing operating systems, compilers, monitors and other systems software. Maintaining and modifying existing operating systems and "tuning" system to maximum efficiency. Providing technical support in the effective use of software to applications programmers. (Do not include application programming.)

33 **DATA CONTROL SUPERVISOR:** Maintaining of records or source documents for data input. Checking of accuracy and appropriateness of both input and output data by visual examination and/or balancing to control figures and insuring of satisfactory condition of data input and output. May provide for distribution of reports after they are prepared.

34 **DATA ENTRY SUPERVISOR:** Operating key entry devices to record a variety of alpha/numeric data onto various storage media and/or utilizing automatic edit parameters.

35 **SYSTEMS ANALYSIS SUPERVISOR:** Analyzing and evaluating present or proposed business procedures or problems to define data and convert it to programmable form for electronic data processing. Obtaining detailed specifications from user to ascertain specific output information requirements. Preparing detailed flow-charts and diagrams from which program will be written. May also correlate interface between programmer and user.

The Nation and Five Regions

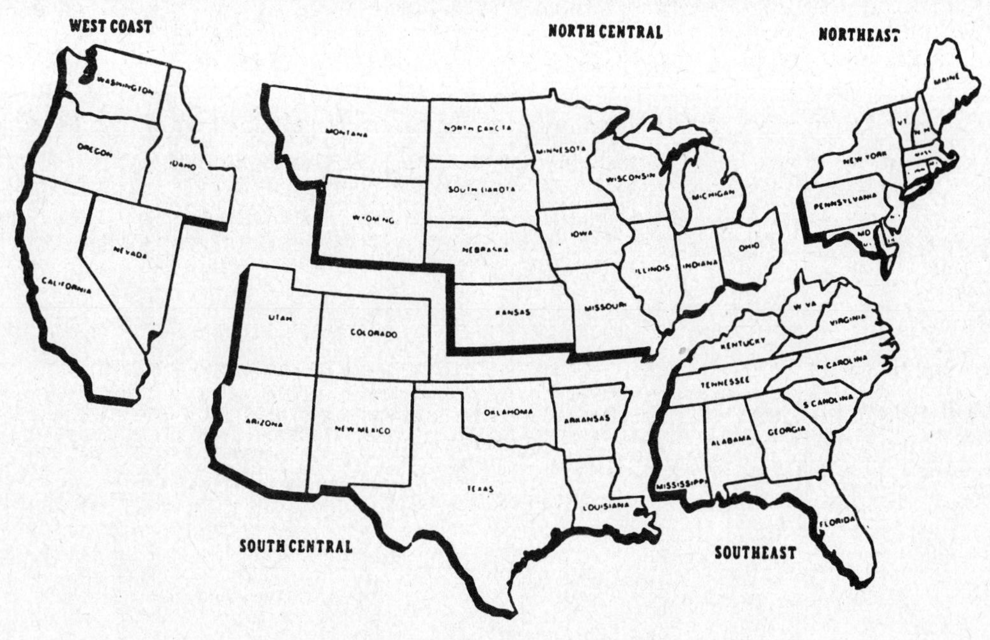

Region: Southeast

SUPERVISOR OF:	NO OF FIRMS	NO IN POS	WTD AVG SALARY	AVERAGE SALARY	1ST QRTL	MEDIAN	3RD QRTL	RATIO OF MEDIAN SALARY TO U.S. MEDIAN	AVG SAL RANGE MINIMUM	AVG SAL RANGE MAXIMUM	AVG NO EMP SUPV'D EXMPT	AVG NO EMP SUPV'D NONEXMPT	RATIO OF HIGHEST PAID SUBORDINATE TO SUPERVISOR'S SALARY EXMPT	RATIO OF HIGHEST PAID SUBORDINATE TO SUPERVISOR'S SALARY NONEXMPT
31 EQUIPMENT OPERATIONS														
LEVEL 1	11	42	21.1	21.7	19.2	20.8	24.7	89.5	17.5	25.6		6		81.0
LEVEL 2	25	68	27.4	27.3	24.9	26.6	30.0	92.9	23.7	35.9	5	10	88.3	77.4
LEVEL 3	22	39	35.1	34.7	31.5	34.7	37.4	97.1	29.0	44.3	7	9	81.2	68.2
32 SOFTWARE SYSTEMS														
LEVEL 1	6	29	32.4	31.1	23.8	32.8	36.2	111.4	26.7	39.4				
LEVEL 2	17	54	41.0	39.5	34.3	40.6	44.7	106.6	32.0	48.5	11	2	89.5	49.7
LEVEL 3	17	35	46.7	47.2	42.4	48.1	52.7	100.7	36.3	56.1	6	2	84.2	58.5
33 DATA CONTROL														
LEVEL 1	11	19	21.2	21.4	19.5	21.3	23.5	108.1	18.2	25.9		4		75.6
LEVEL 2	23	39	26.1	26.9	23.5	25.6	31.2	97.7	22.3	33.5	3	7	74.4	74.8
LEVEL 3	11	20	35.0	36.2	27.3	37.2	43.4	106.7	27.8	42.7	4	4	74.8	62.6
34 DATA ENTRY														
LEVEL 1	21	33	18.6	18.6	16.3	18.0	21.0	90.9	15.7	22.5		13		80.7
LEVEL 2	20	34	25.1	23.7	20.4	22.5	26.2	93.8	20.2	30.8	2	10		78.9
LEVEL 3	15	15	30.9	30.9	27.4	29.4	32.8	95.8	25.6	39.1	2	10	93.1	64.8
35 SYSTEMS ANALYSIS														
LEVEL 1	6	29	35.6	31.0	23.4	32.2	37.7	102.2	25.0	36.7		4		85.3
LEVEL 2	19	47	38.5	37.9	32.6	38.2	43.1	100.5	31.2	47.4	3	3	85.0	72.1
LEVEL 3	17	54	44.9	44.1	38.0	45.6	48.9	103.6	34.1	52.7	6	2	91.5	48.1

ECS

Two Executive Drive
Fort Lee, New Jersey 07024
(201) 585 - 9808

a subsidiary of THE *Wyatt* COMPANY

Professional and Scientific Personnel Report

(Geographic Edition)

Volume I

Fourteenth edition **1987/88**

Data in Effect: March 1, 1987
Publication Date: August, 1987

LEVEL GUIDE FOR DATA PROCESSING POSITIONS

LEVEL	EXPERIENCE	KNOWLEDGE	FUNCTIONAL RESPONSIBILITY	
			AREA OF SPECIALIZATION	ADMINISTRATION
1 (Trainee)	Entry level for college graduate, with Bachelor's Degree or its equivalent. Employees usually have 0-1 year professional experience.	Knows fundamental concepts, practices and procedures of particular field of specialization.	Using established procedures and working under immediate supervision, performs assigned tasks. Work is routine and instructions are usually detailed. Little evaluation, originality or ingenuity is required.	No administrative duties. Reports in most instances to Senior or Lead Level.
2 (Junior)	May be entering level for Master's Degree. Employees usually have 1-3 years professional experience.	Knows and uses well the fundamental concepts, practices and procedures of particular field of specialization.	Under supervision, performs work that is varied and that may be somewhat difficult in character, but usually involving limited responsibility. Some evaluation, originality or ingenuity is required.	No administrative duties. Reports in most instances to Senior or Lead Level.
3 (Inter-mediate)	Intermediate Level. Employees usually have 3-5 years professional experience.	Possesses and applies to the completion of moderately difficult assignments a broad knowledge of principles, practices, and procedures of particular field of specialization.	Usually works with minimum supervision, conferring with superior on unusual matters. Assignments are broad in nature, usually requiring appreciable originality and ingenuity. Has some latitude for unreviewed action or decision.	In some instances assisted by personnel in Trainee or Junior Levels. Reports in many instances to Lead Level or Section Head.
4 (Senior)	Staff Specialist Level. Employees usually have 5-8 years professional experience.	Possesses and applies to the completion of difficult assignments a comprehensive knowledge of particular field of specialization.	Under general supervision, plans, conducts and supervises assignments. Reviews progress and evaluates results. Recommends changes in procedures. Operates with appreciable latitude for unreviewed action or decision. Reviews progress with management.	Plans and assigns personnel for given projects or tasks. May assist with the review and evaluation of personnel performance. Usually reports to Section Head or Middle Management.
5 (Lead)	Employees usually have more than 8 years professional experience. This may be a first level supervisory position. Management is typically the next higher level position.	Possesses and applies to the completion of complex assignments a comprehensive knowledge of particular field of specialization; also well-developed leadership qualities.	Plans, conducts and may supervise assignments, generally involving the larger and more important projects or more than one project. Evaluates progress and results and recommends major changes in procedures or objectives. Operates with considerable latitude for unreviewed action or decision.	Schedules and may supervise project work. Assists with the review and evaluation of personnel performance. May act in liaison capacity with other departments, divisions, and firms. Reports in most instances to Middle Management.

Position Descriptions

060 **APPLICATIONS PROGRAMMER** - Analyzes business or scientific systems specifications and develops block diagrams and logic flowcharts. Encodes programs, prepares test data, and test and debugs programs. Revises and updates programs as required and provides the necessary documentation for the computer operations department.

061 **METHODS AND PROCEDURES ANALYST** - Coordinates proposed policies, procedures, systems, forms and reports among all locations and departments; analyzes existing forms and methods to promote effective operations through standardization, improvement, simplification, discontinuance or other methods; installs new systems and procedures in various departments and instructs personnel regarding them; recommends installation of office equipment and business machines best suited for work to be performed. May review the functions and structure of organization units to avoid overlapping or duplication; reviews personnel change requisitions to determine their effect upon established organization structures and job functions.

062 **PROGRAMMER/ANALYST** - Analyzes and evaluates existing or proposed systems, and devises computer programs, systems and related procedures to process data. Prepares charts and diagrams to assist in problem analysis, and submits recommendations for solution. Prepares program specifications and diagrams and develops coding logic flowcharts. Encodes, tests, debugs, and installs the operating programs and procedures in coordination with the computer operations and user departments.

063 **SOFTWARE SYSTEMS PROGRAMMER** - Develops, tests, installs, and modifies computer software, such as operating systems, compilers, utilities, multiprogramming, and telecommunications systems. Creates block diagrams and logic flowcharts, and encodes, tests, debugs, and installs programs. Interfaces with, and supports the application programming effort.

064 **SYSTEMS ANALYST** - Analyzes and evaluates existing or proposed systems and devises computer systems to process data. Prepares charts and diagrams to assist in problem analysis and submits recommendations for solution. Prepares detailed program specifications and flowcharts, and coordinates the system's installation with the user department, insuring satisfactory results.

Region Southeast

	NO OF FIRMS	NO IN POSITION	WTD AVG SALARY	AVG SAL.	AVERAGE SALARY 1ST QRTL.	MEDIAN	3RD QRTL.	RATIO OF MEDIAN SALARY TO U.S. MEDIAN	AVG SAL RANGE MINIMUM	MAXIMUM	% RCVG BONUS	AVG $ BONUS
060 APPLICATIONS PROGRAMMER												
LEVEL 1	19	76	19.0	19.4	17.8	19.1	20.2	93.2	17.4	25.4	1.3	1.4
LEVEL 2	37	385	21.6	22.1	20.3	21.8	24.0	94.4	19.2	28.5	5.2	1.3
LEVEL 3	37	412	24.8	25.4	23.1	24.8	27.8	93.8	21.6	32.6	6.1	2.6
LEVEL 4	20	206	30.7	31.2	27.7	28.6	34.7	90.4	25.3	38.0	1.9	.5
LEVEL 5	7	62	40.1	39.4	34.1	39.2	46.0	95.2	32.1	48.9	3.2	.8
061 METHODS - PROCEDURES ANALYST												
LEVEL 1												
LEVEL 2	5	39	23.4	23.0	20.2	23.4	25.6	93.4	19.7	28.8		
LEVEL 3	7	27	27.7	28.2	24.8	27.4	31.2	91.2	23.3	34.5		
LEVEL 4	6	10	33.4	34.5	27.3	36.4	40.6	101.3	28.9	42.5		
LEVEL 5												
062 PROGRAMMER/ANALYST												
LEVEL 1	29	310	24.4	23.2	20.4	23.1	25.9	96.3	20.6	30.8	1.0	2.2
LEVEL 2	55	718	26.3	26.0	24.0	25.8	28.9	96.6	22.3	33.5	2.6	3.0
LEVEL 3	68	938	31.1	30.5	27.4	30.1	33.7	99.2	25.2	38.0	.9	1.8
LEVEL 4	53	597	34.6	34.2	30.6	33.5	38.6	95.4	28.3	42.4	.7	2.9
LEVEL 5	25	272	37.0	40.7	36.1	41.7	45.6	100.5	32.7	50.2	1.1	1.1
063 SOFTWARE SYSTEMS PROGRAMMER												
LEVEL 1												
LEVEL 2	21	152	31.2	28.8	26.2	28.5	31.8	98.6	24.1	36.0	1.3	3.8
LEVEL 3	34	217	34.9	31.2	26.1	31.1	33.8	92.4	26.2	39.7	1.8	1.9
LEVEL 4	26	159	40.5	38.7	35.8	38.1	42.0	96.1	31.2	47.1	3.8	2.1
LEVEL 5	13	49	43.0	43.8	40.7	42.3	47.4	92.4	33.0	50.7		
064 SYSTEMS ANALYST												
LEVEL 1	7	21	27.9	27.4	22.2	27.0	34.5	103.8	23.3	34.2		
LEVEL 2	16	78	29.9	29.8	27.4	28.2	34.0	93.8	24.7	37.8	3.8	3.4
LEVEL 3	50	689	34.8	34.0	31.3	33.3	37.0	96.7	27.9	42.4	1.9	3.4
LEVEL 4	48	479	39.5	38.2	35.4	38.0	40.9	96.9	31.6	48.0	1.5	3.3
LEVEL 5	26	170	43.2	41.6	38.7	41.8	44.8	95.9	32.9	50.8	3.5	1.7

ECS

Two Executive Drive
Fort Lee, New Jersey 07024
(201) 585 - 9808

a subsidiary of THE Wyatt COMPANY

Middle Management Report

Volume I

Thirty-sixth edition **1987/88**

Data in Effect: January 1, 1987
Publication Date: May, 1987

Position Descriptions

215 **ELECTRONIC DATA PROCESSING MANAGER** - Responsible for managing the overall electronic data processing function. Supervises the systems and programming procedures and operation of electronic computer equipment. Coordinates the integration of present office operations and data processing into electronic or automatic data processing. Evaluates studies of the economics of possible alternative methods of processing.

223 **APPLICATIONS PROGRAMMING MANAGER** - Plans, directs and controls the development, installation and maintenance of computer business and scientific applications programs. Develops and establishes departmental standards and procedures, and assigns, directs and coordinates the work of the programming staff, providing technical support and direction.

224 **SOFTWARE SYSTEMS PROGRAMMING MANAGER** - Plans, directs, and controls the development and maintenance of computer software programs and systems. Develops and establishes departmental standards and procedures, and is responsible for the assignment of work to the software programming staff, and the monitoring, directing, and coordination of their efforts, both internally, and in support of the applications programming staff. Evaluates current and projected hardware and software, and coordinates and directs the installation of new operating systems.

225 **SYSTEMS ANALYSIS MANAGER** - Directs and administers the Systems Analysis staff in the study, analysis, and evaluation of current and projected computer-based applications systems and procedures, and in the design, implementation, and maintenance of revised or new systems. Develops and establishes departmental standards and procedures, and coordinates the staff's efforts with the programming and other operating departments, providing technical support and direction.

226 **SYSTEMS AND PROGRAMMING MANAGER** - Responsible for the operation and administration of the systems analysis and computer programming functions. Develops and establishes departmental standards and procedures; directs and coordinates the staff's efforts to maintain and upgrade current operating systems, and directs the systems analysis, procedural development, and programming effort in the study, design, implementation and operation of new systems, and in the evaluation, acquisition, and installation of new equipment.

227 **DATA PROCESSING OPERATIONS MANAGER** - Plans, directs, and controls the activities of data processing operations, exclusive of the systems and programming function. Develops and establishes departmental standards and procedures, and is responsible for the assignment of work to the operations staff. Consults with other sections on the proper integration and correlation of the function assigned. Prepares activity and progress reports regarding the activities of the data processing operations section.

228 **DATA PROCESSING AUDIT MANAGER** - Develops audit software, systems integrity reviews and provides periodic examination of data processing operations controls and security. Interfaces with and supports the needs of the financial audit staff. Sets and monitors standards; prepares activity and progress reports regarding the activities of the data processing audit function.

229 **TELECOMMUNICATIONS MANAGER** - Directs and controls the activities of the telecommunications function including the planning, designing, installation and maintenance of networks in support of data processing systems. Responsible for budgeting and long range planning of telecommunications systems and projects, including various word processing and facsimile equipment systems. Consults with data processing staff to coordinate telecommunications systems capabilities. Prepares activity and progress reports regarding the activities of the telecommunications function.

ALL COMPANIES (EXCLUDING ALL FINANCIAL SERVICE AND NON-PROFIT ORGANIZATIONS)

ELECTRONIC DATA PROCESSING MANAGER

CORPORATE AND DIVISIONAL COMPENSATION ANALYSIS

SALES GROUP ($ MILL)	NO. OF COMPANIES	NO. IN POSITION	WEIGHTED AVERAGE	AVERAGE	FIRST QUARTILE	MEDIAN	THIRD QUARTILE
			SALARY ($000)				
Under 50	93	93	44.8	44.8	37.6	44.0	50.9
50 - 100	76	77	50.6	50.7	44.4	50.3	55.6
100 - 300	138	160	54.6	55.6	47.4	54.0	60.8
300 - 600	52	52	61.8	61.8	50.5	62.0	68.7
600 - 1,200	35	39	63.1	63.9	54.6	64.2	71.9
1,200 & Over	33	38	67.4	69.3	59.1	67.7	77.0
			BONUS ($000)				
Under 50	33	33	5.4	5.4	1.6	2.8	7.0
50 - 100	22	23	4.8	4.9	2.1	4.4	6.0
100 - 300	58	59	8.8	8.8	3.5	7.1	13.6
300 - 600	21	21	11.7	11.7	3.5	8.0	19.3
600 - 1,200	13	17	13.6	15.4	9.3	14.8	19.6
1,200 & Over	17	17	9.3	9.3	5.5	8.2	11.9
			TOTAL CASH COMPENSATION ($000)				
Under 50	93	93	46.7	46.7	37.9	44.5	52.2
50 - 100	76	77	52.0	52.1	45.1	51.0	58.3
100 - 300	138	160	57.8	59.3	48.9	56.9	66.2
300 - 600	52	52	66.5	66.5	50.9	63.5	74.5
600 - 1,200	35	39	69.0	69.6	55.0	66.0	82.0
1,200 & Over	33	38	71.5	74.1	60.7	72.3	84.3
				SALARY RANGE MINIMUM ($000)			
Under 50	73			36.4	30.2	34.0	40.1
50 - 100	61			38.3	34.5	38.6	41.9
100 - 300	122			44.2	38.7	42.6	49.2
300 - 600	49			50.1	42.9	49.0	55.2
600 - 1,200	34			50.1	41.3	49.9	57.2
1,200 & Over	31			56.1	50.0	54.6	67.0
				SALARY RANGE MAXIMUM ($000)			
Under 50	73			54.4	45.7	51.1	59.9
50 - 100	61			57.9	52.0	59.0	63.0
100 - 300	122			67.2	58.3	64.6	73.7
300 - 600	49			76.5	67.1	73.8	83.1
600 - 1,200	34			76.3	64.7	75.5	85.7
1,200 & Over	31			86.5	75.0	83.5	101.3

ALL COMPANIES (EXCLUDING ALL FINANCIAL SERVICE AND NON-PROFIT ORGANIZATIONS)

SYSTEMS ANALYSIS MANAGER

CORPORATE AND DIVISIONAL COMPENSATION ANALYSIS

SALES GROUP	NO. OF COMPANIES	NO. IN POSITION	WEIGHTED AVERAGE	AVERAGE	FIRST QUARTILE	MEDIAN	THIRD QUARTILE
			SALARY ($000)				
Under 50 ($ MILL)	17	20	41.2	41.2	35.8	41.3	46.4
50 - 100	11	17	48.6	47.1	38.4	48.1	52.0
100 - 300	39	51	45.0	45.4	39.5	44.6	50.4
300 - 600	18	33	48.9	49.8	45.5	49.9	57.2
600 - 1,200	14	78	57.4	51.9	43.3	53.8	60.0
1,200 & Over	29	124	53.4	57.7	49.0	55.6	64.2
			BONUS ($000)				
Under 50	3	3	3.8	3.8		3.5	
50 - 100	3	3	1.8	1.8		1.7	
100 - 300	9	12	8.6	7.0	2.9	4.9	10.9
300 - 600	7	9	8.0	7.4	2.8	6.0	13.3
600 - 1,200	2	6	7.3	6.9		6.9	
1,200 & Over	10	18	8.3	10.8	5.5	8.0	15.8
			TOTAL CASH COMPENSATION ($000)				
Under 50	17	20	41.7	41.9	35.8	42.0	48.0
50 - 100	11	17	48.9	47.6	38.4	49.8	52.0
100 - 300	39	51	47.1	47.0	39.6	48.4	53.9
300 - 600	18	33	51.1	52.6	45.5	51.3	60.3
600 - 1,200	14	78	57.9	52.5	43.3	53.8	60.0
1,200 & Over	29	124	54.6	61.1	49.0	59.2	71.9
				SALARY RANGE MINIMUM ($000)			
Under 50	16			33.0	28.3	34.3	38.6
50 - 100	10			33.5	28.0	34.2	36.5
100 - 300	35			36.5	34.0	36.2	38.7
300 - 600	17			40.3	35.3	40.2	43.2
600 - 1,200	14			42.4	37.4	41.4	47.8
1,200 & Over	26			45.3	39.9	44.0	52.0
				SALARY RANGE MAXIMUM ($000)			
Under 50	16			48.8	43.1	49.5	57.9
50 - 100	10			50.6	44.3	49.0	55.3
100 - 300	35			54.7	50.5	55.8	59.8
300 - 600	17			62.0	54.0	60.4	66.7
600 - 1,200	14			64.2	57.7	62.7	71.7
1,200 & Over	26			70.0	59.9	68.4	78.0

ALL COMPANIES (EXCLUDING ALL FINANCIAL SERVICE AND NON-PROFIT ORGANIZATIONS)

DATA PROCESSING OPERATIONS MANAGER

CORPORATE AND DIVISIONAL COMPENSATION ANALYSIS

SALES GROUP	NO. OF COMPANIES	NO. IN POSITION	WEIGHTED AVERAGE	AVERAGE	FIRST QUARTILE	MEDIAN	THIRD QUARTILE
			SALARY ($000)				
Under 50 ($ MILL)	69	75	36.7	37.7	30.2	35.9	44.1
50 - 100	63	64	40.4	40.3	34.5	38.4	45.7
100 - 300	124	130	41.5	41.6	35.9	41.2	46.3
300 - 600	75	81	44.6	45.0	37.8	43.7	52.0
600 - 1,200	59	70	49.9	50.3	42.5	48.3	57.5
1,200 & Over	70	124	54.0	53.4	44.6	51.5	58.7
			BONUS ($000)				
Under 50	19	19	4.4	4.4	2.1	3.9	5.8
50 - 100	5	5	3.0	3.0	.9	1.8	5.8
100 - 300	26	27	3.9	4.0	1.4	2.7	5.2
300 - 600	16	16	6.3	6.3	2.6	4.9	9.7
600 - 1,200	14	24	5.6	7.8	4.0	5.6	13.3
1,200 & Over	26	54	7.6	7.7	2.9	7.0	10.2
			TOTAL CASH COMPENSATION ($000)				
Under 50	69	75	37.8	38.9	31.3	37.0	45.5
50 - 100	63	64	40.6	40.5	34.5	38.4	45.7
100 - 300	124	130	42.3	42.4	35.9	42.0	47.2
300 - 600	75	81	45.9	46.4	38.2	43.9	52.5
600 - 1,200	59	70	51.8	52.2	42.9	50.8	59.2
1,200 & Over	70	124	57.3	56.1	46.4	53.8	62.0
				SALARY RANGE MINIMUM ($000)			
Under 50	55			30.5	25.7	29.2	33.9
50 - 100	52			32.5	27.9	30.7	35.2
100 - 300	110			33.8	29.2	34.0	37.3
300 - 600	72			36.0	31.4	35.0	39.8
600 - 1,200	57			41.3	33.6	41.1	48.8
1,200 & Over	64			43.1	36.8	42.6	47.[illegible]
				SALARY RANGE MAXIMUM ($000)			
Under 50	55			45.3	39.7	42.6	50.0
50 - 100	52			48.8	42.0	46.3	52.8
100 - 300	110			51.0	43.6	50.8	56.5
300 - 600	72			54.6	47.9	53.2	59.7
600 - 1,200	57			62.4	50.6	62.1	72.4
1,200 & Over	64			67.1	57.3	66.4	72.8

ECS

Two Executive Drive
Fort Lee, New Jersey 07024
(201) 585 - 9808

a subsidiary of THE Wyatt COMPANY

Top Management Report

Volume I

Thirty-eighth edition 1987/88

Data in Effect: May 1, 1987
Publication Date: September, 1987

Corporate Position Descriptions

001 **CHIEF EXECUTIVE OFFICER** - May serve as presiding officer of the Board of Directors, and in that capacity, guides the deliberations and activities of that group. The Chief Executive of the company is responsible for directing the business with the objective of providing maximum profit and return on invested capital; establishing current and long-range objectives, plans, and policies subject to the approval of the Board of Directors; and representing the company with its major customers, the financial community and the public.

002 **CHIEF OPERATING OFFICER** - Directs, administers and coordinates the activities of the corporation in accordance with policies, goals and objectives established by the Chief Executive Officer and the Board of Directors. Assists the Chief Executive Officer in the development of corporate policies and goals that cover company operations, personnel, financial performance and growth.

003 **EXECUTIVE VICE PRESIDENT** - Directs and coordinates broad corporate activities toward achieving corporate objectives in accordance with policies established by the Chief Executive Officer and the Board of Directors and with instructions issued by the Chief Operating Officer. Responsible for effective operation of the corporation.

090 **ADMINISTRATIVE VICE PRESIDENT** - Directs and coordinates broad corporate activities having as their purpose the planning, development and implementation of policies, programs and practices in support of the production, operating, and marketing functions of the organization. Provides counsel and assistance to other officers and to operating divisions through specialized service departments.

006 **TOP MARKETING AND SALES EXECUTIVE** - Develops objectives, policies and programs for marketing activities of the corporation. Plans, directs, and coordinates the efforts of marketing and sales personnel toward the accomplishment of corporate objectives. Maintains and constantly improves the corporation's competitive position. Insures maximum sales volume at minimum cost. Supplies advice and assistance to the Chief Executive Officer and other company operating units in the field of sales activity.

506 **TOP MARKETING EXECUTIVE (EXCLUDING SALES)** - Plans, directs and coordinates the marketing of the company's products and services. Ensures that products are marketed in accordance with budgeted objectives to obtain maximum profitability and volume in relation to pre-set standards and to general and specific trends within the industry and economy. Continually evaluates the timely adjustment of marketing strategy and plans to meet changing market and competitive conditions. Recommends changes in marketing philosophy and policy when such changes serve the best interests of the company. Provides marketing advice and guidance to various operating units to insure that overall marketing effectiveness is equal to or better than competitors.

096 **TOP EDP (OR MIS) EXECUTIVE** - Directs the electronic data processing systems and programming activities, including systems design programming of procedures, and operation of computer and tabulating equipment. Provides management with direction and leadership in computer applications development and computer operations of the corporation. Provides advice and counsel to management concerning the application of computing techniques to corporate requirements.

SELECTED TOP MANAGEMENT COMPENSATION COMPARED TO CEO COMPENSATION (CEO = 100%)

ALL COMPANIES (EXCLUDING FINANCIAL SERVICES AND NON-PROFIT ORGANIZATIONS)

S = Salary
TC = Total Comp.

	SALES GROUP (IN MILLIONS)																	
	Under $25		$25-$50		$50-$100		$100-$200		$200-$500		$500-$1 Billion		$1,000-$2,000		$2,000-$5,000		$5,000-& over	
	% of		% of		% of		% of		% of		% of		% of		% of		% of	
POSITION	S	TC	S	TC	S	TC	S	TC	S	TC	S	TC	S	TC	S	TC	S	TC
Chief Executive Officer	100	100	100	100	100	100	100	100	100	100	100	100	100	100	100	100	100	100
Chief Operating Officer	82	77	80	77	78	76	80	79	68	66	74	74	71	68	63	63	69	66
Executive Vice President	70	66	67	69	60	57	71	68	57	56	61	55	48	41	46	43	–	–
Administrative Vice President	54	57	51	48	47	44	46	43	42	39	40	40	36	35	36	32	44	43
Top Marketing & Sales Exec.	52	49	55	54	46	45	45	44	44	43	40	33	33	28	30	23	–	–
Top EDP (or MIS) Exec.	39	35	34	31	32	29	31	28	27	23	26	23	21	17	20	16	21	17

ALL COMPANIES (Excluding All Financial Service and Non-Profit Organizations)

CHIEF EXECUTIVE OFFICER

SALES GROUP ($ MILL)	NO. OF COMPANIES	AVERAGE	10TH PERCENTILE	FIRST QUARTILE	MEDIAN	THIRD QUARTILE	90TH PERCENTILE
		SALES ($ MILL)					
Under 25	108	13.7	3.5	7.6	14.0	19.7	22.3
25 - 50	89	36.1	26.6	30.0	35.0	41.8	47.1
50 - 100	102	68.3	50.0	55.2	66.3	78.7	91.9
100 - 200	109	141.5	107.6	117.8	139.2	154.0	183.0
200 - 500	145	319.8	213.5	250.0	308.7	396.2	436.6
500 - 1,000	93	704.8	524.9	585.9	664.9	817.0	947.5
1,000 - 2,000	71	1,378.3	1,058.0	1,114.2	1,392.9	1,544.6	1,818.7
2,000 - 5,000	55	3,303.2	2,134.9	2,500.0	3,100.0	3,872.4	4,759.5
5,000 & Over	17	7,584.7	5,080.4	5,283.3	7,938.0	8,951.5	10,804.3
		SALARY ($000)					
Under 25	108	128.5	71.8	86.7	112.5	157.7	220.5
25 - 50	89	153.1	105.0	118.0	140.0	160.5	200.0
50 - 100	102	178.7	112.9	138.0	161.8	200.0	263.5
100 - 200	109	212.0	129.9	158.8	185.0	225.0	304.0
200 - 500	145	266.8	161.8	200.0	255.0	302.5	360.0
500 - 1,000	93	313.9	200.0	245.0	298.9	380.0	434.0
1,000 - 2,000	71	442.0	251.8	300.0	405.0	500.0	704.0
2,000 - 5,000	55	506.9	315.0	400.0	475.0	590.0	750.0
5,000 & Over	17	592.4	421.6	502.5	537.0	717.5	852.8
		BONUS ($000)					
Under 25	53	47.9	5.9	15.3	30.0	64.3	113.4
25 - 50	54	42.7	14.1	23.0	39.1	56.0	74.9
50 - 100	57	64.1	17.9	34.7	52.3	83.6	100.2
100 - 200	69	84.3	20.0	42.5	80.0	103.4	150.0
200 - 500	102	119.7	34.7	65.3	101.3	151.7	230.6
500 - 1,000	59	168.1	53.9	90.0	165.0	219.6	315.0
1,000 - 2,000	51	255.0	55.8	106.9	228.9	332.0	524.0
2,000 - 5,000	45	310.6	62.0	138.6	230.0	383.9	755.4
5,000 & Over	15	364.8	156.6	241.5	312.6	367.5	752.5
		TOTAL COMPENSATION ($000)					
Under 25	108	152.0	76.9	97.9	120.8	180.0	272.4
25 - 50	89	179.0	112.0	135.7	166.0	205.5	262.4
50 - 100	102	214.5	117.8	160.0	196.1	252.0	324.1
100 - 200	109	265.3	150.0	186.5	237.5	308.5	430.0
200 - 500	145	351.0	195.2	246.5	330.0	400.8	534.8
500 - 1,000	93	420.5	216.1	284.1	400.0	527.0	670.8
1,000 - 2,000	71	625.2	276.0	400.0	550.0	730.0	1,140.0
2,000 - 5,000	55	761.0	357.2	500.0	670.0	930.0	1,300.4
5,000 & Over	17	914.3	533.6	743.8	843.2	996.3	1,502.6
		SALARY (WHEN BONUS PAID) ($000)					
Under 25	53	126.9	58.2	85.0	112.0	159.5	230.9
25 - 50	54	147.6	102.5	122.3	142.5	160.3	200.0
50 - 100	57	179.3	120.8	142.5	172.0	201.0	247.1
100 - 200	69	195.3	133.8	156.3	180.0	220.0	290.0
200 - 500	102	265.5	172.3	209.7	265.0	305.8	357.0
500 - 1,000	59	308.4	200.0	250.0	300.0	375.0	425.0
1,000 - 2,000	51	460.5	267.9	320.0	405.0	500.0	723.0
2,000 - 5,000	45	528.0	331.0	405.0	485.0	620.0	770.0
5,000 & Over	15	617.6	500.0	505.0	537.0	735.0	909.6
		SALARY (WHEN NO BONUS PAID) ($000)					
Under 25	55	130.0	76.2	91.5	113.8	150.0	198.8
25 - 50	35	161.7	107.5	115.0	140.0	166.0	326.6
50 - 100	45	177.9	103.0	123.7	160.2	198.5	291.0
100 - 200	40	240.7	126.8	161.3	192.5	237.9	493.0
200 - 500	43	270.1	157.8	195.0	240.0	275.0	376.0
500 - 1,000	34	323.4	182.0	229.3	292.2	400.0	480.0
1,000 - 2,000	20	394.9	236.5	269.9	375.0	528.0	592.3
2,000 - 5,000	10	412.0	219.1	318.8	407.5	506.3	655.5
5,000 & Over	2	404.0			404.0		

ALL COMPANIES (Excluding All Financial Service and Non-Profit Organizations)

TOP EDP (OR MIS) EXECUTIVE

SALES GROUP ($ MILL)	NO. OF COMPANIES	AVERAGE	10TH PERCENTILE	FIRST QUARTILE	MEDIAN	THIRD QUARTILE	90TH PERCENTILE
		SALES ($ MILL)					
Under 25	19	18.2	11.9	15.0	18.5	21.8	22.6
25 - 50	34	36.7	28.1	31.0	36.4	41.0	46.4
50 - 100	48	70.8	50.0	56.0	69.4	80.0	96.9
100 - 200	57	145.3	113.4	121.4	146.0	167.0	185.1
200 - 500	78	317.5	200.0	247.3	307.1	390.6	411.7
500 - 1,000	58	708.0	527.8	587.9	691.4	812.5	931.1
1,000 - 2,000	39	1,348.9	1,045.8	1,093.1	1,344.7	1,527.7	1,813.4
2,000 - 5,000	33	3,060.0	2,117.9	2,292.8	2,959.7	3,619.5	4,489.4
5,000 & Over	12	7,028.8	5,060.8	5,324.9	6,724.3	8,656.3	9,677.8
		SALARY ($000)					
Under 25	19	50.6	39.6	44.2	49.0	55.2	65.0
25 - 50	34	51.8	31.6	42.5	47.4	56.6	65.6
50 - 100	48	57.1	44.1	46.5	54.0	59.8	76.7
100 - 200	57	65.6	49.0	55.9	63.4	72.1	82.0
200 - 500	78	72.2	52.9	60.0	69.5	80.1	95.9
500 - 1,000	58	83.0	66.5	72.0	81.9	93.4	105.0
1,000 - 2,000	39	91.4	63.5	80.0	90.5	100.0	115.0
2,000 - 5,000	33	102.3	76.8	86.2	96.2	122.5	143.8
5,000 & Over	12	122.5	70.0	91.9	115.0	157.6	175.6
		BONUS ($000)					
Under 25	6	7.7		2.9	7.7	11.9	
25 - 50	18	7.9	1.3	1.5	3.7	7.6	21.3
50 - 100	21	9.6	3.0	4.5	8.2	11.6	15.2
100 - 200	33	13.2	4.0	6.1	12.0	15.4	25.4
200 - 500	45	12.8	2.5	6.1	10.0	16.8	29.1
500 - 1,000	37	21.0	5.9	10.1	16.8	27.3	48.1
1,000 - 2,000	30	22.5	3.6	7.8	18.4	30.1	45.8
2,000 - 5,000	27	22.8	10.1	13.0	21.6	30.0	42.0
5,000 & Over	11	38.8	15.0	23.5	30.7	52.5	83.5
		TOTAL COMPENSATION ($000)					
Under 25	19	53.1	43.4	45.6	50.5	58.2	65.0
25 - 50	34	55.9	32.2	44.3	47.7	63.5	69.8
50 - 100	48	61.3	44.1	50.1	59.0	67.9	90.5
100 - 200	57	73.2	51.8	58.2	72.1	82.1	96.4
200 - 500	78	79.5	52.9	63.9	76.1	87.6	115.1
500 - 1,000	58	96.4	68.3	79.8	93.8	113.3	134.6
1,000 - 2,000	39	108.8	70.3	86.9	102.5	125.9	159.3
2,000 - 5,000	33	121.0	86.6	100.0	116.0	137.6	169.5
5,000 & Over	12	158.0	78.2	115.2	152.7	204.3	245.6
		SALARY (WHEN BONUS PAID) ($000)					
Under 25	6	54.2		43.3	52.4	61.7	
25 - 50	18	57.0	39.3	43.5	52.5	59.6	80.0
50 - 100	21	57.5	45.0	48.5	55.0	59.0	81.2
100 - 200	33	68.1	50.6	58.7	65.0	73.5	83.8
200 - 500	45	75.1	57.3	64.4	70.0	80.3	108.5
500 - 1,000	37	84.5	70.9	73.2	82.5	93.5	105.0
1,000 - 2,000	30	92.8	62.8	79.3	91.3	104.3	116.8
2,000 - 5,000	27	99.7	74.8	85.0	92.2	103.0	141.6
5,000 & Over	11	127.9	87.0	97.7	120.0	157.8	178.1
		SALARY (WHEN NO BONUS PAID) ($000)					
Under 25	13	49.0	33.9	44.1	47.2	55.4	63.2
25 - 50	16	45.9	26.2	40.4	46.4	52.5	66.0
50 - 100	27	56.7	41.0	45.3	52.5	60.0	79.0
100 - 200	24	62.1	43.2	52.9	61.2	71.9	81.2
200 - 500	33	68.2	46.4	55.3	67.3	78.2	91.2
500 - 1,000	21	80.3	51.7	67.7	78.6	92.5	113.2
1,000 - 2,000	9	87.1		76.0	86.9	96.2	
2,000 - 5,000	6	114.0		97.0	110.5	131.3	
5,000 & Over							

National Survey of Professional, Administrative, Technical, and Clerical Pay: Private Service Industries, March 1987

U.S. Department of Labor
Bureau of Labor Statistics
December 1987

Bulletin 2290

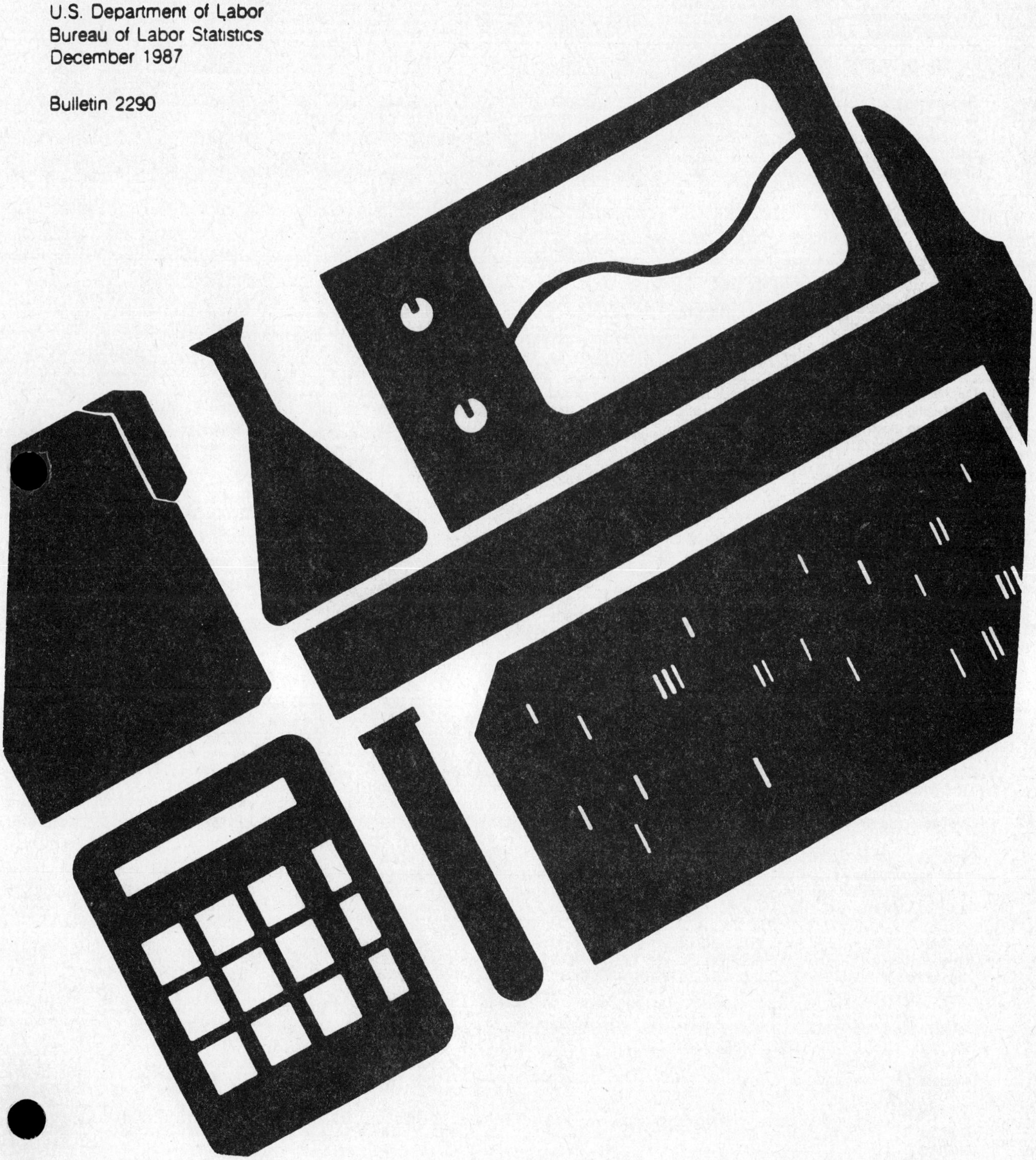

TABLE B-2. Average Salaries for Selected Occupations, National Survey of Professional, Administrative, Technical, and Clerical Pay, All Private Industries Surveyed in March 1986 and March 1987[1]

Occupational Classification	Number of workers	Annual mean salary	Annual median salary
Accounting clerks I	41,656	$12,831	$12,247
Accounting clerks II	160,540	15,102	14,630
Accounting clerks III	94,900	18,296	17,871
Accounting clerks IV	26,486	22,223	21,623
File clerks I	30,054	10,984	10,535
File clerks II	16,100	12,821	12,047
Key entry operators I	80,597	13,408	12,962
Key entry operators II	39,231	16,931	16,207
Messengers	14,754	12,197	11,585
Secretaries I	80,024	16,448	15,890
Secretaries II	94,752	18,769	18,125
Secretaries III	127,130	21,745	21,082
Secretaries IV	55,527	24,603	24,203
Secretaries V	16,948	29,090	28,417
Stenographers I	6,847	19,011	18,764
Stenographers II	5,443	22,603	23,189
Typists I	28,030	13,098	12,895
Typists II	14,381	17,218	16,379
Personnel clerks/asst. I	3,708	14,310	14,392
Personnel clerks/asst. II	5,487	17,343	16,633
Personnel clerks/asst. III	4,041	20,158	19,879
Personnel clerks/asst. IV	1,482	24,457	23,883
Purchasing clerk/asst. I	5,090	14,285	14,046
Purchasing clerk/asst. II	6,651	17,689	17,072
Purchasing clerk/asst. III	4,271	22,832	22,629
Purchasing clerk/asst. IV	1,037	30,524	29,288
General clerks I	16,537	10,702	10,405
General clerks II	82,850	12,907	12,463
General clerks III	89,708	15,700	15,149
General clerks IV	37,750	19,987	19,325
Accountants I	15,604	21,527	21,291
Accountants II	34,887	25,984	25,445
Accountants III	50,828	32,074	31,482
Accountants IV	25,661	40,611	40,272
Accountants V	8,388	51,144	50,152
Accountants VI	1,411	63,977	62,975
Auditors I	1,748	22,354	22,226
Auditors II	3,046	27,007	26,276
Auditors III	4,836	33,302	33,071
Auditors IV	2,037	41,250	40,505
Chief accountants I	937	40,198	41,144
Chief accountants II	1,484	49,531	49,852
Chief accountants III	515	65,564	65,400
Chief accountants IV	230	83,883	82,725
Public accountants I	14,233	21,006	21,000
Public accountants II	14,443	23,044	22,991
Public accountants III	15,563	27,537	26,789
Public accountants IV	6,849	33,989	33,300
Job analysts I	110	22,642	22,137
Job analysts II	448	25,615	24,259
Job analysts III	760	30,749	29,222
Job analysts IV	488	39,326	38,469
Directors of personnel I	2,258	40,229	38,775
Directors of personnel II	2,767	47,021	46,713
Directors of personnel III	1,302	65,106	64,392
Directors of personnel IV	406	78,123	75,090
Attorneys I	1,421	32,022	31,188
Attorneys II	3,070	41,319	40,667
Attorneys III	4,519	52,158	50,620

TABLE B-2. Average Salaries for Selected Occupations, National Survey of Professional, Administrative, Technical, and Clerical Pay, All Private Industries Surveyed in March 1986 and March 1987[1]—Continued

Occupational Classification	Number of workers	Annual mean salary	Annual median salary
Attorneys IV	3,924	$65,944	$64,992
Attorneys V	1,960	80,856	79,995
Attorneys VI	609	105,658	106,235
Chemists I	3,833	23,205	23,003
Chemists II	6,685	28,238	28,042
Chemists III	10,140	35,504	34,910
Chemists IV	8,869	43,480	43,015
Chemists V	7,176	52,927	52,569
Chemists VI	3,539	63,548	63,499
Chemists VII	871	78,605	75,921
Engineers I	40,460	28,958	29,392
Engineers II	75,123	32,295	32,205
Engineers III	147,085	37,235	37,006
Engineers IV	160,817	44,360	44,083
Engineers V	112,374	52,698	52,303
Engineers VI	50,605	61,807	61,440
Engineers VII	12,223	71,475	70,291
Engineers VIII	2,755	81,060	80,517
Registered nurses I	38,257	21,012	20,830
Registered nurses II	366,888	24,127	23,835
Registered nurses III	20,402	31,216	31,073
Registered nurses IV	392	34,383	33,735
Licensed practical nurses I	31,195	14,636	14,559
Licensed practical nurses II	165,049	16,487	16,285
Licensed practical nurses III	2,061	18,837	18,836
Nursing assistants I	148,366	8,558	8,111
Nursing assistants II	269,803	10,872	10,248
Nursing assistants III	22,075	14,369	14,394
Engineering technicians I	5,524	17,577	17,288
Engineering technicians II	17,215	21,131	20,792
Engineering technicians III	32,443	24,857	24,627
Engineering technicians IV	35,064	29,732	29,475
Engineering technicians V	18,367	34,380	34,186
Buyers I	8,119	21,779	21,610
Buyers II	24,706	27,184	26,939
Buyers III	18,459	34,818	34,035
Buyers IV	4,953	42,772	42,139
Computer operators I	10,476	14,339	14,162
Computer operators II	44,318	17,690	17,288
Computer operators III	28,475	22,207	21,657
Computer operators IV	9,011	25,441	25,098
Computer operators V	1,457	30,295	30,522
Photographers III	1,079	27,712	27,558
Photographers IV	410	33,452	34,317
Photographers V	81	37,961	39,484
Computer programmers I	16,995	21,398	21,387
Computer programmers II	42,721	25,056	24,936
Computer programmers III	52,523	30,320	30,048
Computer programmers IV	23,412	36,422	36,143
Computer programmers V	9,763	44,693	44,698
Systems analysts I	23,249	30,111	29,849
Systems analysts II	53,410	36,103	35,960
Systems analysts III	39,382	43,592	43,070
Systems analysts IV	14,342	51,537	50,912
Systems analysts V	2,685	61,673	60,582
Systems analysts VI	246	74,632	74,378
Drafters I	3,645	13,258	13,086
Drafters II	13,523	16,479	16,064
Drafters III	27,346	21,071	20,759
Drafters IV	25,978	25,621	25,185
Drafters V	13,747	32,117	31,539

[1] This tabulation combines the results of the March 1987 survey in the service industries with updated results from the March 1986 survey of private industries, excluding services. The BLS Employment Cost Index component for wages and salaries of private industry white-collar occupations, excluding sales, was used for updating. This adjustment factor was a 3.9 percent increase between March 1986 and March 1987.

Table D-1. Comparison of average annual salaries in private industry w[illegible]alary rates for Federal employees under the General Schedule, March 1987

Occupation and level surveyed by BLS[1]	Average annual salary in private industry[2]	Salary rates for Federal employees under the General Schedule[3]											
		Grade[4]	Average[5]	Step[6]									
				1	2	3	4	5	6	7	8	9	10
File clerks I	$10,984	GS 1	$9,980	9,619	9,940	10,260	10,579	10,899	11,087	11,403	11,721	11,735	12,036
General clerks I	$10,702												
Messengers	$12,197												
Accounting clerks I	$12,831	GS 2	$11,112	10,816	11,073	11,430	11,735	11,866	12,215	12,564	12,913	13,262	13,611
Drafters I	$13,258												
File clerks II	$12,821												
General clerks II	$12,907												
Key entry operators I	$13,408												
Typists I	$13,016												
Accounting clerks II	$15,102	GS 3	$12,691	11,802	12,195	12,588	12,981	13,374	13,767	14,160	14,553	14,946	15,339
Drafters II	$16,479												
Engineering technicians I	$17,577												
General clerks III	$15,700												
Key entry operators II	$16,931												
Personnel clerks/assistants I	$14,310												
Purchasing clerks/assistants I	$14,285												
Typists II	$17,218												
Accounting clerks III	$18,296	GS 4	$14,727	13,248	13,690	14,132	14,574	15,016	15,458	15,900	16,342	16,784	17,226
Computer operators I	$14,339												
Drafters III	$21,027												
Engineering technicians II	$21,131												
General clerks IV	$19,987												
Personnel clerks/assistants II	$17,343												
Purchasing clerks/assistants II	$17,689												
Secretaries I	$16,448												
Accounting clerks IV	$22,223	GS 5	$16,783	14,822	15,316	15,810	16,304	16,798	17,292	17,786	18,280	18,744	19,268
Accountants I	$21,527												
Auditors I	$22,354												
Buyers I	$21,779												
Chemists I	$23,205												
Computer operators II	$17,690												
Drafters IV	$25,621												
Engineers I	$28,958												
Engineering technicians III	$24,857												
Job analysts I	$22,642												
Personnel clerks/assistants III	$20,158												
Computer programmers I	$21,398												
Purchasing clerks/assistants III	$22,832												
Secretaries II	$18,769												
Computer operators III	$22,207	GS 6	$18,980	16,521	17,072	17,623	18,174	18,725	19,276	19,827	20,378	20,929	21,480
Personnel clerks/assistants IV	$24,457												
Purchasing clerks/ assistants IV	$30,524												
Secretaries III	$21,745												

Table D-1. Comparison of average annual salaries in private industry with salary rates for Federal employees under the General Schedule, March 1987 —Continued

Occupation and level surveyed by BLS[1]	Average annual salary in private industry[2]	Salary rates for Federal employees under the General Schedule[3]											
		Grade[4]	Average[5]	Step[6]									
				1	2	3	4	5	6	7	8	9	10
Accountants II	$25,984	GS 7	$20,817	18,358	18,970	19,582	20,194	20,806	21,418	22,030	22,642	23,254	23,866
Auditors II	$27,007												
Buyers II	$27,184												
Chemists II	$28,238												
Computer operators IV	$25,441												
Drafters V	$32,117												
Engineers II	$32,295												
Engineering technicians IV	$29,732												
Job analysts II	$25,615												
Photographers III	$27,712												
Computer programmers II	$25,056												
Public accountants I	$21,006												
Secretaries IV	$24,603												
Computer operators V	$30,295	GS 8	$23,618	20,333	21,011	21,689	22,367	23,045	23,723	24,401	25,079	25,757	26,435
Secretaries V	$29,090												
Accountants III	$32,074	GS 9	$25,289	22,458	23,207	23,956	24,705	25,454	26,203	26,952	27,701	28,450	29,199
Attorneys I	$32,022												
Auditors III	$33,302												
Buyers III	$34,818												
Engineers III	$37,235												
Engineering technicians V	$34,380												
Job analysts III	$30,749												
Photographers IV	$33,452												
Computer programmers III	$30,320												
Public accountants II	$23,044												
Systems analysts I	$30,111												
Accountants IV	$40,611	GS 11	$30,811	27,172	28,078	28,984	29,890	30,796	31,702	32,608	33,514	34,420	35,326
Attorneys II	$41,319												
Auditors IV	$41,250												
Buyers IV	$42,772												
Chemists IV	$43,480												
Directors of personnel I	$40,229												
Engineers IV	$44,360												
Job analysts IV	$39,326												
Photographers V	$37,961												
Computer programmers IV	$36,422												
Public accountants III	$27,537												
Systems analysts II	$36,103												
Accountants V	$51,144	GS 12	$37,243	32,567	33,653	34,73	35,825	36,911	37,997	39,083	40,169	41,255	42,341
Attorneys III	$52,158												
Chemists V	$52,927												
Chief accountants II	$49,531												
Directors of personnel II	$47,021												
Engineers V	$52,698												

Table D-1. Comparison of average annual salaries in private industry with salary rates for Federal employees under the General Schedule, March 1987 —Continued

Occupation and level surveyed by BLS[1]	Average annual salary in private industry[2]	Salary rates for Federal employees under the General Schedule[3]											
		Grade[4]	Average[5]	Step[6]									
				1	2	3	4	5	6	7	8	9	10
Computer programmers V	$44,693												
Public accountants IV	$33,989												
Systems analysts III	$43,592												
Attorneys IV	$65,944	GS 13	$44,797	38,727	40,018	41,309	42,600	43,891	45,182	46,473	47,764	49,055	50,346
Chemists VI	$63,548												
Chief accountants III	$65,564												
Directors of personnel III	$65,106												
Engineers VI	$61,807												
Systems analysts IV	$51,537												
Attorneys V	$80,856	GS 14	$53,309	45,763	47,288	48,813	50,338	51,863	53,388	54,913	56,438	57,963	59,488
Chemists VII	$78,605												
Chief accountants IV	$83,883												
Directors of personnel IV	$78,123												
Engineers VII	$71,475												
Systems analysts V	$61,673												
Attorneys VI	$105,658	GS 15	$63,725	53,830	55,624	57,418	59,212	61,006	62,800	64,594	66,388	68,182	69,976
Engineers VIII	$81,060												
Systems analysts VI	$74,632												

[1] For definitions, see appendix C.

[2] Survey findings as summarized in table B-2 of this bulletin. For scope of 1986 and 1987 surveys, see appendix B.

[3] General schedule rates in effect in March 1987, the reference date of the PATC survey.

[4] Corresponding grades in the General Schedule were supplied by the Office of Personnel Management.

[5] Mean salary of all General Schedule employees in each grade as of March 31, 1987. Not limited to Federal employees in occupations surveyed by BLS.

[6] Section 5335 of title 5 of the U.S. Code provides for within-grade increases on condition that the employee's work is of an acceptable level of competence as defined by the head of the agency. For employees who meet this condition, the service requirements are 52 calendar weeks for each advancement to salary rates 2, 3, and 4; 104 weeks for advancement to salary rates 5,6, and 7; and 156 weeks for each advancement to salary rates 8, 9, and 10. Section 5336 provides that an additional within-grade increase may be granted within any 52-week period in recognition of high quality performance above that ordinarily found in the type of position concerned.

NOTE: Under Section 5303 of title 5 of the U.S. Code, higher minimum rates (but not exceeding the maximum salary rate prescribed in the General Schedule for the grade or level) and a corresponding new salary range may be established for positions or occupations under certain conditions. The conditions include a finding that the Government's recruitment or retention of well-qualified persons is significantly handicapped because the salary rates in private industry are substantially above the salary rates of the statutory pay schedules. As of March 1987, special higher salary rates were authorized for professional engineers at the entry grades (GS-5 and GS-7), and at GS-9 through GS-12. In addition, special rates were authorized for petroleum engineers at GS-5 through GS-13. Information on special salary rates, including the occupations and the areas to which they apply, may be obtained from the Office of Personnel Management, Washington, D.C. 20415, or its regional offices.

Appendix C. Occupational Definitions

The primary purpose of preparing job definitions for the Bureau's wage surveys is to assist its field staff in classifying into appropriate occupations, or levels within occupations, workers who are employed under a variety of payroll titles and different work arrangements from establishment to establishment and from area to area. This permits the grouping of occupational wage rates representing comparable job content. To secure comparability of job content, some occupations and work levels are defined to include only those workers meeting specific criteria as to training, job functions, and responsibilities. Because of this emphasis on inter-establishment and interarea comparability of occupational content, the Bureau's occupational definitions may differ significantly from those in use in individual establishments or those prepared for other purposes.

Computer Systems Analysts[1]

Analyzes business or scientific problems for resolution through electronic data processing. Gathers information from users, defines work problems, and, if feasible, designs a system of computer programs and procedures to resolve the problems. Develops complete specifications to enable computer programmers to prepare required programs: Analyzes subject-matter operations to be automated; specifies number and types of records, files, and documents to be used and outputs to be produced; prepares work diagrams and data flow charts; coordinates tests of the system and participates in trial runs of new and revised systems; and recommends computer equipment changes to obtain more effective operations. May also write the computer programs.

Excluded are:

(a) Trainees who receive detailed directives and work plans, select authorized procedures for use in specific situations, and seek assistance for deviations and problems;

(b) Positions which require a bachelor's degree in a specific scientific field (other than computer science), such as an engineering, mathematics, physics, *or* chemistry degree; however, positions are potential matches where the required degree may be from *any* of several possible scientific fields;

(c) Computer programmers who write computer programs and solve user problems not requiring systems modification;

(d) Workers who primarily analyze and evaluate problems concerning *computer equipment* or its selection or utilization; and

(e) Computer systems programmers or analysts who primarily write programs or analyze problems concerning the system software, e.g., operating systems, compilers, assemblers, system utility routines, etc., which provide basic services for the use of all programs and provide for the scheduling of the execution of programs; however, positions matching this definition may develop a "total package" which includes not only analyzing work problems to be processed but also selecting the computer equipment and system software required.

Positions are classified into levels on the basis of the following definitions.

Computer Systems Analysts I

At this level, *initial assignments* are designed to *expand* practical experience in applying systems analysis techniques and procedures. Provides *several phases* of the required systems analysis where the nature of the system is predetermined. Uses established factfinding approaches, knowledge of pertinent work processes and procedures, and familiarity with related computer programming practices, system software, and computer equipment.

Carries out factfinding and analysis as assigned, usually of a single activity or a routine problem; applies established procedures where the nature of the system,

[1] For publication purposes, data for Computer Systems Analysts and Computer Systems Analysts Supervisors/Managers were combined into a six level series as follows:

Level	Systems Analysts: Nonsupervisory	Systems Analysts: Supervisory/Managerial
I	I	-
II	II	-
III	III	I
IV	IV	II
V	V	III
VI	-	IV

feasibility, computer equipment, and programming language have already been decided; may assist a higher level systems analyst by preparing the detailed specifications required by computer programmers from information developed by the higher level analyst; may research routine user problems and solve them by modifying the existing system when the solutions follow clear precedents. When costs and deadline estimates are required, results receive close review.

The supervisor defines objectives, priorities, and deadlines. Incumbents work independently; adapt guides to specific situations; resolve problems and deviations according to established practices; and obtain advice where precedents are unclear or not available. Completed work is reviewed for conformance to requirements, timeliness, and efficiency. May supervise technicians and others who assist in specific assignments.

Computer Systems Analysts II

Applies systems analysis and design skills in an area such as a recordkeeping or scientific operation. A system of several varied sequences or formats is usually developed, e.g., develops systems for maintaining depositor accounts in a bank, maintaining accounts receivable in a retail establishment, maintaining inventory accounts in a manufacturing or wholesale establishment, or processing a limited problem in a scientific project. Requires competence in most phases of systems analysis and knowledge of pertinent system software and computer equipment and of the work processes, applicable regulations, workload, and practices of the assigned subject-matter area. Recognizes probable interactions of related computer systems and predicts impact of a change in assigned system.

Reviews proposals which consist of objectives, scope, and user expectations; gathers facts, analyzes data, and prepares a project synopsis which compares alternatives in terms of cost, time, availability of equipment and personnel, and recommends a course of action; and, upon approval of synopsis, prepares specifications for development of computer programs. Determines and resolves data processing problems and coordinates the work with programmers, users, etc.; orients user personnel on new or changed procedures. May conduct special projects such as data element and code standardization throughout a broad system, working under specific objectives and bringing to the attention of the supervisor any unusual problems or controversies.

Works independently under overall project objectives and requirements; apprises supervisor about progress and unusual complications. Guidelines usually include existing systems and the constraints imposed by related systems with which the incumbent's work must be meshed. Adapts design approaches successfully used in precedent systems. Completed work is reviewed for timeliness, compatibility with other work, and effectiveness in meeting requirements. May provide functional direction to lower level assistants on assigned work.

OR

Works on a segment of a complex data processing scheme or broad system, as described for computer systems analysts, level III. Works independently on routine assignments and receives instructions and guidance on complex assignments. Work is reviewed for accuracy of judgment, compliance with instructions, and to insure proper alignment with overall system.

Computer Systems Analysts III

Applies systems analysis and design techniques to complex computer systems in a *broad* area such as manufacturing; finance management; engineering, accounting, or statistics; logistics planning; material management; etc. Usually, there are multiple users of the system; however, there may be complex single-user systems, e.g., for engineering or research projects. Requires competence in all phases of available systems analysis techniques, concepts, and methods and knowledge of available systems software, computer equipment, and the regulations, structure, techniques, and management practices of one or more subject-matter areas. Since *input data usually come from diverse sources,* is responsible for recognizing probable conflicts and integrating diverse data elements and sources. Produces innovative solutions for a variety of complex problems.

Maintains and modifies complex systems or develops new subsystems such as an integrated production scheduling, inventory control, cost analysis, and sales analysis record in which every item of each type is automatically processed through the full system of records. Guides users in formulating requirements; advises on alternatives and on the implications of new or revised data processing systems; analyzes resulting user project proposals, identifies omissions and errors in requirements, and conducts feasibility studies; recommends optimum approach and develops system design for approved projects. Interprets information and informally arbitrates between system users when conflicts exist. May serve as lead analyst in a design subgroup, directing and integrating the work of one or two lower level analysts, each responsible for several programs.

Supervision and nature of review are similar to level II; existing systems provide precedents for the operation of new subsystems.

Computer Systems Analysts IV

Applies expert systems analysis and design techniques to complex *systems development* in a specialized design area and/or resolves unique or unyielding problems in existing complex systems by *applying new technology.* Work requires a broad knowledge of data sources and flow, interactions of existing complex systems in the organization, and the capabilities and limitations of the systems software and computer equipment. Objectives and overall requirements are defined in organization EDP policies and standards; the primary constraints typically are those imposed by the need for compatibility with existing systems or processes. Supervision and nature of review are similar to levels II and III.

Typical duties and responsibilities. One or more of the following:

1. As team project leader, provides systems design *in a specialized and highly complex design area,* e.g., interrelated business statistics and/or projections, scientific systems, mathematical models, or similar unprecedented computer systems. *Establishes the framework of new computer systems* from feasibility studies to postimplementation evaluation. Devises new sources of data and develops new approaches and techniques for use by others. May serve as technical authority for a design area. At least one or two team members perform work at level III; one or two team members may also perform work as a level IV staff specialist or consultant as described below.

2. As staff specialist or consultant, with expertise in a specialty area (e.g., data security, telecommunications, systems analysis techniques, EDP standards development, etc.), plans and conducts analyses of unique or unyielding problems in a broad system. Identifies problems and specific issues in assigned area and prepares overall project recommendations from an EDP standpoint, including feasible advancements in EDP technology; upon acceptance, determines a design strategy that anticipates directions of change; designs and monitors necessary testing and implementation plans. Performs work such as: Studies broad areas of projected work processes which cut across established organization EDP systems; conducts continuing review of computer technological developments applicable to systems design and prepares long-range forecasts; develops EDP standards where new and improved approaches are needed; or develops recommendations for a management information system where new concepts are required.

Computer Systems Analysts V

As a top technical expert, develops broad unprecedented computer systems and/or conducts critical studies central to the success of large organizations having extensive technical or highly diversified computer requirements. Considers such requirements as broad company policy, and the diverse user needs of several organization levels and locations. Works under general administrative direction.

Typical duties and responsibilities. One or more of the following:

1. As team or project leader, guides the development of broad unprecedented computer systems. The information requirements are complex and voluminous. Devises completely new ways to locate and develop data sources; establishes new factors and criteria for making subject-matter decisions. Coordinates fact-finding, analysis, and design of the system and applies the most recent developments in data processing technology and computer equipment. Guidelines consist of state-of-the-art technology and general organization policy. *At least one team member performs work at level IV.*

2. As staff specialist or consultant, is a recognized leader and authority in a large organization (as defined above). Performs at least *two* of the following: (a) Has overall responsibility for evaluating the significance of technological advancement and developing EDP standards where new and improved approaches are needed, e.g., programming techniques; (b) conceives and plans exploratory investigations critical to the overall organization where useful precedents do not exist and new concepts are required, e.g., develops recommendations regarding a comprehensive management information system; or (c) evaluates existing EDP organizational policy for effectiveness, devising and formulating changes in the organization's position on broad policy issues. May be assisted on individual projects by other analysts.

COMPUTER SYSTEMS ANALYSTS SUPERVISORS/MANAGERS

Supervises three or more employees, two of whom perform systems analysis. Work requires substantial and recurring use of systems analysis skills in directing staff. May also supervise programmers and related clerical and technical support personnel.

Excluded are:

a. Positions also having significant responsibility for the management or supervision of functional areas (e.g., system software development, data entry, or computer operations) *not* related to the Computer Systems Analyst and Computer Programmer definitions.

b. Supervisory positions having base levels below Computer Systems Analyst II or Computer Programmer IV.

c. Managers who supervise two or more subordinates performing at Computer Systems Analyst Supervisor/Manager level IV.

Supervisory jobs are matched at 1 of 4 levels according to two factors: (a) Base level of work supervised, and (b) level of supervision. Table C-3 indicates the level of the supervisor for each combination of factors.

Excludes secretaries performing any of the following duties:

a. Acts as office manager for the executive's organization, e.g., determines when new procedures are needed for changing situations and devises and implements alternatives; revises or clarifies procedures to eliminate conflict or duplication; identifies and resolves various problems that affect the orderly flow of work in transactions with parties outside the organization.

b. Prepares agenda for conferences; explains discussion topics to participants; drafts introductions and develops background information and prepares outlines for executive or staff members(s) to use in writing speeches.

c. Advises individuals outside the organization on the executive's views on major policies or current issues facing the organization; contacts or responds to contacts from high-ranking outside officials (e.g., city or State officials, Members of Congress, presidents of national unions or large national or international firms, etc.) in unique situations. These officials may be relatively inaccessible, and each contact typically must be handled differently, using judgment and discretion.

Table C-5. Criteria for matching secretaries by level

Level of secretary's supervisor	Level of secretary's responsibility			
	LR-1	LR-2	LR-3	LR-4
LS-1	I	II	III	IV
LS-2	I	III	IV	V
LS-3	I	IV	V	V

MESSENGERS

Performs various routine duties such as running errands, operating minor office machines such as sealers or mailers, opening mail, distributing mail on a regularly scheduled route or in a familiar area, and other minor clerical work. May deliver mail that requires some special handling, e.g., mail that is insured, registered, or marked for special delivery.

***Excluded* are positions which include any of the following as *significant* duties:**

a. Operating motor vehicles;

b. Delivering valuables or security-classified mail when the work requires a continuing knowledge of special procedures for handling such items;

c. Weighing mail, determining postage, or recording and controlling registered, insured, and certified mail in the mail room;

d. Making deliveries to unfamiliar or widely separated buildings or points which are not part of an established route; or

e. Directing other workers.

FILE CLERKS

Files, classifies, and retrieves material in an established filing system. May perform clerical and manual tasks required to maintain files. Positions are classified into levels on the basis of the following definitions.

File Clerks I

Performs routine filing of material that has already been classified or which is easily classified in a simple serial classification system (e.g., alphabetical, chronological, or numerical). As requested, locates readily available materials in files and forwards material; may fill out withdrawal charge. May perform simple clerical and manual tasks required to maintain and service files.

File Clerks II

Sorts, codes, and files unclassified material by simple (subject-matter) headings or partly classified material by finer subheadings. Prepares simple related index and cross-reference aids. As requested, locates clearly identified material in files and forwards material. May perform related clerical tasks required to maintain and service files.

File Clerks III

Classifies and indexes file material such as correspondence, reports, technical documents, etc., in an established filing system containing a number of varied subject matter files. May also file this material. May keep records of various types in conjunction with the files. May lead a small group of lower level file clerks.

KEY ENTRY OPERATORS

Operates keyboard-controlled data entry device such as keypunch machine or key-operated magnetic tape or disc encoder to transcribe data into a form suitable for computer processing. Work requires skill in operating an alphanumeric keyboard and an understanding of transcribing procedures and relevant data entry equipment.

Positions are classified into levels on the basis of the following definitions.

Key Entry Operators I

Work is routine and repetitive. Under close supervision or following specific procedures or detailed instructions, works from various standardized source documents which have been coded and require little or no selecting, coding, or interpreting of data to be entered. Refers to supervisor problems arising from erroneous items, codes, or missing information.

Key Entry Operators II

Work requires the application of experience and judgment in selecting procedures to be followed and in searching for, interpreting, selecting, or coding items to be entered from a variety of source documents. On occasion, may also perform some routine work as described for level I.

NOTE: Excluded are operators above level II using the key entry controls to access, read, and evaluate the substance of specific records to take substantive actions, or to make entries requiring a similar level of knowledge.

instructions. May write routine new programs using prescribed specifications; may confer with EDP personnel to clarify procedures, processing logic, etc.

In addition and as continued training, computer programmers may evaluate simple interrelationships in the immediate programming area, e.g., whether a contemplated change in one part of a simple program would cause unwanted results in a related part; confers with user representatives to gain an understanding of the situation sufficient to formulate the needed change; implements the change upon approval of the supervisor or higher level staff. The incumbent is provided with charts, narrative descriptions of the functions performed, an approved statement of the product desired (e.g., a change in a local establishment report), and the inputs, outputs, and record formats.

Reviews objectives and assignment details with higher level staff to insure thorough understanding; uses judgment in selecting among authorized procedures and seeks assistance when guidelines are inadequate, significant deviations are proposed, or when unanticipated problems arise. Work is usually monitored in progress; all work is reviewed upon completion for accuracy and compliance with standards.

Computer Programmers III

As a fully qualified computer programmer, applies standard programming procedures and detailed knowledge of pertinent subject matter (e.g., work processes, governing rules, clerical procedures, etc.) in a programming area such as: A recordkeeping operation (supply, personnel and payroll, inventory, purchasing, insurance payments, depositor accounts, etc.); a well-defined statistical or scientific problem; or other standardized operation or problem. Works according to approved statements of requirements and detailed specifications. While the data are clear cut, related, and equally available, there may be substantial interrelationships of a variety of records, and several varied sequences or formats are usually produced. The programs developed or modified typically are linked to several other programs in that the output of one becomes the input for another. Recognizes probable interactions of other related programs with the assigned program(s) and is familiar with related system software and computer equipment. Solves conventional programming problems. (In small organizations, may maintain programs which concern or combine several operations, i.e., users, or develop programs where there is one primary user and the other gives input.)

Performs such duties as: Develops, modifies, and maintains assigned programs; designs and implements modifications to the interrelation of files and records within programs in consultation with higher level staff; monitors the operation of assigned programs and responds to problems by diagnosing and correcting errors in logic and coding; and implements and/or maintains assigned portions of a scientific programming project, applying established scientific programming techniques to well-defined mathematical, statistical, engineering, or other scientific problems usually requiring the translation of mathematical notation into processing logic and code. (Scientific programming includes assignments such as: Using predetermined physical laws expressed in mathematical terms to relate one set of data to another; the routine storage and retrieval of field test data; and using procedures for real-time command and control, scientific data reduction, signal processing, or similar areas.) Tests and documents work and writes and maintains operator instructions for assigned programs. Confers with other EDP personnel to obtain or provide factual data.

In addition, computer programmers may carry out factfinding and programming analysis of a single activity or routine problem, applying established procedures where the nature of the program, feasibility, computer equipment, and programming language have already been decided. May analyze present performance of the program and take action to correct deficiencies based on discussion with the user and consultation with and approval of the supervisor or higher level staff. May assist in the review and analysis of detailed program specifications and in program design to meet changes in work processes.

Works independently under specified objectives; applies judgment in devising program logic and in selecting and adapting standard programming procedures; resolves problems and deviations according to established practices; and obtains advice where precedents are unclear or not available. Completed work is reviewed for conformance to standards, timeliness, and efficiency. May guide or instruct lower level programmers; may supervise technicians and others who assist in specific assignments.

OR

Works on complex programs (as described in level IV) under close direction of higher level staff or supervisor. May *assist* higher level staff by independently performing less difficult tasks assigned, and performing more difficult tasks under close supervision.

Computer Programmers IV

Applies expertise in programming procedures to complex programs; recommends the redesign of programs, investigates and analyzes feasibility and program requirements, and develops programming specifications. Assigned programs typically affect a broad multiuser computer system which meets the data processing needs of a broad area (e.g., manufacturing, logistics planning, finance management, human resources, material management, etc.) or a computer system for a project in engineering, research, accounting, statistics, etc. Plans the full range of programming actions to produce several interrelated but different products from numerous and diverse data elements which are usually from different sources; solves difficult programming problems. Uses knowledge of pertinent system software, computer equipment, work processes, regulations, and management practices.

Performs such duties as: Develops, modifies, and maintains complex programs; designs and implements the interrelation of files and records within programs which will effectively fit into the overall design of the project; working with problems or concepts, develops programs for the solution to major scientific computational problems requiring the analysis and development of logical or mathematical descriptions of functions to be programmed; and develops occasional special programs, e.g., a critical path analysis program to assist in managing a special project. Tests, documents, and writes operating instructions for all work. Confers with other EDP personnel to secure information, investigate and resolve problems, and coordinate work efforts.

In addition, performs such programming analysis as: Investigates the feasibility of alternate program design approaches to determine the best balanced solution, e.g., one that will best satisfy immediate user needs, facilitate subsequent modification, and conserve resources; on typical maintenance projects and smaller scale, limited new projects, assists user personnel in defining problems or needs and determines how the work should be organized, the necessary files and records, and their interrelation within the program; and on large or more complicated projects, usually participates as a team member along with other EDP personnel and users and is typically assigned a portion of the project.

Works independently under overall objectives and direction, apprising the supervisor about progress and unusual complications. Modifies and adapts precedent solutions and proven approaches. Guidelines include constraints imposed by the related programs with which the incumbent's programs must be meshed. Completed work is reviewed for timeliness, compatibility with other work, and effectiveness in meeting requirements. May function as team leader or supervise a few lower level programmers or technicians on assigned work.

Computer Programmers V

At level V, workers are typically either supervisors, team leaders, staff specialists, or consultants. Some programming analysis is included as a part of the programming assignment. Supervision and review are similar to level IV.

Typical duties and responsibilities. One or more of the following:

1. *In a supervisory capacity,* plans, develops, coordinates, and directs a large and important programming project (finance, manufacturing, sales/marketing, human resources, or other broad area) or a number of small programming projects with complex features. A substantial portion of the work supervised (usually two to three workers) is comparable to that described for level IV. Supervises, coordinates, and reviews the work of a small staff, normally not more than 15 programmers and technicians; estimates personnel needs and schedules, assigns, and reviews work to meet completion date. These day-to-day supervisors evaluate performance, resolve complaints, and make recommendations on hiring and firing. They do not make final decisions on curtailing projects, reorganizing, or reallocating resources.

2. *As team leader, staff specialist, or consultant,* defines complex scientific problems (e.g., computational) or other highly complex programming problems (e.g., generating overall forecasts, projections, or other new data fields widely different from the source data or untried at the scale proposed) and directs the development of computer programs for their solution; or designs improvements in complex programs where existing precedents provide little guidance, such as an interrelated group of mathematical/statistical programs which support health insurance, natural resources, marketing trends, or other research activities. In conjunction with users (scientists or specialists), defines major problems in the subject-matter area. Contacts coworkers and user personnel at various locations to plan and coordinate project and gather data; devises ways to obtain data not previously available; and arbitrates differences between various program users when conflicting requirements arise. May perform simulation studies to determine effects of changes in computer equipment or system software or may assess the feasibility and soundness of proposed programming projects which are novel and complex. Typically, develops programming techniques and procedures where few precedents exist. May be assisted on projects by other programmers or technicians.

SECRETARIES

Provides principal secretarial support in an office, usually to one individual, and, in some cases, also to the subordinate staff of that individual. Maintains a close and highly responsive relationship to the day-to-day activities of the supervisor and staff. Works fairly independently receiving a minimum of detailed supervision and guidance. Performs varied clerical and secretarial duties requiring knowledge of office routine and an understanding of the organization, programs, and procedures related to the work of the office.

Exclusions: Not all positions titled "secretary" possess the above characteristics. Examples of positions which are excluded from the definition are as follows:

a. Clerks or secretaries working under the direction of secretaries or administrative assistants as described in *e*;

b. Stenographers not fully performing secretarial duties;

c. Stenographers or secretaries assigned to two or more professional, technical, or managerial persons of equivalent rank;

d. Assistants or secretaries performing any kind of technical work, e.g., personnel, accounting, or legal work;

e. Administrative assistants or supervisors performing duties which are more difficult or more responsible than the secretarial work described in LR-1 through LR-4;

f. Secretaries receiving additional pay primarily for maintaining confidentiality of payroll records or other sensitive information;

g. Secretaries performing routine receptionist, typing, and filing duties following detailed instructions and guidelines; these duties are less responsible than those described in LR-1 below; and

h. Trainees.

Classification by Level

Secretary jobs which meet the required characteristics are matched at one of five levels according to two factors: a) Level of the secretary's supervisor within the overall organizational structure, and (b) level of the secretary's responsibility. Table C-5 indicates the level of the secretary for each combination of factors.

Level of secretaries' supervisor (LS)

Secretaries should be matched at one of the three LS levels below best describing the organization of the secretary's supervisor.

LS-1. Organizational structure is not complex and internal procedures and administrative controls are simple and informal; supervisor directs staff through face-to-face meetings.

LS-2. Organizational structure is complex and is divided into subordinate groups that usually differ from each other as to subject matter, function, etc.; and supervisor usually directs staff through intermediate supervisors; internal procedures and administrative controls are formal. An entire organization (e.g., division, subsidiary, or parent organization) may contain a variety of subordinate groups which meet the LS-2 definition. Therefore, it is not unusual for one LS-2 supervisor to report to another LS-2 supervisor.

The presence of subordinate supervisors does not by itself mean LS-2 applies, e.g., a clerical processing organization divided into several units, each performing very similar work, is placed in LS-1.

In smaller organizations or industries such as retail trade, with relatively few organizational levels, the supervisor may have an impact on the policies and may deal with important outside contacts, as described in LS-3.

LS-3. Organizational structure is divided into two or more subordinate supervisory levels (of which at least one is a managerial level) with several subdivisions at each level. Executive's program(s) are usually interlocked on a direct and continuing basis with other major organizational segments, requiring constant attention to extensive formal coordination, clearances, and procedural controls. Executive typically has: Financial decisionmaking authority for assigned program(s);considerable impact on the entire organization's financial position or image; and responsibility for, or has staff specialists in, such areas as personnel and administration for assigned organization. Executive plays an important role in determining the policies and major programs of the entire organization, and spends considerable time dealing with outside parties actively interested in assigned program(s) and current or controversial issues.

Level of secretaries' responsibility (LR)

This factor evaluates the nature of the work relationship between the secretary and the supervisor or staff, and the extent to which the secretary is expected to exercise initiative and judgment. Secretaries should be matched at the level best describing their level of responsibility. When a position's duties span more than one LR level, the introductory paragraph at the beginning of each LR level should be used to determine which of the levels best matches the position. (Typically, secretaries performing at the higher levels of responsibility also perform duties described at the lower levels.)

LR-1. Carries out *recurring* office procedures independently. Selects the guideline or reference which fits the specific case. Supervisor provides specific instructions on new assignments and checks completed work for accuracy. Performs varied duties including or comparable to the following:

a. Responds to routine telephone requests which have standard answers; refers calls and visitors to appropriate staff. Controls mail and assures timely staff response; may send form letters.

b. As instructed, maintains supervisor's calendar, makes appointments, and arranges for meeting rooms.

c. Reviews materials prepared for supervisor's approval for typographical accuracy and proper format.

d. Maintains recurring internal reports, such as: Time and leave records, office equipment listings, correspondence controls, training plans, etc.

e. Requisitions supplies, printing, maintenance, or other services. Types, takes and transcribes dictation, and establishes and maintains office files.

LR-2. Handles differing situations, problems, and deviations in the work of the office according to the supervisor's general instructions, priorities, duties, policies, and program goals. Supervisor may assist secretary with special assignments. Duties include or are comparable to the following.

a. Screens telephone calls, visitors, and incoming correspondence; personally responds to requests for information concerning office procedures; determines which requests should be handled by the supervisor, appropriate staff members, or other offices. May prepare and sign routine, nontechnical correspondence in own or supervisor's name.

b. Schedules tentative appointments without prior clearance. Makes arrangements for conferences and meetings and assembles established background materials, as directed. May attend meetings and record and report on the proceedings.

c. Reviews outgoing materials and correspondence for internal consistency and conformance with supervisor's procedures; assures that proper clearances have been obtained, when needed.

d. Collects information from the files or staff for routine inquiries on office program(s) or periodic reports. Refers nonroutine requests to supevisor or staff.

e. Explains to subordinate staff supervisor's requirements concerning office procedures. Coordinates personnel and administrative forms for the office and forwards for processing.

LR-3. Uses greater judgment and initiative to determine the approach or action to take in nonroutine situations. Interprets and adapts guidelines, including unwritten policies, precedents, and practices, which are not always completely applicable to changing situations. Duties include or are comparable to the following:

a. Based on a knowledge of the supervisor's views, composes correspondence on own initiative about administrative and general office policies for supervisor's approval.

b. Anticipates and prepares materials needed by the supervisor for conferences, correspondence, appointments, meetings, telephone calls, etc., and informs supervisor on matters to be considered.

c. Reads publications, regulations, and directives and takes action or refers those that are important to the supervisor and staff.

d. Prepares special or one-time reports, summaries, or replies to inquiries, selecting relevant information from a variety of sources such as reports, documents, correspondence, other offices, etc., under general direction.

e. Advises secretaries in subordinate offices on new procedures; requests information needed from the subordinate office(s) for periodic or special conferences, reports, inquiries, etc. Shifts clerical staff to accommodate workload needs.

LR-4. Handles a wide variety of situations and conflicts involving the clerical or administrative functions of the office which often cannot be brought to the attention of the executive. The executive sets the overall objectives of the work. Secretary may participate in developing the work deadlines. Duties include or are comparable to the following:

a. Composes correspondence requiring some understanding of technical matters; may sign for executive when technical or policy content has been authorized.

b. Notes commitments made by executive during meeting and arranges for staff implementation. On own initiative, arranges for staff members to represent organization at conferences and meetings, establishes appointment priorities, or reschedule or refuses appointments or invitations.

c. Reads outgoing correspondence for executive's approval and alerts writers to any conflict with the file or departure from policies or executives's viewpoints; gives advice to resolve the problems.

d. Summarizes the content of incoming materials, specially gathered information, or meetings to assist executive; coordinates the new information with background office sources; and draws attention to important parts or conflicts.

e. In the executive's absence, ensures that requests for action or information are relayed to the appropriate staff member; as needed, interprets requests and helps implement action; makes sure that information is furnished in timely manner; decides whether executive should be notified of important or emergency matters.

Atlanta, Georgia, Metropolitan Area May 1987

Area Wage Survey

U.S. Department of Labor
Bureau of Labor Statistics

Bulletin 3040-18

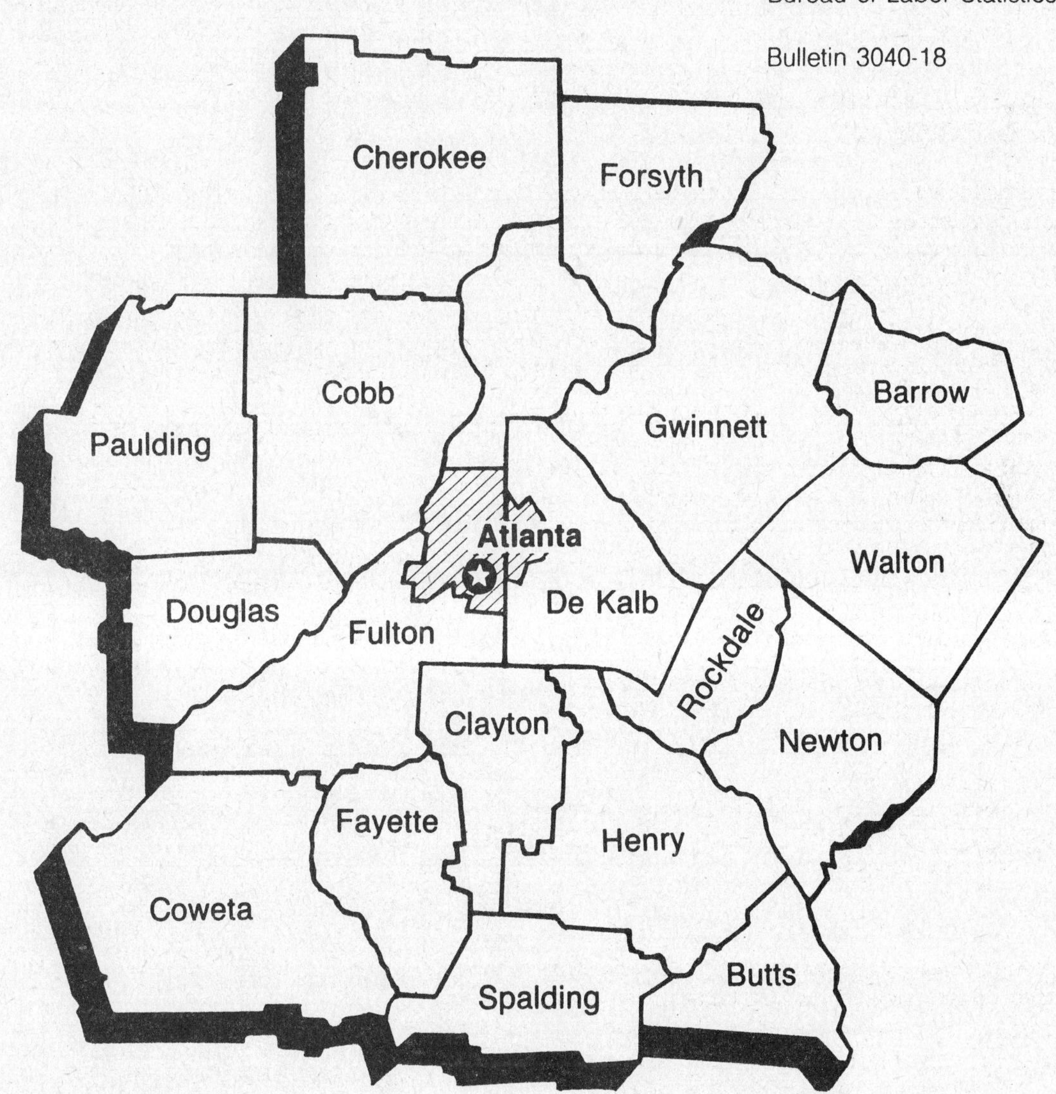

Table A-1. Weekly earnings of office workers in Atlanta, GA, May 1987

Occupation and industry division	Number of workers	Average weekly hours[1] (standard)	Weekly earnings (in dollars)[2]			Number of workers receiving straight-time weekly earnings (in dollars) of —																			
			Mean[3]	Median[3]	Middle range[3]	Under 180	180 and under 200	200 – 220	220 – 240	240 – 260	260 – 280	280 – 300	300 – 320	320 – 340	340 – 360	360 – 380	380 – 400	400 – 420	420 – 440	440 – 460	460 – 480	480 – 520	520 – 560	560 – 600	600 – 640
Secretarial and keyboarding occupations																									
Secretaries	5,317	39.0	403.50	384.00	328.00– 467.50	–	1	2	22	59	247	388	329	502	569	442	599	239	239	276	183	420	427	209	78
Manufacturing	1,009	39.5	432.50	422.00	354.50– 559.00	–	–	–	17	27	49	39	32	45	64	85	68	70	47	71	26	80	251	14	10
Nonmanufacturing	4,308	39.0	396.50	377.00	326.50– 450.00	–	1	2	5	32	198	349	297	457	505	357	531	169	192	205	157	340	176	195	68
Transportation and utilities	708	39.0	483.00	484.00	418.00– 544.00	–	–	–	1	1	–	23	15	13	25	30	46	27	40	47	71	124	107	66	34
Secretaries I	1,442	39.0	341.50	326.00	300.00– 350.00	–	1	2	6	53	142	148	241	341	210	56	92	11	18	21	3	7	2	83	5
Manufacturing	120	40.0	318.50	310.50	265.00– 379.50	–	–	–	1	27	5	13	16	18	5	20	12	2	1	–	–	–	–	–	–
Nonmanufacturing	1,322	38.5	343.50	326.00	303.50– 349.50	–	1	2	5	26	137	135	225	323	205	36	80	9	17	21	3	7	2	83	5
Transportation and utilities	60	40.0	323.00	328.50	288.00– 348.00	–	–	–	1	1	–	19	3	13	17	3	2	–	–	1	–	–	–	–	–
Secretaries II	1,078	39.0	346.00	349.50	291.00– 386.00	–	–	–	16	3	104	190	48	61	183	169	179	35	37	28	7	11	6	1	–
Manufacturing	182	39.0	340.50	327.50	274.50– 400.00	–	–	–	16	–	44	16	10	8	18	18	6	4	11	26	–	4	1	–	–
Nonmanufacturing	896	39.0	347.00	349.50	297.00– 386.00	–	–	–	–	3	60	174	38	53	165	151	173	31	26	2	7	7	5	1	–
Secretaries III	1,792	39.0	440.00	425.00	369.50– 510.00	–	–	–	–	–	1	47	39	92	163	182	202	135	121	167	71	160	327	38	22
Manufacturing	462	40.0	489.00	559.00	404.00– 559.00	–	–	–	–	–	–	10	5	14	29	23	28	31	12	22	3	35	234	3	3
Nonmanufacturing	1,330	39.0	423.00	412.00	364.00– 466.00	–	–	–	–	–	1	37	34	78	134	159	174	104	109	145	68	125	93	35	19
Transportation and utilities	417	39.0	478.50	482.50	427.00– 531.50	–	–	–	–	–	–	–	8	–	8	22	38	16	34	37	42	81	87	32	10
Secretaries IV	681	39.0	472.00	472.00	397.00– 519.00	–	–	–	–	–	–	–	1	5	12	31	126	43	51	37	61	144	65	58	29
Manufacturing	173	38.0	425.50	415.50	381.00– 467.50	–	–	–	–	–	–	–	1	5	11	24	22	27	20	16	16	20	7	1	3
Nonmanufacturing:																									
Transportation and utilities	138	39.0	507.00	487.50	464.50– 578.00	–	–	–	–	–	–	–	–	–	–	5	6	8	5	8	24	33	10	20	10
Secretaries V:																									
Nonmanufacturing:																									
Transportation and utilities	71	38.0	620.00	622.50	566.50– 673.00	–	–	–	–	–	–	–	–	–	–	–	–	1	1	–	–	6	8	14	14
Stenographers:																									
Nonmanufacturing	100	39.0	347.00	349.00	260.00– 411.00	–	–	–	–	–	41	–	–	8	2	9	6	14	5	9	1	1	3	1	–
Transportation and utilities	49	38.0	398.00	396.50	364.50– 427.00	–	–	–	–	–	1	–	–	8	2	8	6	11	1	9	–	–	2	1	–
Typists	1,017	39.5	269.00	244.00	221.00– 315.00	–	11	212	151	165	118	83	155	40	7	18	10	2	16	5	4	10	10	–	–
Manufacturing	114	39.0	297.00	278.50	243.00– 338.50	–	–	7	9	27	15	7	10	13	6	14	–	2	–	–	–	–	4	–	–
Nonmanufacturing	903	39.5	265.50	242.00	221.00– 303.00	–	11	205	142	138	103	76	145	27	1	4	10	–	16	5	4	10	6	–	–
Typists II:																									
Nonmanufacturing	136	39.0	308.00	280.00	240.00– 302.50	–	–	1	1	43	13	43	3	3	–	1	6	–	1	5	4	8	4	–	–
Key entry operators	2,790	39.5	293.50	275.00	248.00– 320.00	12	9	38	428	688	339	368	205	180	66	112	38	75	116	73	1	12	8	22	–
Manufacturing	464	40.0	295.50	290.00	276.50– 305.50	–	–	15	2	66	90	158	53	24	21	19	3	4	1	–	–	–	7	1	–
Nonmanufacturing	2,326	39.5	293.00	267.00	242.00– 321.50	12	9	23	426	622	249	210	152	156	45	93	35	71	115	73	1	12	1	21	–
Transportation and utilities	251	39.0	358.50	370.00	292.00– 427.00	–	5	8	5	6	10	41	14	17	8	19	15	23	58	8	1	12	1	–	–

Table A-1. Weekly earnings of office workers in Atlanta, GA, May 1987 —Continued

Occupation and industry division	Number of workers	Average weekly hours[1] (standard)	Weekly earnings (in dollars)[2] Mean[3]	Median[3]	Middle range[3]	Number of workers receiving straight-time weekly earnings (in dollars) of — Under 180	180 and under 200	200 - 220	220 - 240	240 - 260	260 - 280	280 - 300	300 - 320	320 - 340	340 - 360	360 - 380	380 - 400	400 - 420	420 - 440	440 - 460	460 - 480	480 - 520	520 - 560	560 - 600	600 - 640
Key entry operators I	2,050	39.5	279.50	255.50	240.00- 293.00	12	9	37	425	588	222	276	119	115	23	27	15	17	98	65	-	-	2	-	-
Manufacturing	372	40.0	284.00	290.00	276.50- 293.00	-	-	15	2	50	89	150	52	5	2	2	2	2	-	-	-	-	1	-	-
Nonmanufacturing	1,678	39.5	278.00	252.50	236.00- 296.00	12	9	22	423	538	133	126	67	110	21	25	13	15	98	65	-	-	1	-	-
Transportation and utilities	125	38.5	355.00	370.00	300.00- 427.00	-	5	8	4	-	5	5	8	12	7	14	9	6	41	-	-	-	1	-	-
Key entry operators II	724	40.0	332.00	318.50	270.50- 377.00	-	-	1	2	94	117	92	86	65	43	84	23	57	14	6	1	11	6	22	-
Manufacturing	92	40.0	342.50	341.50	284.00- 368.00	-	-	-	-	16	1	8	1	19	19	17	1	2	1	-	-	-	6	1	-
Nonmanufacturing	632	40.0	330.50	312.00	270.50- 377.00	-	-	1	2	78	116	84	85	46	24	67	22	55	13	6	1	11	-	21	-
Transportation and utilities	110	40.0	364.00	370.00	286.00- 427.50	-	-	-	-	-	5	36	6	5	1	4	6	16	13	6	1	11	-	-	-
Other clerical occupations																									
Accounting clerks	5,661	39.0	330.00	307.00	267.00- 382.50	1	25	175	369	652	686	630	715	467	261	189	173	222	172	256	74	544	23	26	1
Manufacturing	669	39.5	330.00	310.00	265.00- 377.50	-	-	16	76	40	124	50	65	78	37	19	22	16	19	39	11	29	1	26	1
Nonmanufacturing	4,992	39.0	330.00	307.00	268.00- 382.50	1	25	159	293	612	562	580	650	389	224	170	151	206	153	217	63	515	22	-	-
Transportation and utilities	1,235	37.5	429.50	455.50	399.00- 484.50	-	3	8	7	43	49	61	15	28	22	31	43	36	132	193	37	512	15	-	-
Accounting clerks I	489	40.0	260.50	254.00	242.00- 277.00	1	-	6	97	153	127	85	6	9	-	3	-	2	-	-	-	-	-	-	-
Nonmanufacturing	463	40.0	259.50	254.00	241.00- 277.00	1	-	6	97	153	107	82	4	8	-	3	-	2	-	-	-	-	-	-	-
Accounting clerks II	2,863	39.5	297.50	286.00	258.00- 318.50	-	25	160	216	363	518	438	457	106	151	34	28	172	119	55	15	1	5	-	-
Manufacturing	443	39.5	291.50	278.50	255.50- 323.00	-	-	16	76	39	102	47	45	47	27	5	8	5	8	18	-	-	-	-	-
Nonmanufacturing	2,420	39.5	298.50	286.50	259.00- 318.50	-	25	144	140	324	416	391	412	59	124	29	20	167	111	37	15	1	5	-	-
Transportation and utilities	345	39.0	347.50	348.00	280.00- 427.00	-	3	8	7	30	28	61	13	13	14	22	16	17	93	14	1	-	5	-	-
Accounting clerks III	1,409	39.5	339.50	329.50	307.00- 369.00	-	-	8	50	127	30	100	236	331	89	130	113	23	24	28	51	66	3	-	-
Manufacturing	155	39.5	404.00	406.00	326.50- 464.50	-	-	-	-	-	-	-	18	29	8	11	8	9	10	21	11	29	1	-	-
Nonmanufacturing	1,254	39.5	332.00	329.00	300.00- 363.00	-	-	8	50	127	30	100	218	302	81	119	105	14	14	7	40	37	2	-	-
Transportation and utilities	118	40.0	441.00	478.00	397.50- 482.00	-	-	-	-	-	-	-	1	12	3	4	10	4	14	6	28	36	-	-	-
Accounting clerks IV	874	37.0	462.50	484.50	455.50- 484.50	-	-	-	1	2	3	4	14	21	21	22	32	25	29	173	8	477	15	26	-
Nonmanufacturing	832	37.0	460.50	484.50	455.50- 484.50	-	-	-	1	2	3	4	14	20	19	19	26	23	28	173	8	477	15	-	-
Transportation and utilities	736	36.5	474.00	484.50	455.50- 484.50	-	-	-	-	-	-	-	1	2	5	5	17	14	25	173	8	476	10	-	-
Payroll clerks	734	39.5	328.00	322.00	277.00- 365.00	-	-	5	7	17	221	47	66	132	43	31	77	22	23	12	11	18	-	2	-
Manufacturing	202	39.0	343.50	355.50	276.50- 390.00	-	-	1	3	10	39	19	9	13	8	8	53	13	16	10	-	-	-	-	-
Nonmanufacturing	532	39.5	322.00	308.00	277.00- 338.00	-	-	4	4	7	182	28	57	119	35	23	24	9	7	2	11	18	-	2	-
Transportation and utilities	66	40.0	361.50	374.00	292.00- 396.00	-	-	-	-	-	8	11	5	3	3	3	18	5	6	-	-	2	-	2	-
File clerks	1,473	39.0	221.50	211.00	195.00- 237.50	88	380	455	186	163	90	54	1	11	6	30	2	2	1	1	-	-	3	-	-
Manufacturing	205	39.0	273.50	243.00	234.00- 338.50	-	1	36	34	61	18	-	-	11	6	30	2	2	1	-	-	-	3	-	-
Nonmanufacturing	1,268	39.5	213.00	200.00	195.00- 228.50	88	379	419	152	102	72	54	1	-	-	-	-	-	-	1	-	-	-	-	-
File clerks I	1,176	39.5	212.00	200.00	195.00- 223.00	88	380	389	116	95	50	51	-	1	2	4	-	-	-	-	-	-	-	-	-
Manufacturing	101	40.0	242.50	234.00	216.00- 249.50	-	1	36	20	20	17	-	-	1	2	4	-	-	-	-	-	-	-	-	-
Nonmanufacturing	1,075	39.5	209.00	200.00	195.00- 216.00	88	379	353	96	75	33	51	-	-	-	-	-	-	-	-	-	-	-	-	-
File clerks II	287	38.5	255.50	243.00	225.00- 267.00	-	-	66	69	66	40	1	-	10	4	26	2	2	1	-	-	-	-	-	-
Nonmanufacturing	186	39.0	233.50	231.00	219.00- 248.50	-	-	66	55	25	39	1	-	-	-	-	-	-	-	-	-	-	-	-	-
Messengers	118	39.5	240.00	216.50	198.50- 268.00	3	39	22	8	10	9	12	1	10	1	-	-	-	-	2	-	1	-	-	-
Manufacturing	54	39.5	241.00	198.50	194.00- 292.00	-	32	2	-	2	2	4	-	10	1	-	-	-	-	1	-	-	-	-	-
Nonmanufacturing	64	39.5	239.50	233.00	204.00- 266.00	3	7	20	8	8	7	8	1	-	-	-	-	-	-	1	-	1	-	-	-

Table A-2. Weekly earnings of professional and technical workers in Atlanta, GA, May 1987

Occupation and industry division	Number of workers	Average weekly hours[1] (standard)	Weekly earnings (in dollars)[2]: Mean[3]	Median[3]	Middle range[3]	Number of workers receiving straight-time weekly earnings (in dollars) of —: Under 260	260 and under 280	280 - 300	300 - 320	320 - 360	360 - 400	400 - 440	440 - 480	480 - 520	520 - 560	560 - 600	600 - 640	640 - 680	680 - 720	720 - 760	760 - 800	800 - 840	840 - 880	880 - 920	920 - 960	960 and over
Computer systems analysts	1,780	39.0	698.50	713.00	631.00– 761.50	3	1	–	–	6	8	1	33	99	95	78	185	239	216	342	264	95	32	16	14	53
Manufacturing	224	39.0	735.00	745.00	649.50– 813.50	1	–	–	–	–	–	–	–	–	9	23	18	28	19	33	26	28	11	10	12	6
Nonmanufacturing	1,556	39.0	693.00	713.00	631.00– 759.50	2	1	–	–	6	8	1	33	99	86	55	167	211	197	309	238	67	21	6	2	47
Computer systems analysts I	161	39.0	510.50	500.00	481.00– 538.50	–	–	–	–	6	–	1	32	68	34	10	6	1	–	–	1	2	–	–	–	–
Nonmanufacturing	146	39.0	499.50	493.50	473.00– 524.00	–	–	–	–	6	–	1	32	68	34	2	2	–	–	–	1	–	–	–	–	–
Computer systems analysts II	1,107	39.0	684.00	690.00	633.50– 753.50	3	1	–	–	–	–	–	1	31	60	59	165	199	168	193	210	16	1	–	–	–
Manufacturing	100	38.5	681.50	681.50	634.00– 758.00	1	–	–	–	–	–	–	–	–	9	7	10	23	10	16	15	9	–	–	–	–
Nonmanufacturing	1,007	39.0	684.50	691.00	633.50– 753.50	2	1	–	–	–	–	–	1	31	51	52	155	176	158	177	195	7	1	–	–	–
Computer systems analysts III	455	39.0	757.50	749.00	714.00– 808.00	–	–	–	–	–	8	–	–	–	1	9	14	39	48	148	52	75	28	12	10	11
Manufacturing	102	39.0	795.00	799.00	720.00– 874.50	–	–	–	–	–	–	–	–	–	–	8	4	4	9	17	10	17	8	9	10	6
Nonmanufacturing	353	39.0	746.50	746.00	714.00– 798.00	–	–	–	–	–	8	–	–	–	1	1	10	35	39	131	42	58	20	3	–	5
Computer programmers	1,261	39.0	548.50	556.00	468.00– 614.50	2	–	3	20	3	99	99	117	157	155	183	166	136	54	38	18	6	3	–	2	–
Nonmanufacturing	1,016	38.5	541.00	555.50	465.00– 608.00	–	–	–	20	2	95	96	68	143	122	160	136	103	30	27	9	4	–	–	1	–
Transportation and utilities	185	39.5	500.50	478.00	428.00– 554.00	–	–	–	–	–	25	36	32	28	24	6	8	17	6	3	–	–	–	–	–	–
Computer programmers II	393	38.5	472.50	461.00	422.50– 505.00	2	–	–	17	1	44	80	87	78	28	16	14	11	7	6	2	–	–	–	–	–
Manufacturing	68	40.0	451.50	461.00	441.50– 461.00	2	–	–	–	1	3	3	47	5	5	–	1	1	–	–	–	–	–	–	–	–
Nonmanufacturing	325	38.5	477.00	470.50	408.00– 515.00	–	–	–	17	–	41	77	40	73	23	16	13	10	7	6	2	–	–	–	–	–
Computer programmers IV	464	38.5	642.00	633.00	595.00– 668.50	–	–	–	–	–	–	–	–	1	14	114	126	107	45	31	16	6	3	–	1	–
Computer operators	1,484	39.0	412.50	404.00	325.00– 481.00	63	77	70	87	236	188	178	214	110	99	63	71	19	2	–	7	–	–	–	–	–
Manufacturing	224	39.5	402.50	372.00	324.00– 450.50	8	3	22	15	57	34	27	9	5	1	16	27	–	–	–	–	–	–	–	–	–
Nonmanufacturing	1,260	38.5	414.50	416.00	330.00– 486.00	55	74	48	72	179	154	151	205	105	98	47	44	19	2	–	7	–	–	–	–	–
Transportation and utilities	435	38.0	459.00	455.00	403.50– 508.50	7	3	7	26	39	22	23	157	47	31	22	44	5	2	–	–	–	–	–	–	–
Computer operators I	293	38.5	342.50	320.50	286.00– 367.00	18	44	39	41	69	38	5	1	14	21	3	–	–	–	–	–	–	–	–	–	–
Manufacturing	68	39.5	325.50	324.00	293.50– 345.00	1	–	17	6	36	7	1	–	–	–	–	–	–	–	–	–	–	–	–	–	–
Nonmanufacturing	225	38.0	347.50	316.00	276.50– 370.00	17	44	22	35	33	31	4	1	14	21	3	–	–	–	–	–	–	–	–	–	–
Computer operators II	731	38.5	396.50	390.00	337.00– 454.00	45	33	28	43	108	136	59	180	35	2	34	28	–	–	–	–	–	–	–	–	–
Manufacturing	114	39.5	391.50	390.00	356.00– 407.50	7	3	2	9	20	27	26	5	1	–	14	–	–	–	–	–	–	–	–	–	–
Nonmanufacturing	617	38.5	397.50	388.50	334.00– 455.00	38	30	26	34	88	109	33	175	34	2	20	28	–	–	–	–	–	–	–	–	–
Transportation and utilities	294	37.5	437.50	443.00	371.50– 455.00	7	3	4	18	38	22	7	144	3	–	20	28	–	–	–	–	–	–	–	–	–
Computer operators III	315	39.5	450.00	429.00	401.00– 527.50	–	–	3	3	59	13	99	27	22	53	4	28	4	–	–	–	–	–	–	–	–
Nonmanufacturing	280	39.5	435.50	424.00	386.50– 510.00	–	–	–	3	58	13	99	24	22	53	3	1	4	–	–	–	–	–	–	–	–
Computer data librarians	52	38.0	378.00	403.00	293.50– 404.50	–	11	3	–	–	7	25	1	4	1	–	–	–	–	–	–	–	–	–	–	–

Occupational Descriptions

The primary purpose of preparing job descriptions for the Bureau's wage surveys is to assist its field representatives in classifying into appropriate occupations workers who are employed under a variety of payroll titles and different work arrangements from establishment to establishment and from area to area. This permits grouping of occupational wage rates representing comparable job content. Because of this emphasis on comparability of occupational content, the Bureau's job descriptions may differ significantly from those in use in individual establishments or those prepared for other purposes. In applying these job descriptions, the Bureau's field representatives are instructed to exclude working supervisors; apprentices; and part-time, temporary, and probationary workers. Handicapped workers whose earnings are reduced because of their handicap are also excluded. Learners, beginners, and trainees, unless specifically included in the job description, are excluded.

Listed below are three occupations for which new or revised descriptions or titles are being introduced in this survey:

Computer systems analyst
Computer programmer
Computer operator

The titles and numerical codes below the job titles in this appendix are taken from the 1980 edition of the *Standard Occupational Classification Manual* (SOC), issued by the U.S. Department of Commerce, Office of Federal Statistical Policy and Standards.

In general, the Bureau of Labor Statistics' occupational descriptions are much more specific than those found in the SOC manual. The BLS occupation, "Registered Industrial Nurse," for example, is limited to workers providing medical assistance and other related services (e.g., health education) to persons who are ill or become ill or suffer an injury in a factory or other establishment. The SOC occupation (code 29) includes a variety of registered nurses (e.g., school nurse, head nurse, general duty nurse, private duty nurse) that are excluded from the BLS description.

Thus, in comparing the results of this survey with other sources, factors such as differences in occupational definitions and survey scope should be taken into consideration.

See job summaries in preceding PATC Survey to establish comparability based on job content. Summary of Computer Operator occupation follows.

The following table provides FES point scores for Federal Government GS Grades - See Table D-1 in PATC Survey.

FACTOR EVALUATION GRADE CONVERSION TABLE

GS Grade	FES Point Range
1	190 - 250
2	255 - 450
3	455 - 650
4	655 - 850
5	855 - 1100
6	1105 - 1350
7	1355 - 1600
8	1605 - 1850
9	1855 - 2100
10	2105 - 2350
11	2355 - 2750
12	2755 - 3150
13	3155 - 3600
14	3605 - 4005
15	4055 - up

COMPUTER OPERATOR

(4612:Computer operator)

Monitors and operates the control console of either a main-frame digital computer or a group of mini-computers, in accordance with operating instructions, to process data. Work is characterized by the following:

- Studies operating instructions to determine equipment setup needed;
- Loads equipment with required items (tapes, cards, paper, etc.);
- Switches necessary auxiliary equipment into system;
- Starts and operates console;
- Diagnoses and corrects equipment malfunctions;
- Reviews error messages and makes corrections during operation or refers problems;
- Maintains operating record.

May test run new or modified programs and assist in modifying systems or programs. Included within the scope of this definition are fully qualified computer operators, trainees working to become fully qualified operators, and lead operators providing technical assistance to lower level positions.

Excluded are:

a. Workers operating small computer systems where there is little or no opportunity for operator intervention in program processing and few requirements to correct equipment malfunctions;

b. Peripheral equipment operators and remote terminal or computer operators who do not run the control console of either a main-frame digital computer or a group of mini-computers (see peripheral equipment operator); and

c. Workers using the computer for scientific, technical, or mathematical work when a knowledge of the subject matter is required.

Positions are classified into levels on the basis of the following definitions:

Computer Operator I

Receives on-the-job training in operating the control console (sometimes augmented by classroom training). Works under close personal supervision and is provided detailed written or oral guidance before and during assignments. As instructed, resolves common operating problems. May serve as an assistant operator working under close supervision or performing a portion of a more senior operator's work.

Computer Operator II

Processes scheduled routines which present few difficult operating problems (e.g., infrequent or easily resolved error conditions). In response to computer output instructions or error conditions, applies standard operating or corrective procedure. Refers problems which do not respond to preplanned procedure. May serve as an assistant operator, working under general supervision.

Computer Operator III

Processes a range of scheduled routines. In addition to operating the system and resolving common error conditions, diagnoses and acts on machine stoppage and error conditions not fully covered by existing procedures and guidelines (e.g., resetting switches and other controls or making mechanical adjustments to maintain or restore equipment operations). In response to computer output instructions or error conditions may deviate from standard procedures if standard procedures do not provide a solution. Refers problems which do not respond to corrective procedures.

Computer Operator IV

Resolves a variety of nonstandard problems (e.g., frequent new programs, applications, and procedures). Problems may require unusual equipment connections and channel configurations. May also provide technical assistance to lower level operators and use knowledge of program languages, computer features, and software systems in assisting programmers, systems analysts, and other users in resolving problems. Completed work is usually submitted to users without supervisory review.

PERIPHERAL EQUIPMENT OPERATOR

(4613: Peripheral equipment operator)

Operates peripheral equipment which directly supports digital computer operations. Such equipment is uniquely and specifically designed for computer applications, but need not be physically or electronically connected to a computer. Printers, plotters, card read/punches, tape readers, tape units or drives, disk units or drives, and data display units are examples of such equipment.

The following duties characterize the work of a peripheral equipment operator:

a. Loading printers and plotters with correct paper; adjusting controls for forms, thickness, tension, printing density, and location; and unloading hard copy;

b. Labeling tape reels, disks, or card decks;

c. Checking labels and mounting and dismounting designated tape reels or disks on specified units or drives;

d. Setting controls which regulate operation of the equipment;

e. Observing panel lights for warnings and error indications and taking appropriate action;

f. Examining tapes, cards, or other material for creases, tears, or other defects which could cause processing problems.

COMPUTER DATA LIBRARIAN

(4696: File clerk)
(4754: Stock and inventory clerk)

Maintains library of media (tapes, disks, cards, cassettes) used for automatic data processing applications. The following or similar duties characterize the work of a computer data librarian: Classifying, cataloging, and storing media in accordance with a standardized system; upon proper requests, releasing media for processing; maintaining records of releases and returns; inspecting returned media for damage or excessive wear to determine whether or not they need replacing. May perform minor repairs to damaged tapes.

MODULE 11

PERFORMANCE APPRAISAL AND MERIT PAY AT OLYMPIA DATA DESIGN (ODD)

Senior management at ODD has informed Personnel that they want all pay increases to be based strictly on merit. Most jobs at ODD are "knowledge" directed, and it is not easy to determine or measure differences in performance among employees who perform a wide variety of assignments. It is impossible to observe an applications programmer and know whether or not that individual is doing acceptable work. It is also not always possible to review results of a work assignment and be able to give a precise rating or score to an output. However, over a period of time -- one year or less, it is possible to make a sufficient number of observations of performance, reviews of demonstrated workplace behaviors, and analyses of results to generate objective and supportable performance ratings.

Currently, Olympia uses the "blank sheet of paper" method for performance appraisal. At the start of each year, each supervisor is supposed to interview each direct subordinate, and together they set goals for the subordinate for the coming year. At the end of the year, the supervisor describes on a blank sheet of paper how well the employee has achieved his or her goals. The results of these reviews have been very uneven. Some supervisors provide excellent reviews and supportable ratings, while many other supervisors provide ratings that are at best worthless and could even be damaging if they ever had to be used in a court case.

Alma Jenkins has recently reviewed a number of performance appraisal instruments and she has identified two very different kinds that may be more useful than the blank sheet of paper method now being used. The appraisal instruments Alma has identified follow this module.

Instrument A is an example of possibly the most commonly used kind of appraisal instrument -- one in which general qualities, behaviors, or traits are measured. The second kind of instrument is an example of one that uses a job description for each employee. In this case, in Instrument B, it uses the job description of an office secretary. This instrument requires the supervisor and subordinate to (1) update and approve the job definition section (responsibilities and duties) of the job description before each rating period, and (2) establish performance standards for measuring levels of performance for each identified duty or each responsibility.

Whatever performance appraisal instrument is finally selected, Personnel must be able to use the rating score generated by the performance appraisal instrument to assign a merit increase to each deserving employee. During the budget process, Finance and Personnel will establish a certain amount of merit increase funds for each unit. Personnel will then be responsible for allocating the budgeted merit increase funds among the employees of each unit. Each employee's allocation will be based on that individual's performance rating.

ASSIGNMENT

Review the two performance appraisal instruments selected by Alma.

1. Identify the strengths and weaknesses of each instrument.

2. Describe which instrument would be most useful in making merit budget allocations.

3. If you were involved in defending your organization in a performance appraisal-based court case relative to sex or age discrimination, what would be the benefits and liabilities related to each performance appraisal instrument?

INSTRUMENT A - **ANNUAL EMPLOYEE PERFORMANCE EVALUATION**

Employee:______________________________ **Evaluator:**______________________________

Job Title:______________________________

Place a check in the column which most accurately reflects your evaluation in each category of the above-named person. (See reverse side for rating definitions.)

	Outstanding	Exceeds Job Requirements	Meets Job Requirements	Needs Improvement	Unsatisfactory
1. **KNOWLEDGE OF JOB:** Rate overall knowledge and understanding of assigned duties, responsibilities, relevant policies and procedures					
2. **QUALITY OF WORK:** Rate the accuracy, thoroughness and neatness of work in comparison to the requirements or expectations for the position					
3. **QUANTITY OF WORK:** Rate the amount of work successfully completed on a timely basis in comparison to the requirements or expectations for the position					
4. **ORGANIZATIONAL SKILLS:** Consider how employee effectively manages time, properly sets priorities, and follows up on projects as necessary					
5. **COOPERATION AND FLEXIBILITY:** Rate the extent to which the employee is willing to help others during peak work periods and how he/she responds to changing work requirements					
6. **JUDGMENT:** Rate effectiveness in responding to problems with appropriate courses of action					
7. **EMPLOYEE/PUBLIC RELATIONS:** Rate employee's communication skills, courtesy and effective interaction with firm personnel, clients and vendors, if applicable					
8. **ATTENDANCE AND PUNCTUALITY:** Consider whether employee has a good attendance record, is basically on time, or has an attendance problem and is frequently late					

(Principal Strengths and/or Areas Needing Improvement): ______________________________

____

____

____

____

____

SUMMARY RATING - (to be completed by evaluator) Place a check in the box next to the appropriate overall rating of the employee's performance based on your evaluation of all relevant factors.

☐ **OUTSTANDING** - Performance far surpasses job requirements and/or expectations and outstanding results are attained consistently. This rating is to be reserved exclusively for those individuals who have displayed excellence on a consistent and sustained basis.
Note: In order for an employee to receive a summary overall rating of "Outstanding," no factor should have received an evaluation lower than "Meets Job Requirements."

☐ **EXCEEDS JOB REQUIREMENTS** - Performance almost always exceeds job requirements and/or expectations and results attained in day-to-day activities are frequently superior.
Note: In order for an employee to receive a summary rating of "Exceeds Job Requirements," no factor should have received an evaluation of "Needs improvement."

☐ **MEETS JOB REQUIREMENTS** - Performance consistently meets job requirements and/or expectations.
Note: In order for an employee to receive a summary rating of "Meets Job Requirements," no factor should have received an evaluation of "Unsatisfactory."

☐ **NEEDS IMPROVEMENT** - Performance is such that an employee may still require considerable supervision and learning due to newness and inexperience in his/her current position. In the case of a long-term employee, this evaluation indicates that serious deficiencies exist. Performance at this level for any extended period of time is unacceptable.

☐ **UNSATISFACTORY** - Performance is unacceptable and requires immediate improvement. A specified time period will be established for the employee to improve performance.
Note: An employee evaluated at this level will not receive a salary increase and termination will occur unless there is an improvement in job performance.

______________________________ **Date:** ______________________

Evaluator Signature

INSTRUMENT B - JOB DEFINITION OF OFFICE SECRETARY

			UO	1	2	3	4	5	PO	IR
1.0	Performs administrative assignments for the Manager.	1.0								
1.1	Schedules and maintains Manager's appointment calendar.	.1								
1.2	Maintains business and personal files for Manager.	.2								
1.3	Receives and screens Manager's calls, responding to questions in her absence.	.3								
1.4	Calculates budgetary expenses, including salaries, benefits, rent, and utilities.	.4								
1.5	Submits budget to Manager for revision and approval.	.5								
1.6	Monitors budget throughout year to ensure availability of funds.	.6								
1.7	Interacts with Headquarter's Budget Analyst to stay abreast of budgeting requirements.	.7								
1.8	Composes and types correspondence for the Manager and three supervisors.	.8								
1.9	Coordinates activities of Electrical Wholesale Distributor's Association, taking and typing minutes, updating membership register, typing and mailing correspondence, taking applications, and performing accounting procedures.	.9								
2.0	Supervises three office clerks.	2.0								
2.1	Establishes procedures for clerical assignments.	.1								
2.2	Schedules work for clerical staff.	.2								
2.3	Counsels clerks on job-related performance and behaviors.	.3								
2.4	Assists clerks in resolving difficult situations and answering questions regarding policies and procedures.	.4								
2.5	Monitors clerical assignments.	.5								
3.0	Processes personnel records and other forms.	3.0								
3.1	Prepares, tabulates, and maintains time cards.	.1								
3.2	Maintains attendance records for sick pay, vacation, and personal holidays, correcting and updating monthly computer printout of each employee's record.	.2								
3.3	Completes and submits various personnel forms.	.3								
4.0	Performs clerical assignments.	4.0								
4.1	Completes purchase requisitions for approval by Budget Department, Division of Accounts, and Purchasing Department.	.1								
4.2	Notifies Purchasing Department of receipt of goods by sending them a copy of the Purchase Order.	.2								
4.3	Receives and distributes mail to appropriate clerks.	.3								
4.4	Develops and summarizes complaint and repair reports.	.4								
4.5	Dispatches service calls.	.5								
4.6	Completes payment requests for services.	.6								
4.7	Totals number of miles driven by each employee from daily speedometer readings.	.7								
4.8	Computes amount to be paid for mileage at end of month.	.8								
4.9	Maintains Coke fund and Coke machine.	.9								

UO - Unable to observe. Unable to measure performance relative to this activity.
1 - Completely unacceptable level of performance.
2 - Minimally acceptable level of performance.
3 - Fully acceptable level of performance.
4 - Above acceptable level of performance.
5 - Outstanding level of performance.
PO - If performance of this activity was observed ✓ this column.
IR - If performance of this activity was inferred from results achieved or observed performance of others ✓ this column.

MODULE 12

SCHEDULING SHIFTS AND WEEKEND WORK AT ODD COMPUTER OPERATIONS

Recently, Personnel has noted a significant increase in turnover in the Computer Operations Center at ODD. Also, a number of the more senior employees have been complaining to Personnel about their work schedules and the pay they receive.

Currently, 12 employees cover computer operations 24 hours a day, 365 days a year. Normally, there are three employees on the 8 to 4 shift and two employees on the 4 to 12 shift. Two employees work the 12 to 8 ("graveyard") shift, and two employees work on weekends. One employee is available as a "floater" (to fill in as needed). The employees who work on weekends work a 12-hour shift. The weekend shifts are from 8:00 a.m. to 8:00 p.m. and 8:00 p.m. to 8:00 a.m. There must always be at least one senior operator on the day shift. A rather complex 6-week schedule has been developed by the supervisor of computer operations that rotates all workers through all shifts.

Among the 12 employees, six are in the senior computer operator job and six are in the computer operator job. The pay ranges for the two jobs are:

	Minimum	Maximum
Computer Operator - PG 9	$16,233	$21,103
Senior Computer Operator - PG 11	$17,811	$24,935

Each employee receives a rate of pay based on movement through the assigned pay grade.

The rotating schedule requires each employee to work two 8:00 a.m. to 4:00 p.m. day shifts, then rotate to the 4:00 p.m. to 12:00 midnight second shift, then one week on the midnight shift (12:00 midnight to 8:00 a.m.), and one week on the weekend shift. On one weekend shift, the employee works the 8:00 a.m. to 8:00 p.m. shift and on the next six-week cycle the employee works the 8:00 p.m. to 8:00 a.m. shift. Employees working the midnight and weekend shifts receive a premium of $50 a week.

The computer operators complain that the 6-week rotating shift cycle requires a constant rearranging of sleeping patterns and that they have to learn how to cope with disruptions in their personal lives. All of the operators except two senior computer operators are under 35 and three of the 12 are female. Almost all of them complain that the rotating shifts have destroyed their social lives. Among the 12 operators, two have been in computer operations more than seven years; two have been on the staff four years; four, between one and three years; and four have been on the job less than a year.

ASSIGNMENT

What recommendations would you make regarding pay and scheduling to reduce some of the complaints and turnover that is resulting from the 6-week rotating shift schedule?

MODULE 13

GAINSHARING AT OLYMPIA CENTRAL SERVICES

Olympia Central Services is a profit-center operation within Olympia, Inc. Central Services is responsible for designing and operating data production services. Various Olympia, Inc., units have extremely large paper (records)-based data inputs that are then electronically stored and transferred into a wide variety of informational outputs. The inputs include recording credit card transactions for Olympia Financial Services and recording all orders coming from sales representatives of Olympia Personal Care Products. The jobs at Olympia Central Services range from relatively low-skilled clerical, data entry, and computer operator jobs to medium-skilled electronic machine servicing and repair and data transmission jobs to highly skilled systems analyst jobs.

Central Services has given considerable thought to placing its data entry operators on piece rates. Each operator's terminal is programmed to count the operator's daily input (strokes per 8-hour day) and the actual number of items processed (credit card transactions, sales orders). The reason Central Services has not already traveled the piece rate route is that there are significant differences in forms used and those who initially complete the forms make a relatively large number of errors. The data entry operators are trained to catch certain kinds of errors, but looking for errors tends to reduce the quantity of work performed. Quality of input, however, is more important than quantity of input, and Central Services has not been able to reconcile its quality concerns with quantity requirements. In addition, placing data entry people on piece rates might alienate the clerks and other support personnel who can critically influence the work of the data entry people.

George Waters, staff compensation analyst, has been given the assignment of reviewing options available to Central Services for providing monetary incentives that can lead to improved performance. George has been particularly interested in gainsharing plans and has visited different organizations that use Scanlon, Rucker, and Improshare Plans. During his visits, George noted at least four advantages for these kinds of incentive plans:

1. The plans include all or a significant number of employees in an organization.

2. Output measurement uses some overall organizational standard that is easier to identify and administer (maintain records) than many individual standards.

3. Meeting or beating the standard requires the cooperative effort of all employees (it does not foster an us/them attitude between workers on an incentive and those not on an incentive).

4. Standard setting frequently involves all members of the organization, granting both management and employees the opportunity to understand how the standard was established, why it must be at a specific level, and what everyone (not just a few employees) can do to

improve operations that will lead to meeting or exceeding the standard.

George obtained the various mathematical processes used in the Scanlon, Rucker, and Improshare Plans, and now, in addition to recognizing the way each plan is typically designed, he also understands the basic philosophy and concepts of each plan.

George began collecting payroll and various kinds of performance-related data at Central Services over a time period spanning the past 5 years. He collected sufficient data to perform the necessary calculations to determine potential bonuses under each gainsharing plan. The following data were developed and the operating concepts underlying each method were kept as similar as possible so that comparisons could be made under similar operating conditions.

The Improshare and Rucker Plans normally call for a 50/50 split of all cost savings, while the Scanlon Plan's bonus calculations are slightly more complex. A typical Scanlon Plan calls for a 75/25 split of all savings, with the employees receiving the 75 percent share. However, the employees receive only 50 percent of the savings in their monthly bonus. The remaining 25 percent is placed in a special fund. Any month the costs are greater than the standard, money is removed from the fund to make up the difference. At the end of the year, all money remaining in the 25 percent fund is disbursed among all plan participants. Each employee's total annual earnings is divided by the total payroll. This value is that employee's share of the bonus.

After conducting his research of company records, George came up with the following base period data for use in calculating standard values under the Scanlon, Rucker, and Improshare Plans:

ASSIGNMENT

1. Calculate the monthly bonus (if any) Mary Jane -- a representative data entry operator would have earned under (1) the Scanlon Plan, (2) the Rucker Plan, and (3) the Improshare Plan.

2. After reviewing the data requirements and results of each plan, which one would you recommend for adoption by Olympia Central Services?

3. What kind of documentation would you use to support your specific recommendation? (This analysis could include a strength-weakness review of each gainsharing method.)

Forms for calculating each gainsharing plan follow this module.

(See Chapter 11 in Henderson's Compensation Management: Rewarding Performance, 5th edition, for examples and detailed descriptions on procedures for calculating Scanlon, Rucker, and Improshare bonuses.)

BASE PERIOD DATA

Sales/Sales Value of Production			$12,250,500
(There is no inventory in this operation. All data products are, for all intents and purposes, transmitted instantaneously to the client organization.)			
Payroll Cost (Cost of Labor)			7,656,250
Cost of Materials, Supplies, Services			612,500
Units Produced (In Millions of Units)			
Credit Card Transactions	150		
Sales Orders	5		
		155	
Production Workers (Credit Card)	120		
Support Workers (Credit Card)	208		
		328	
Production Workers (Sales Orders)	40		
Support Workers (Sales Orders)	70		
		110	
Base Period Labor Force		338	
Hours worked in base period per employee - 2,000			

MONTHLY BONUS PERIOD CALCULATION DATA

Sales Value of Production		$1,531,250
Actual Monthly Payroll (Cost of Labor)		696,245
Mary Jane's Monthly Earnings		1,154
Hours Worked by Mary Jane	168	
Cost of Materials and Supplies		76,200
Days Worked by Each Employee	21	
Hours Worked Per Day by Each Employee	8	
Credit Card Transactions -	19,600,000 units	
Sales Orders	580,000 units	
Total Production and Support Personnel During Bonus Period	449	

SCANLON PLAN

Base Period Calculation

Ratio	=	Payroll (Labor) Costs for Base Period / Sales for Base Period
	=	

Bonus Period Calculation

Sales Value of Production	=	$1,531,250
Bonus Period Allowed Labor Cost	=	Bonus Period Sales Value of Production x Ratio
	=	
Monthly Bonus Pool	=	Allowed Labor Cost - Actual Monthly Bonus Pool
	=	
50% to Monthly Employee Bonus	=	
25% to Reserve	=	
25% to Employer	=	

Mary Jane's Bonus

Mary Jane's Pay as Percentage of Total Payroll	=	
Mary Jane's Share of Bonus Pool	=	
Mary Jane's Bonus as % of her Monthly Pay	=	
Bonus as Additional Hourly Earning	=	
Additional Earning if Total Reserve Returned to Employee, Mary Jane's Reserve Bonus	=	
Mary Jane's Potential Total Bonus	=	
Mary Jane's Total Potential Bonus as % of her Monthly Pay	=	

RUCKER PLAN

Base Period Calculation

Sales Value of Production (SVP	=	
Cost of Materials, Supplies, Services (COM)	=	
Cost of Labor (COL)	=	
Value Added (VA) = SVP − COM	=	
Labor Contribution to Value Added (LCVA = $\frac{COL}{VA}$	=	
Economic Productivity Index (EPI) = $\frac{1.000}{LCVA}$	=	

Bonus Period Calculation

SVP	=	$1,531,250
COM	=	$ 76,200
COL	=	$ 696,245
VA	=	
Actual Value of Production (AVP)	=	SVP - (COM + COL)
AVP	=	
Economic Value of Production (EVP)	=	EPI x COL (for bonus period)
EVP	=	
Savings = EVP - AVP	=	
LCVA	=	
Money Placed in Bonus Pool for Labor Contribution to Savings	=	Savings x LCVA
LC to Savings	=	
Mary Jane's percentage share of bonus pool	=	$\frac{\text{Mary Jane's earnings (bonus period)}}{\text{Total Payroll (bonus period)}}$
	=	
Mary Jane's Share of Bonus	=	Mary Jane's % of Payroll x Bonus
	=	
Mary Jane's Bonus as % of her Monthly Pay	=	

IMPROSHARE

Base Period Calculation

Base Period Labor Force (per employee)	=	
Base Period Hours Worked	=	
Base Period Units Produced	=	
Credit Card Output	=	
Sales Order Output	=	
Standard Value Hours (SV) per product	=	$\frac{\text{Total Production Employees}}{\text{Units Produced}}$
SV Credit Cards	=	
	=	
SV Sales Orders	=	
	=	
Total Standard Value Hours	=	SV x Output
Total SV Credit Card Hours	=	
Total SV Sales Order Hours	=	
Total SV Output Hours	=	
Base Productivity Factor (BPF)	=	$\frac{\text{Total Hours Worked}}{\text{Total Standard Value Hours}}$
	=	

Monthly Bonus Calculation

Credit Card Transactions	=	
Sales Orders	=	
Total Production - Support Personnel	=	
Hours Worked per Employee	=	
Total Actual Hours Worked	=	

Total ImproShare Hours During Bonus Period

Credit Cards = SV (Credit Cards) x Units Produced x BPF

x x =

Sales Orders = SV (Sales Orders) x Units Produced x BPF

x x =

Total ImproShare Hours =

Total Actual Hours Worked =

Total Bonus Hours =

50/50 Split Bonus Hours =

Bonus Percentage $= \frac{\text{50\% Bonus Hours}}{\text{Total Hours Worked}} =$

Mary Jane's Share of Bonus =

Mary Jane's Bonus as % of Her Monthly Pay =

MODULE 14

ESTABLISHING A SHORT- AND LONG-TERM COMPENSATION PACKAGE FOR EMPLOYEES OF ODD

The Board of Directors has become extremely interested in the compensation packages provided to all employees. The Board members want to treat all employees fairly. They recognize that, traditionally, different groups of employees receive many different kinds of compensation. They also realize that the great majority of compensation components are short-term related. The kind and amount of the component relate both to short-term employee performance and to organizational performance. The Board feels that more long-term components should be made available to all employee groups and that these components, if at all possible, should be linked to employee and organizational short- and long-term performance. The Board also realizes that there are definite limits to the compensation it can offer employees. They know that compensation costs consume about 48 percent of total revenues. They also feel very strongly that a committed and involved work force can produce a significant increase in total output. These increases can be the result of innovative ways to reduce cost and extended effort to improve both quantity and quality of output.

In response to a request from the Board, Compensation developed the following list of compensation components that are currently provided to the major employee groups at Olympia. The Board members wanted to review the list and make recommendations to Senior Management regarding their views as to the direction compensation should take at Olympia.

ASSIGNMENT

Review the list of compensation components provided to the Board (the list follows this module) and complete the included Compensation Package Analysis Form. Develop a brief summary of your justification including costs and benefits for your package for each employee group.

COMPENSATION PACKAGE ANALYSIS FORM FOR MAJOR EMPLOYEE GROUPS

Compensation Components	Top Executives (CEO, President, COO, EVPs)	Sr. Mgt. (Sr.VPs, Div.VPs)	Sr. Operating Mgt (VP, General Mgr., Regional or District Mgr.)	Mid-Level Operating Mgt. and Mid-Level Professionals and Administrators (Department Heads)	Lower-Level Operating Mgt., Professionals and Administrators	Higher-Paid Nonexempt	Lower-Paid Nonexempt
Base Pay	$200,000+ - $1 million+	$125,000 - $250,000	$80,000 - $175,000	$30,000 - $80,000	$20,000 - $40,000	$18,000 - $60,000	$10,000 - $18,000
Annual Short-Term Bonus	40% Target - 100%+ Maximum	35% Target; 60% Maximum	30% Target; 45% Maximum	10% Target; 20% Maximum			
Social Security	X	X	X	X	X	X	X
Olympia Defined Ben. Pl.	X	X	X	X	X	X	X
401(k)	X	X	X	X	X	X	X
Non-qual. stock option	X	X	X				
Olympia Hosp. Insur. Pl.	X	X	X	X	X	X	X
Olympia [illegible] Plan	X	X	X	X	X	X	X
" Grp. Life Ins.	X	X	X	X	X	X	X
5 wks. ANNUAL VACATION	X	4 wks	3-4 wks	2-4 wks	2-4 wks	1-4 wks	1-4 wks
12 pd. holidays	X	X	X	X	X	X	X
10 days sick leave	X	X	X	X	X	X	X
401(k) based on annual profits	X	X	X	X	X	X	X
Supp. Ex Medical Pl.	X	X					
" " Disab. Insur. Pl.	X	X					
" " Life Insur.	X	X					
" " Retirement Pl.	X	X					
Rabbi Trust	X						
Employment Contract	X						
Golden Parachute	X						
Co.-provided AUTO.	X LUXURY	X					
" " Club memb.'s	X	X					
FINANCIAL COUNSELING	X	X	X				
1st class travel	X	X					
Spouse Travel Allow.	X	X					

COMPENSATION COMPONENTS CURRENTLY PROVIDED BY OLYMPIA FOR EACH MAJOR EMPLOYEE GROUP

TOP EXECUTIVES

Base Pay
Annual Short-Term Bonus
Social Security
Olympia Defined Benefit Retirement Plan
401(k) Salary Reduction Plan
Nonqualified Stock Option
Olympia Hospital, Surgical, Medical Insurance Plan
Olympia Disability Insurance Plan
Olympia Group Life Insurance (2 X Base with $50,000 Cap)
5 Weeks Annual Vacation
12 Paid Holidays
10 Days Sick Leave

401(k) Olympia Contributions based on Annual Profits
Supplemental Executive Medical Plan
Supplemental Executive Disability Insurance Plan
Supplemental Executive Life Insurance
Supplemental Executive Retirement Plan
Rabbi Trust
Employment Contract
Golden Parachute
Company-Provided Luxury Automobile
Company-Provided City and Country Club Memberships
Financial Counseling
First-Class Travel
Spouse Travel Allowance

SENIOR MANAGEMENT

Base Pay
Annual Short-Term Bonus
Social Security
Olympia Defined Benefit Retirement Plan
401(k) Salary Reduction Plan
Nonqualified Stock Option
Olympia Hospital, Surgical, Medical Insurance Plan
Olympia Disability Insurance Plan
Olympia Group Life Insurance (2 X Base with $50,000 Cap)
4 Weeks Annual Vacation
12 Paid Holidays
10 Days Sick Leave

401(k) Olympia Contribution based on Annual Profits
Supplemental Executive Medical Plan
Supplemental Executive Disability Insurance Plan
Supplemental Executive Life Insurance Plan
Supplemental Executive Retirement Plan
Company-Provided Automobile
Company-Provided City and Country Club Membership
Financial Counseling
First-Class Travel
Spouse Travel Allowance

SENIOR OPERATING MANAGEMENT

Base Pay
Annual Short-Term Bonus
Social Security
Olympia Defined Benefit Retirement Plan
401(k) Salary Reduction Plan
Nonqualified Stock Option
Olympia Hospital, Surgical, Medical Insurance Plan
Olympia Disability Insurance Plan

Olympia Group Life Insurance (2 X Base with $50,000 Cap)
3-4 Weeks Vacation Depending on Service
12 Paid Holidays
10 Days Sick Leave
401(k) Olympia Contributions based on Annual Profits
Financial Counseling

MID-LEVEL OPERATING MANAGEMENT AND MID-LEVEL PROFESSIONALS AND ADMINISTRATORS

Base Pay
Annual Short-Term Bonus
Social Security
Olympia Defined Benefit Retirement Plan
401(k) Salary Reduction Plan
Olympia Hospital, Surgical, Medical Insurance Plan
Olympia Disability Insurance Plan
Olympia Group Life Insurance (2 X Base with $50,000 Cap)
2-4 Weeks Vacation Depending on Service
12 Paid Holidays
10 Days Sick Leave
401(k) Olympia Contributions based on Annual Profits

LOWER-LEVEL OPERATING MANAGEMENT, PROFESSIONALS, AND ADMINISTRATORS

Base Pay
Social Security
Olympia Defined Benefit Retirement Plan
401(k) Salary Reduction Plan
Olympia Hospital, Surgical, Medical Insurance Plan
Olympia Disability Insurance Plan
Olympia Group Life Insurance (2 X Base with $50,000 Cap)
2-4 Weeks Vacation Depending on Service
12 Paid Holidays
10 Days Sick Leave
401(k) Olympia Contributions based on Annual Profits

HIGHER- AND LOWER-PAID NONEXEMPT EMPLOYEES

Base Pay
Social Security
Olympia Defined Benefit Retirement Plan
401(k) Salary Reduction Plan
Olympia Hospital, Surgical, Medical Insurance Plan
Olympia Disability Insurance Plan
Olympia Group Life Insurance (2 X Base with $50,000 Cap)
1-4 Weeks Vacation Depending on Service
12 Paid Holidays
10 Days Sick Leave
401(k) Olympia Contributions based on Annual Profits

MODULE 15

CONTAINING THE COSTS OF BENEFITS

For the past 5 years, Murray Kaufman has spent a number of hours of every working day involved in activities related to controlling benefits costs. Over these past years, Olympia began to require employees to pay a part of the premiums for their hospital, surgical, medical, and major medical insurance. Family coverage premiums have almost doubled. Deductibles on the medical plan have increased for the employee from $50 to $ 200 and for family coverage from $100 to $300. Even with this sharing of the premium costs, the overall cost of medical insurance continues to rise.

Murray has been reviewing an HMO option. HMOs, however, seem to be having the same problems as his current carrier. Murray has tracked the HMO premium structure for the past 3 years, and their premiums have also escalated.

Murray has also given thought to developing a flexible benefits opportunity in the selection of various kinds of medical benefits. However, he is also concerned that if selection for various medical options is provided, the young and healthy employees will gravitate toward the cheaper plans, leaving the old and the sick in plans with constantly increasing costs. What then could happen is that no plan could offer benefits in such critical areas as mental health, drug abuse, and nursing care. If a plan did offer these options, they would be chosen only by those in need of such assistance, and the plan would be immediately inundated with claims. Murray feels that health-care cost containment must recognize the need to spread the risk of illness among as large a group of employees as possible.

Murray recognizes that in addition to HMOs other possibilities for reducing the cost of medical benefits include (1) requiring second opinions on surgery; (2) making use of PROs and PPOs; and (3) even further increasing employee paid premiums and raising the deductible limits.

In the past, Murray had frequently considered using a 501(c)(9) trust or Voluntary Employee Benefits Association (VEBA) for funding some special programs. He thought that day care, recreation, and long-term disability programs could make use of such a trust. However, he realized that there was too much uncertainty regarding IRS's interpretation of what was or was not an acceptable practice and he never implemented and made use of a 501(c)(9) trust.

All is not lost, however. The Deficit Reduction-Act of 1984 and the Tax Reform Act of 1986 clarified many issues regarding the use of benefits provided under Section 125 of the IRC. Employees can reduce their taxable income (including applicable Social Security tax) if they elect to use an Employee Spending Account (if arranged by their employer) for such uses as

1. medical expense reimbursements
2. premiums for accident, health, hospitalization, disability, and group term life insurance
3. dependent care
4. legal services
5. personal financial planning

When using an Employee Spending Account, the employees place money in an account for a specified purpose at the beginning of the year. The money placed in the account comes from an equal reduction in the employee's wages. The employee can then draw upon the funds to pay for the cost of the specified benefit. The money used to pay the benefit cost is pre-tax money and thus allows the employee to escape income tax on the money spent on paying for the predefined benefit. However, unspent money is lost to the employee. Murray thinks this should be an option presented to employees who have day care problems.

In the past decade, the composition of the work force at Olympia has witnessed dramatic change. Nowhere is the change more evident than with female employees in the age bracket of 25 to 35. Child-bearing and child-raising no longer keep women out of the workplace. In the past, many women in the 25 to 35 age range dropped out of the work force soon after becoming pregnant. Now they work until a month or two before delivery and are frequently back at work 10 weeks after giving birth.

This situation has given rise to one of the biggest problems facing Murray and Olympia -- that is, day care. Whether they like it or not, day care has become an Olympia problem as much as it is a parent problem.

Another change in the benefits program considered by Murray is to switch the Olympia retirement program to a 401(k) plan. Olympia currently requires employees to contribute 6 percent to their pension plan. Olympia also offers a thrift plan and matches 50 cents for each employee's dollar up to 6 percent of the employee's salary.

Murray is thinking of recommending that Olympia study the possibility of eliminating their current pension and thrift plans and offering employees a 401(k) salary reduction plan with a corporate matching of employee contributions. Murray would like to place a corporate floor of 50 cents for each employee dollar contributed with a ceiling based on corporate profits. He would like to see a formula developed that would permit the corporation to match up to as much as $2.00 for each employee dollar depending on profit.

ASSIGNMENT

1. What benefits do an HMO provide to employers and employees that may not be provided by conventional Blue Cross-Blue Shield or insurance company-based medical plans?

2. The "use it or lose it" requirement when allowing employees to set aside money at the beginning of the year may discourage the use of such a plan for medical benefits, but may also be an inducement for day-care benefits. Why? Explain your answer.

3. What are the advantages of using a 401(k) plan to replace a traditional savings and thrift plan or even for using it to replace an existing pension plan (especially a defined benefits plan)?

4. What options would you recommend to Murray for restricting continued increases in health-care costs while providing employees with the best health-care protection possible?

(Chapters 12 and 13 in Compensation Management: Rewarding Performance, 5th edition, provide valuable information on this module. In particular, see section in Chapter 12 -- Qualified Deferred Arrangements and its subsection, Cash or Deferred Arrangement (CODA)-401(k) Plans -- and in Chapter 13, sections within Health and Accident Protection, Limiting the Rise of Health Care and Other Benefit Component Costs, Child Care, Elderly Care, Funding Benefits Through A VEBA, and Flexible Benefits -- in particular, Changes in Legislation and Employee Spending Accounts - IRC, Section 125, Plans.)

MODULE 16

USING COMPA-RATIO TO ANALYZE PAY INCREASE REQUESTS

John Truelove, Manager of Applications Programming, has recently submitted his proposed pay recommendations for the coming year. Review the recommendations that John has made, considering length of service and prior performance ratings of the 20 programmers in his department.

ASSIGNMENT

1. Calculate the current and proposed compa-ratios for each job group and each employee.

2. What conclusions can be made from the computed compa-ratios and from the information provided in the proposed pay adjustments?

3. List any review comments and recommendations you think Personnel should make in responding to the proposed pay adjustments.

Job Title / Pay Grade Data				Name	Length of Service Years	Length of Service Months	Last 2 Performance Ratings	Current Rates of Pay	Proposed Rate of Pay
Job Title - Applications Programmer I			1.	Stan Miller	-	7	Satis	$18,018	$19,100
Job Code - 141			2.	Charlotte Kimball	-	11	Satis	19,100	21,400
Pay Grade - 7			3.	Tom Lee	1	1	Ab.Av.;Ab.Av.	19,488	22,100
Pay Grade Data	Current	Proposed	4.	Myrtle Peterson	1	8	Needs Imp.;Satis	18,275	20,920
Max.	$22,365	$23,278	5.	Louise Elder	2	-	Ab.Av.;Satis	22,636	23,995
Mid.	$19,800	$20,592	6.	Lauri Clayton	2	9	Needs Imp.;Satis	20,800	21,985
Min.	$17,217	$17,906							
Job Title - Applications Programmer II			1.	Wayne Erwin	-	11	Satis	$21,120	$22,300
Job Code - 142			2.	Joy King	1	6	Satis;Satis	22,972	24,350
Pay Grade - 8			3.	Sharon Woods	1	9	Satis;Satis	23,100	24,390
Pay Grade Data	Current	Proposed	4.	Howard Niles	2	-	Sat;Needs Imp.	23,500	23,785
Max.	$26,565	$27,696	5.	Candy McDonald	2	2	Ab.Av.;Ab.Av.	22,800	25,000
Mid.	$23,500	$24,500	6.	Robert Bryant	3	1	Needs Imp; Needs Imp;	22,900	22,900
Min.	$20,435	$21,304	7.	Rex Deaton	3	1	Satis;Satis	25,090	26,590
			8.	Debbie Forrest	3	4	Ab.Av.;Ab.Av.	25,390	27,480
			9.	Rick Wallace	4	1	Ab.Av.;Satis	26,020	27,480
Job Title - Applications Programmer III			1.	Sam Ketch	1	10	Ab.Av.; Satis	$28,260	$28,955
Job Code - 143			2.	Brenda Sawyer	2	11	Satis;Satis	27,620	29,000
Pay Grade - 9			3.	Dale Chambers	3	2	Satis;Ab.Av.	28,417	30,975
Pay Grade Data	Current	Proposed	4.	Phyllis Jones	3	7	Satis;Satis	27,905	29,610
			5.	William Cole	5	1	Satis;Needs Imp.	29,000	29,210
Max.	$29,270	$30,450							
Mid.	$25,900	$26,936							
Min.	$22,522	$23,423							

MODULE 17

MERIT GUIDE CHART AND PAY-FOR-PERFORMANCE ALLOCATIONS

Alma Jenkins is reviewing the performance ratings given by John Truelove to the applications programmers in his department. Alma has developed a merit pay spreadsheet to help her review the variables involved in the merit pay decisions and the merit pay recommendations she must make. The merit pay guide chart following this module is the one ODD has been using for the past two years in determining merit pay allocations.

ASSIGNMENT

1. Using the merit pay guide chart, complete the merit pay spreadsheet. Calculate the recommended pay adjustments and proposed new base pay for the six applications programmers.

2. What merit pay recommendations would you make if Alma had $10,000 to allocate among the six employees?

3. What merit pay recommendations would you make if Alma had $4,000 to allocate among the six employees?

4. In reviewing the merit guide chart, what changes do you think should be made to treat the employees more fairly?

Location in Pay Grade / Performance Rating	0 - 25 Percentile	26 - 50 Percentile	51 - 75 Percentile	76 - 100 Percentile
Superior (5)	10	8	6	4
Commendable (4)	6	4	3	2
Fully Proficient (3)	5	3	2	0
Marginal (2)	2	0	0	0
Unsatisfactory (1)	0	0	0	0

Applications Programmers

Pay Grade Designation:

Max.	$39,000
75th	35,750
50th	32,500
25th	29,250
Min	26,000

MERIT PAY ALLOCATION
SPREADSHEET

② Split the $10,000 up according to percents. That would use $8800 of the $10,000. Put the extra $1200 aside and use later. Can use as bonus, reward, whatever. Can even save it to add later as a pay raise.

#2

Employees	Gender	Years with ODD	Performance Rating	Current Base Pay	Guide Chart % Inc.	Recommended Pay Adjustment	Proposed New Base Pay	EXTRA $10,000
Branch, John	M	3	4	$29,640	4	$1186	$30,826	+$1600
Coleman, Martha	F	3	5	27,400	10	$2740	$30,140	+$4000
Firm, William	M	11	3	34,500	2	$690	$35,190	+$800
May, Cynthia	F	8	4	31,850	4	$1274	$33,124	+$1600
O'Brien, Cecilia	F	1	2	26,100	2	$522	$26,622	+$800
Thorn, James	M	15	3	37,200	Ø	Ø	$37,200	+ Ø

MODULE 18

USING MATURITY CURVES TO MAKE PAY DECISIONS

In late 1986 , Olympia, Inc., purchased the Valley Laboratory from BMI, Ltd. After purchase, the laboratory was renamed Olympia Electronics Laboratory, and plans are underway to eventually fully integrate it with Olympia Electronics. Currently, it is operating as an independent division of Olympia.

The laboratory is relatively small with only 54 employees. Of these 54 employees, 2 are in senior management, 37 are scientists and engineers in nonsupervisory positions, 8 are scientists and engineers in supervisory positions, and 7 are secretaries and clerks. All scientists and engineers are graduates of accredited universities and colleges, 3 have earned Ph.D. degrees, 7 have MS degrees, and 35 have BS degrees.

In the past, salaries were set by Harry Nakkon, the past president of the lab. Harry knows little about salary administration, and his way of setting a salary is to "do whatever is necessary." If a person complained and Harry liked the individual, an adjustment was made. When hiring a new employee, he would offer whatever was necessary to obtain the individual if he wanted the person badly enough.

Rick Elman has recently been hired by Olympia Electronics Laboratory as Personnel Director and Manager of Compensation. After receiving numerous complaints from the engineers and scientists in the laboratory, Rick reviewed the current salary of each employee. In his review, he checked each employee's personnel file, noting the last two performance ratings received by each employee and the employee's current rate of pay. He then compared the salaries with the Professional Income of Engineers 1987 Annual Salary survey produced by the Engineering Manpower Commission of the American Association of Engineering.

After reviewing the salaries of all professionals, Rick recognized that the current salary schedule was chaotic and changes must be made. The first announcement he made was that all 1988 salary adjustments will be dependent on (1) the employee's current salary; (2) 1988 performance ratings; and (3) professional development. (Since Rick was new to the laboratory, he would be using year since receipt of BS degree as a proxy for professional development.) He also established guidelines for determining salary adjustments:

5 - Superior - '5' performance rating - maximum increase in salary is 9 percent. No salary may go higher than the upper decile (90th percentile) on the Engineers' Report.

4 - Commendable - '4' performance rating - maximum increase in salary is 7 percent. No salary may go higher than the upper quartile (75th percentile) on the Engineers' Report.

3 - Fully Satisfactory - '3' performance rating - maximum salary increase is 5 percent. No salary may go higher than the median (50th percentile) on the Engineers' Report.

2 - Marginal - '2' performance rating - maximum salary increase is 2 percent. No salary may go higher than the lower quartile (25th percentile) on the Engineers' Report.

1 - Unsatisfactory - '1' performance rating - no increase.

Under no circumstances will an employee's pay be reduced, but those receiving no increase shall be told the reason for such action, e.g., their current pay level and their most recent performance rating.

ASSIGNMENT

Using the salary curves and associated salary statistics in the Electronic Equipment Engineers from the 1987 Professional Engineers Annual Salary, what pay recommendations would you make on the following six engineers?

Incumbent	Past Two Performance Ratings	Years Since BS Degree	1987 Salary	Proposed 1988 Salary
1. Axtell, Josephine	3,3	10	$36,300	
2. Coleman, George	3,5	5	34,912	
3. Faulkner, Larry	2,3	11	40,450	
4. Gomez, Luis	3,4	10	41,750	
5. Oxfelt, Carol	2,2	1	26,752	
6. Sturgeon, Hall	3,2	17	45,925	

SALARY CURVES FOR ENGINEERS IN ELECTRONIC EQUIPMENT
ALL ENGINEERS, ALL DEGREE LEVELS

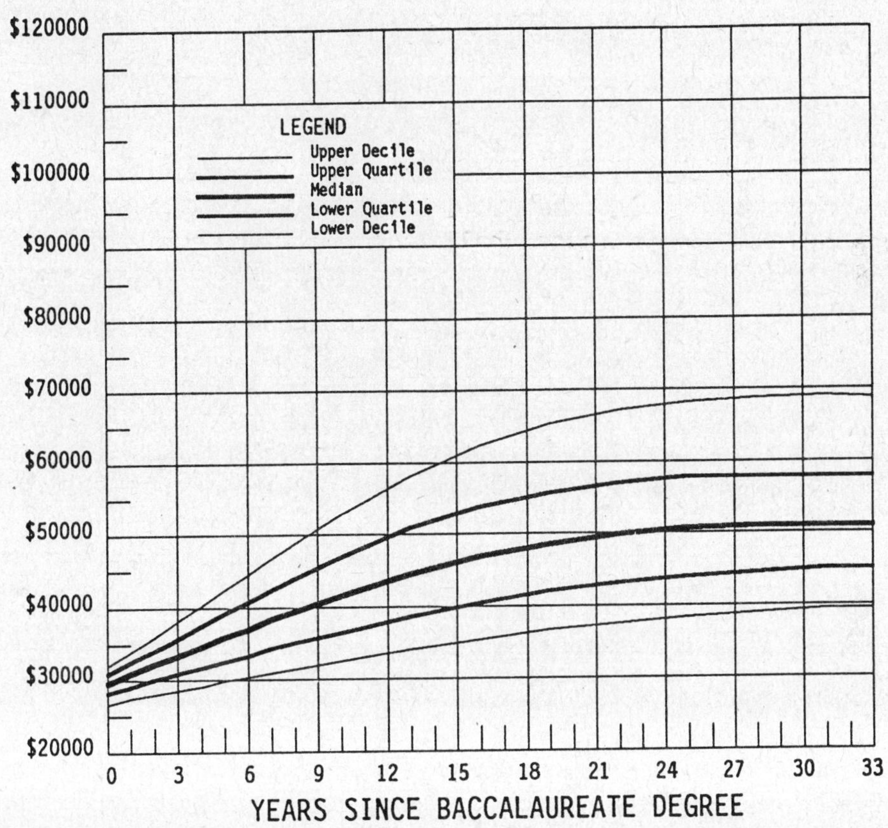

ENGINEERING SALARY STATISTICS: ELECTRONIC EQUIPMENT

Years Since B.S.	0	1	2	3	4	5	6	7	8	9-11	12-14	15-17	18-20	21-23	24-26	27-29	30-32	33+	Totals
Smooth Curve Data																			
Upper Decile	32000	34000	36100	38200	40350	42500	44650	46800	48900	52900	58200	62350	65350	67250	68300	68800	68950	68850	59650
Upper Quartile	30900	32500	34200	35850	37550	39200	40850	42450	44050	47000	50850	53800	55850	57100	57750	57950	57900	57500	50700
Median	29700	30950	32200	33450	34650	35900	37100	38300	39450	41650	44500	46850	48600	49800	50550	50900	51050	50950	41000
Lower Quartile	28300	29200	30050	30900	31750	32600	33450	34300	35100	36600	38700	40550	42050	43200	44050	44650	45050	45450	33550
Lower Decile	26750	27350	28000	28550	29150	29750	30350	30900	31500	32600	34150	35500	36700	37700	38450	39000	39400	39600	30100
Mean	29600	30900	32200	33500	34800	36100	37400	38700	39950	42300	45550	48200	50300	51800	52750	53350	53600	53700	43800
Raw (Unsmoothed) Statistics																			
Upper Decile	32350	33850	35900	38200	40350	42750	45550	46900	48600	51200	55900	62850	67800	69250	70350	72200	66300	67100	59650
Upper Quartile	31250	32350	34050	35800	37250	39700	41550	42850	43950	45550	49050	53800	57850	58150	59200	59650	57100	55900	50700
Median	29800	30900	32200	33250	34600	36650	38050	38300	39300	39900	42550	47600	50300	50350	51250	52550	50600	49650	41000
Lower Quartile	28250	29350	30400	30750	31500	32850	34400	34200	34700	35050	37250	40850	43550	43500	45100	46350	44900	43900	33550
Lower Decile	26650	27950	28450	28550	28900	30200	30600	30650	31050	30550	32450	35900	38200	38850	39800	39550	39350	38450	30100
Mean	29700	30950	32300	33400	34600	36550	38200	38800	39700	40700	43700	48550	52250	52500	53950	55250	53000	52050	43800
Supporting Data																			
Total Number	702	877	925	809	670	687	645	596	450	956	852	1150	921	953	943	934	1368	1028	15461
$125,000 or More	0	0	0	0	0	0	0	0	0	0	0	0	3	0	3	7	13	5	30
Less Than $22000	2	5	3	3	5	2	2	4	0	4	1	0	1	1	0	0	0	0	32

MODULE 19

REQUEST FOR PAY ADJUSTMENT

John Truelove, Data Processing Software Manager, has just sent a number of requests for changes in pay to the compensation department. It is the responsibility of Janice James to review all requests for changes in pay to check compliance with existing compensation policy. Janice is not required to approve or disapprove any request, but she must note any variances in a request relative to existing policies or procedures. Janice dreads receiving pay change requests from John because past experience has made her extremely wary of exceptions that arise when John makes pay adjustment requests for his employees. John is constantly fighting with compensation administration regarding policies that limit the timing and amount of pay increases he may offer his people. In the past, John has been able to negotiate a number of exceptions regarding changes in pay when taking his pay-related problems before the Salary Administration Committee and higher levels of management. This module includes Excerpt From Compensation Policy and Administrative Manual for Olympia, Inc., a copy of the Request for Pay Adjustment, and copies of Request for Pay Adjustment completed by John Truelove.

ASSIGNMENT

1. Review the requests submitted by John and a copy of the pertinent sections of the compensation policy and procedures manual. After reviewing John's requests and the relative sections of the policy and administration manual, what information would you note for special attention by your boss, Sam Thomas, who has to make a pay adjustment recommendation in each case?

EXCERPT FROM COMPENSATION POLICY AND ADMINISTRATION MANUAL FOR OLYMPIA, INC.

PAY RANGES

It is the policy of Olympia that the range of pay for each pay grade reflect the current competitive rates of pay for jobs in the relevant labor market.

Minimum of Range

The minimum rate of pay for each pay grade will be sufficient to attract qualified applicants to fill job vacancies. An incumbent possessing minimum job qualifications will be paid at least the minimum rate of pay.

First Quartile

The first quartile represents the lower quarter of the pay grade. New hires or newly promoted employees should normally be paid a rate of pay within the first quartile.

Second Quartile

Incumbents who are satisfactorily progressing toward complete fulfillment of job requirements should be advanced toward midpoint of the pay grades.

Midpoint of Pay Grade

The midpoint represents the competitive market or "going" rate of pay for jobs in a given pay grade. A fully experienced employee who consistently functions at a satisfactory or acceptable level of performance will receive this rate of pay. A new hire possessing sufficient education, experience, and skill qualifications may be offered a starting rate of pay up to midpoint. A new hire may not be hired at a rate of pay between the 25th percentile and midpoint unless prior written approval has been granted by the Salary Administration Committee.

Third Quartile

Only those employees who consistently perform at a level above that normally demonstrated by employees of Olympia should receive rates of pay at this level.

Fourth Quartile

Only those employees who make outstanding contributions and demonstrate consistently outstanding performance should receive rates of pay in the 75th percentile to the maximum of the pay grade.

Maximum of the Range

Olympia, Inc. establishes the maximum of the pay grade as that amount that should be sufficient to recognize the full worth of a job, to reward the outstanding contributor, and to stimulate above average performance by employees of Olympia. Only those employees who have consistently performed in an exceptional manner over an extended period of time can expect to be paid at the maximum of the pay grade. It is expected that employees reaching the maximum of a pay grade will be eligible for promotion to higher level jobs that will permit continued growth in pay and other compensation opportunities.

KINDS OF PAY ADJUSTMENTS

Employees may receive pay adjustments because of change in job content, job change, job performance, physical location of job, and economic conditions.

Job Content

Where differences in job responsibilities and duties are sufficient to change the evaluated worth of the job and the assigned pay grade, the pay of all affected incumbents will be recognized by such changes.

Job Changes

When transfer, promotion, or demotion occurs, change in pay should relate to changes made in kind and level of work in the new assignment.

Job Performance

Employee contributions and changes in performance will be recognized through adjustments in pay. Job performance and employee pay will be reviewed at least once a year to ensure fair treatment and consistent relationship between pay and performance.

Physical Location of Job

The "going" rate of pay for all jobs at Olympia will reflect competitive market conditions. Those jobs that relate to regional and national labor markets will reflect changes in their respective labor markets.

Economic Changes

Economic changes, or what is frequently termed "cost-of-living" adjustments will be recognized through changes in the pay structure. Through the use of pay and compensation surveys conducted by compensation personnel of Olympia and respected Third Parties, pay structure adjustments will be made. These changes in pay structure permit employees performing in an acceptable manner to expect their rates of pay to be fully competitive.

FACTORS LIMITING PAY ADJUSTMENTS

No employee shall receive pay adjustments that increase their base pay by more than 25 percent within one calendar year. Employees paid below minimum of the pay grade will have their pay reviewed in six month intervals. Where performance warrants, a manager may recommend a merit increase at each six month interval until the employee reaches the minimum of the pay grade. At that time, normal review procedures take effect.

Employees paid above the maximum may not receive any kind of pay increases unless such an increase has been approved by the Salary Administration Committee. Any request for a pay increase that places the recipient in an above-maximum situation must be justified by the requesting manager.

An employee receiving a promotion should be rewarded with an increase in pay that normally ranges from 5 to 15 percent of that previously earned. The actual amount of the increase depends on the level of the new job and the kind of work required in the performance of the new job.

A competent employee demonstrating acceptable work performance should normally expect to reach the midpoint of the pay grade within three years.

Approximately six weeks prior to the annual pay review of each employee, the immediate supervisor will appraise the performance of the employee. Upon completion of the performance appraisal, the compensation department will review the rating and recommend a pay adjustment.

Those managers having personnel budget allocation authority will recommend annual pay adjustments. All recommendations will be reviewed by the compensation department and final approval will be granted by the Salary Administration Committee.

All performance ratings and budget allocations that relate directly to pay adjustments will be reviewed by the compensation department. This review will focus specifically on distribution of pay adjustments by job, functional area, and category of employee. Any questionable ratings or recommended pay adjustments will be discussed with the involved managers. Extreme care must be taken to ensure that the ratings of performance are accurate and that pay adjustments are equitable within a department and between departments. The Salary Administration Committee has the responsibility of resolving any conflict that relates to pay adjustments.

REQUEST FOR PAY ADJUSTMENT

All managers will receive from the compensation department for each subordinate employee information regarding job evaluation, pay grade assignment, and current rate of pay. Each manager is responsible for notifying the compensation department when

- grade assignment for a specific job based on job evaluation appears to be inconsistent in relationship to other jobs;

- job assignments require differences in job responsibilities, duties, knowledge, and skills than those identified in the current job description;

- difficulties are experienced in hiring and retaining qualified and competent personnel;

- existing pay guidelines would result in overpaying an employee in the judgment of the manager.

Managers requesting pay adjustments will complete a Request for Pay Adjustment form and submit the completed form to the Compensation Manager. The Compensation Department will institute all necessary reviews and prepare all necessary changes including possible job analysis and the rewriting of the job description, reevaluation of the job, and review of relevant pay practices. Findings and final recommendations and conclusions will be discussed with the requesting manager. The Salary Administration Committee has responsibility for final approval of all pay adjustments.

TIME IN GRADE REQUIREMENTS

All employees must spend a specified period of time within a certain segment of their assigned pay grade before being eligible for a pay increase that moves them to the next sector of the pay grade. Employees of Olympia must demonstrate an acceptable or better level of performance over a specified period of time prior to being eligible for a pay increase.

Time on Job	Maximum Employee Rate of Pay
0 to 24 months	Within First Quartile of Pay Grade
25 to 48 months	Between First Quartile and Midpoint of Pay Grade
48 to 84 months	Between Midpoint and Third Quartile of Pay Grade
Beyond 7 years	Between Third Quartile and Maximum of Pay Grade

REQUEST FOR PAY ADJUSTMENT
(All Pay Figures Should Be In Annual Amounts)

Date of Request ________________

Name of Employee ____

Job Title ________________________________ Job Code ____________

Department _____________________

Assigned Pay Grade _____________ Current Rate of Pay _____________

Grade Minimum _________________ Grade Maximum _________________

Length of Service in Present Job _____________________________

Length of Service at Olympia __________________________________

Date of Last Pay Adjustment __________________ Kind ______________

Amount of Last Pay Adjustment ________________________________

Percent Increase Through Last Pay Adjustment _________________

Requested Adjustment $___________ Date To Be Effective ____________

Percent Increase If Adjustment Is Approved ___________________

Reasons for Request (check appropriate item):

Change in Job Content ___ Transfer Adjustment ___
Meritorious Performance ___ Promotion Adjustment ___
Cost-of-Living Adjustment ___ Demotion Adjustment ___
Location (geographic/area) New Hire ___
Differential Adjustment ___

Brief Description of Reason for Request: __________________________

____

____

To Be Completed By Compensation Department

Amount Current Rate of Pay Is Below Grade Minimum $_____________

Amount Current Rate of Pay Is Above Grade Maximum $_____________

Amount Requested Increase Would Place Recipient's
Pay Above Grade $_____________

Last Three Performance Appraisal Ratings _______________________

If Job Was Reevaluated:

Current Evaluation			Revised Evaluation		
Compensable Factors	Degrees	Points	Compensable Factors	Degrees	Points

Comments:

____________ ____________________________________

Date Compensation Department Manager

Salary Administration Committee Approval

Approval _____________ Disagreement ______________

Date _________________ _________________________, Secretary
Compensation Administration Comm.

REQUEST FOR PAY ADJUSTMENT
(All Pay Figures Should Be In Annual Amounts)

Date of Request 4/17/88

Name of Employee DUANE BICKERSTAFF

Job Title Application Programmer Trainee Job Code 140

Department Data Processing

Assigned Pay Grade 11 Current Rate of Pay $18,701

Grade Minimum $17,811 Grade Maximum $24,935

Length of Service in Present Job 1 year 5 months

Length of Service at Olympia 1 year 5 months

Date of Last Pay Adjustment 9/1/87 Kind Merit Per.

Amount of Last Pay Adjustment $890

Percent Increase Through Last Pay Adjustment 5%

Requested Adjustment $ $800 Date To Be Effective 9/1/88

Percent Increase If Adjustment Is Approved 4.3%

Reasons for Request (check appropriate item):

Change in Job Content ___
Meritorious Performance x
Cost-of-Living Adjustment ___
Location (geographic/area) Differential Adjustment ___
Transfer Adjustment ___
Promotion Adjustment ___
Demotion Adjustment ___
New Hire ___

Brief Description of Reason for Request: Duane has demonstrated above-average performance in current assignments and is doing the same work as junior applications programmers. He has to be in this job two years before he can be promoted to junior applications programmer and if he doesn't get the increase, I feel he will resign and get a job elsewhere.

John Truelove
D.P. Software Mgr.

To Be Completed By Compensation Department

Amount Current Rate of Pay Is Below Grade Minimum $

Amount Current Rate of Pay Is Above Grade Maximum $

Amount Requested Increase Would Place Recipient's Pay Above Grade $

Last Three Performance Appraisal Ratings

If Job Was Reevaluated:

Current Evaluation			Revised Evaluation		
Compensable Factors	Degrees	Points	Compensable Factors	Degrees	Points

Comments:

Date

Compensation Department Manager

Salary Administration Committee Approval

Approval ______ Disagreement ______

Date ______

, Secretary
Compensation Administration Comm.

REQUEST FOR PAY ADJUSTMENT
(All Pay Figures Should Be In Annual Amounts)

Date of Request 4/15/88

Name of Employee MYRTLE PETERSON

Job Title Applications Programmer-Junior Job Code 141

Department Data Processing

Assigned Pay Grade 13 Current Rate of Pay $21,411

Grade Minimum $20,391 Grade Maximum $28,548

Length of Service in Present Job 2 years

Length of Service at Olympia 4 years 9 months

Date of Last Pay Adjustment 8/15/87 Kind Merit Per.

Amount of Last Pay Adjustment $1,020

Percent Increase Through Last Pay Adjustment 5.0%

Requested Adjustment $1,600 Date To Be Effective 9/1/88

Percent Increase If Adjustment Is Approved 7.5%

Reasons for Request (check appropriate item):

Change in Job Content ___
Meritorious Performance x
Cost-of-Living Adjustment ___
Location (geographic/area) Differential Adjustment ___
Transfer Adjustment ___
Promotion Adjustment ___
Demotion Adjustment ___
New Hire ___

Brief Description of Reason for Request: · Myrtle's performance in her past two assignments has been outstanding. She has been a loyal, hard-working employee and deserves the recommended pay adjustment.

John Lullove
Requesting Authority
D.P. Software Mgr.

To Be Completed By Compensation Department

Amount Current Rate of Pay Is Below Grade Minimum $

Amount Current Rate of Pay Is Above Grade Maximum $

Amount Requested Increase Would Place Recipient's Pay Above Grade $

Last Three Performance Appraisal Ratings

If Job Was Reevaluated:

Current Evaluation			Revised Evaluation		
Compensable Factors	Degrees	Points	Compensable Factors	Degrees	Points

Comments:

Date

Compensation Department Manager

Salary Administration Committee Approval

Approval

Disagreement

Date

, Secretary
Compensation Administration Comm.

REQUEST FOR PAY ADJUSTMENT
(All Pay Figures Should Be In Annual Amounts)

Date of Request 4/19/88

Name of Employee WILLIAM COLE

Job Title Applications Programmer - Senior Job Code 143

Department Data Processing

Assigned Pay Grade 15 Current Rate of Pay $32,100

Grade Minimum $23,565 Grade Maximum $32,991

Length of Service in Present Job 5 years 1 month

Length of Service at Olympia 9 years 10 months

Date of Last Pay Adjustment 1/1/87 Kind ______

Amount of Last Pay Adjustment $1,235

Percent Increase Through Last Pay Adjustment 4.5%

Requested Adjustment $2,000 Date To Be Effective 7/1/88

Percent Increase If Adjustment Is Approved 6.2%

Reasons for Request (check appropriate item):

Change in Job Content ___ Transfer Adjustment ___
Meritorious Performance ___ Promotion Adjustment ___
Cost-of-Living Adjustment ___ Demotion Adjustment ___
Location (geographic/area) Differential Adjustment ___ New Hire ___
Failure to be competitive with other employers *

Brief Description of Reason for Request: The present maximum pay on this job is completely out of line with reality and what is happening in the labor market to programmers. If we don't give better increases, I will be losing all of my programmers.

John [signature]
D.P. Software Mgr.

To Be Completed By Compensation Department

Amount Current Rate of Pay Is Below Grade Minimum $______

Amount Current Rate of Pay Is Above Grade Maximum $______

Amount Requested Increase Would Place Recipient's Pay Above Grade $______

Last Three Performance Appraisal Ratings ______

If Job Was Reevaluated:

Current Evaluation			Revised Evaluation		
Compensable Factors	Degrees	Points	Compensable Factors	Degrees	Points

Comments:

______ Date ______ Compensation Department Manager

Salary Administration Committee Approval

Approval ______ Disagreement ______

Date ______ ______, Secretary
Compensation Administration Comm.

MODULE 20

PERFORMANCE MEASUREMENT, MERIT PAY, AND DUE PROCESS

In recent months, there have been heated discussions at Olympia that have included key executives, senior managers of some of the top-performing divisions of Olympia, and personnel and compensation specialists. The point of discussion focuses on the subject of merit pay. Because pay-for-performance has been a slogan so dear to the heart of most managers and has been an integral part of the overall policy of Olympia, it has, until the last couple of years, been accepted as gospel without thought or consideration.

In recent years, however, the entire issue of pay-for-performance has become extremely hot and it appears that everyone involved with it has been singed, if not burned. The problem is truly not whether merit pay is an appreciated or worthy concept, but, rather, is it viable? Is it workable? In the kind of organizations operating today, is it possible to recognize individual contributions or, in particular, absolute or relative differences in contribution, and then reward people differently relative to quality, quantity, and timeliness of their job-related contributions?

It has also been recognized that employee behavior relative to organizational values is a subject that may not be recognized when focusing strictly on job-related employee performance. Although commonly used procedures for measuring employee traits such as cooperation, integrity, and dependability have been under fire for a number of years from Federal courts, these human characteristics may be the critical elements that lead to organizational success.

Alma Jenkins, Vice President of Human Resources, has been working on merit pay for 5 years and has had over 15 years of experience in designing and implementing performance appraisal programs. She has been under extreme pressure to produce a program that will make it possible for Olympia to recognize differences in employee performance, reward those employees who provide the extra contributions, and be sure the program leads to improved organizational productivity. Over the past 5 years, Alma and her staff have developed a number of different programs that at first appeared to provide a path to success, only to see roadblocks arise.

Alma recently received a rude shock to the use of performance appraisal in Olympia when Harvey Tate, a 49-year old manager in an accounting department of Olympia Life and Casualty Co., filed a suit with the Equal Employment Opportunity Commission in which he claimed that, because of his age, he had not received a duly-earned promotion. He contended that younger male employees with lesser qualifications and seniority received promotions and that he was denied promotion because he was over 40 years old.

After reading the papers she received regarding the suit, Alma contacted the corporate legal department. At that time, she scheduled a meeting with Barry Cohen, corporate attorney, who specializes in discrimination problems. Alma wanted Barry to guide her as to what she should do. Although she felt that, to some degree, it was "closing the barn door after the horse had been stolen," she wanted to make certain that all instruments, procedures, and methods being used by Olympia for promotion purposes were as free as possible of unfair or illegal discrimination practices.

In her discussion with Barry, the issue of corporate liability arose. Barry mentioned that new laws, court interpretations, and amendments to current laws are causing all organizations to take a deeper look at due process and the arbitrary rights of management. There are already strict limitations regarding the rights of management to hire, fire, and promote. These rights are being extended to all employees, not just those in union shops or in government organizations.

Barry told Alma that, very simply, there are six guidelines to due process. "It may be wise," he said, "to review current personnel practices with regard to these guidelines."

The guidelines stated:

All personnel practices will

1. follow set procedures -- prohibit arbitrary actions;
2. be visible and known -- both potential violators of rights and victims of abuse must know it;
3. be institutionalized -- be a relatively permanent part of the organization;
4. be perceived as equitable -- a majority of employees accept the action as fair;
5. be easy to use -- neither complexity in administration nor potential ill effect prohibit its use;
6. be applicable to all employees -- all employees from lowest to highest can expect to receive similar treatment.

"If our performance appraisal system had been designed with due process in mind," Barry continued, "the Tate case would most likely have never occurred. If Tate has a leg to stand on, it relates to the performance appraisal ratings and reviews he has received over the past 5 years. Do you realize, Alma, that Harvey Tate had never received a performance rating of less than Fully Satisfactory over the last 10 years? In fact, less than 5 percent of our employees in any 1 year ever receive performance ratings that cause some kind of formal disciplinary or training actions. I'm not intimately familiar with just how the various units or divisions perform the appraisal function, but I would like to make these recommendations:

"1. All employees have access to their job descriptions and know <u>what</u> is expected of them in the performance of their jobs.

"2. On some regular basis, supervisor and subordinate should mutually review the subordinate's job description to be sure it adequately and accurately reflects <u>what</u> the subordinate is doing and is supposed to be doing.

"3. There is a direct relationship between performance appraisal criteria and job content.

"4. On a regular basis, supervisor and subordinate review the subordinate's demonstrated workplace behavior and results achieved. Employees must know not only what is expected of them but <u>how well</u> they are meeting these expectations.

"5. Either during the regular performance review or in some special development interview, employee strengths, weaknesses, and future career opportunities are discussed.

"6. Any record that goes into an employee's personnel file should be made available for review by the employee. The employee must be notified what is being placed in his or her file. This certainly includes performance appraisal information.

"7. Any management actions that relate to employee workplace behavior should be grievable. It is important that all employees have the opportunity to appeal decisions that may have an adverse impact on their current and future job opportunities."

In addition to legal issues regarding the design and administration of the performance appraisal process, a whole series of organizational issues has arisen regarding merit pay. The Human Resources staff of Olympia has identified 18 questions that must be considered and answered if a merit pay plan is to have a reasonable opportunity for success.

1. In times of high inflation and government controls over pay systems, can merit pay offerings be large enough to recognize the outstanding performers?

2. Which compensation components are best suited for merit pay?

3. What mix of kind and quantity of compensation components can Olympia offer to stimulate and reward above-average performance?

4. Is it possible to measure performance with sufficient accuracy in order to relate merit pay to differences in individual performance?

5. Is it possible to set standards in all kinds of jobs in Olympia so that every employee will have an opportunity for merit pay rewards?

6. Is it wise or necessary to include all employees in a merit pay program or is it best to include only a select group like managers or only managers at a certain level or higher, or only those performing certain types of jobs?

7. Is it possible to incrementalize performance so that specific levels of performance lead to specific differences in merit pay?

8. Isn't it likely that the work of one employee is so dependent on the work of others that it is not possible to identify accurately the contributions of a specific employee?

9. Can particular employees or groups of employees manipulate the merit pay system to such a degree that it provides them with distinct and unfair advantages?

10. Should there be one merit pay plan for Olympia or should there be different plans for different kinds of employee work groups, different jobs, different units, divisions, etc? If different plans are desirable, how would Olympia relate one plan to another with regard to fairness and equal treatment for equal contribution?

11. Do employees truly want merit pay programs that differentiate individual compensation according to variations in performance?

12. Can a quality control program that insures consistent meeting of quantity, quality, and time standards be implemented?

13. Do employees believe that Olympia (or any organization, for that matter) can design and manage a merit pay program that will treat all employees equitably?

14. Do employees want to be placed in a competitive situation with their peers and fellow workers?

15. Doesn't a modern organization like Olympia need to focus attention more on cooperation related programs than on ones that stress competition?

16. Is it possible to link individual merit pay programs with group and organization performance programs?

17. If Olympia broadly implemented a merit pay program, wouldn't the base pay of employees have to be reduced to provide sufficient funds for an effective pay-for-performance program?

18. In a merit pay program, how is the value of non-compensation rewards of a job calculated and how then do these non-compensation rewards combine with the merit pay and other compensation components to develop a motivating total reward package that treats all employees in an equitable manner?

Olympia must recognize the many diverse variables involved in due process and employee rights, including the need to improve productivity, i.e., (1) increase output; (2) maintain high levels of quality in services provided and goods produced; (3) provide goods and services in a timely manner; (4) improve profitability and market standing; and (5) recognize individuals and work units. When an employee is not performing or behaving in an acceptable manner, the employee has the right to expect due notice of deficiencies and support in improving his or her performance.

ASSIGNMENT

What kind of compensation/reward system would you design that you feel would lead to improved organizational performance? In your answer discuss the components of the compensation system that you feel would lead to improved organizational performance recognizing that all organizations have a limited amount of financial resources available for employee compensation and that employee rights to due process must also be considered.